THE CHALLENGE
OF MODERNITY

The Quest for Authenticity in the Arab World

LOUAY M. SAFI

UNIVERSITY
PRESS OF
AMERICA

JAN   '96

Lanham • New York • London

Library of Congress Cataloging-in-Publication Data

Safi, Louay M.
The challenge of modernity : the quest for authenticity in the Arab
world / Louay M. Safi.
p.   cm.
Includes bibliographical references and index.
1. Social change—Arab countries.   2. Arab countries—Economic
conditions.   3. Arab countries—Civilization—20th century.
4. Civilization, arab—Western influences.   5. Arabism.   6. Arab
countries—Intellectual life.   7. Progress.   I. Title.
HN766.A8S24   1994   .
303.4'09174927—dc20   93–41772 CIP

ISBN 0–8191–9375–5 (cloth : alk. paper)
ISBN 0–8191–9376–3 (pbk. : alk. paper)

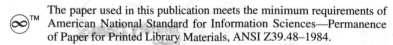

Contents

PART II: THE MODERNIZATION OF THE ARAB WORLD

Preface

This study has two primary purposes. The first, to gain insight into the central aspects of modernity and the underlying factors at work in the process of modernization. The second, to examine major intellectual forces, and to identify underlying patterns of cultural change, in the Arab society. The study begins by examining Western modernity and then uses the insight gained from this examination to study the implications of Western modernity for non-Western societies, taking Middle Eastern development as a case study

I contend that modernization is at bottom a rationalization process, i.e. an emancipatory project, aiming at eliminating the superstitious and irrational elements of culture, and therefore freeing the creative energies of the members of society. The emancipatory project is stimulated by an experienced disorder. The disorder manifests itself in two interrelated ways. On the level of consciousness, the disorder takes the form of cultural distortion, whereby the individual becomes increasingly unable to relate social ideas and values to his life situation. Cultural ideals and values appear to stand in contradiction with the aspirations of an increasing segment of society. On the level of reality, societal structures and institutions are turned into fetters, denying the individual the opportunity to grow and realize his potential. Political institutions cease to be the social embodiment of individual value commitments for an increasing number of people. The replacement of disorder with order is, however, contingent, first, on the people's ability to discover the cultural and social sources of distortion and deformation, as a necessary step for identifying the principles of order, and secondly, on the creation of social consensus on the desirability of the new principles of order.

I conclude, therefore, that the project of modernity emerges as a result of the activities of the universal intellectual who, being equipped with the intellectual skills to analyze, synthesize and reinterpret reality, and the psychological authenticity to resist the pressure to adapt to prevailing societal conditions, endeavors to bring order to his own internal world by redefining the relationship between the part and the whole, the universal and the individual, and then strive to extend the internally achieved peace and order to the surrounding society via discourse.

I want to thank James Chalmers, R. John Kinkel, Charles Parrish, and Jorge Tapia-Videla for making helpful comments on the manuscript. I am especially grateful to Philip Abbott who has read the entire manuscript and provided invaluable suggestions and comments.

Among the many friends and colleagues who have rendered moral and logistical support, I am especially thankful to Mustansir Mir, Mohamed Tahir el-Misawie, Ahmad Azam Abdul Rahman, and Mahuyddin Ismail. Warm thanks are due to Helen Hudson and Julie Krisch of the University Press of America for providing useful guidance and advice in preparing the camera-ready pages.

I am deeply grateful to my parents and wife; my wife's support and understanding have made the pursuit of the demanding task of research and writing bearable; my parents' appreciation of the value of learning, and their encouragement to pursue the path of knowledge, were an important source of inspiration and comfort.

Above all else, I owe my profoundest gratitude to the Source of this all, whose Bounty and Glory have made developing, learning, communicating, and appreciating intrinsic parts of human experience.

Introduction

Modernization is one among a host of terms, including development, change, and industrialization, denoting the movement from one sociopolitical state to another. This movement is usually associated with the improvement of the overall social conditions, and the enhancement of the quality of life in the society which experiences it. The process of modernization itself has acquired its name from the end state it aspires to bring about, i.e. modernity. Yet despite the relentless efforts to understand this phenomenon, modernization continues to be the most bewildering question in social sciences. Since Condorcet addressed the question of progress, countless philosophers, sociologists, psychologists, economists, and most recently political scientists have attempted to shed light on this fascinating, and crucially important, subject. As a result of this tremendous effort, our understanding of the process of modernization, though far from being unproblematic, is greatly enhanced.

The bulk of the information we have today on modernization, and the question of development in general, is primarily based on one specific historical experience, that of the West. Throughout the two centuries passed since Condorcet, the process of modernization has been studied from within the Western cultural milieu, and most of the categories associated with the study of modernity have been abstracted from the social and historical experiences of Western life. The complete reliance on Western society for analyzing modernization is not influenced by the lack of information regarding non-Western societies. For in the last three centuries, Western scholarship (especially in Germany and France, and most recently in the United States) has made an enormous contribution to the study of the cultures and histories of non-Western societies, and produced invaluable works in this area. The exclusive reliance on Western experience to understand modernization is rather influenced by a deeply-held conviction in the universality of Western civilization. This conviction is reinforced partly by the stagnant nature of non-Western society, of course viewed from the dynamism of Western society which has been experiencing a breath-taking growth, and partly by the ever expanding hegemony of Western powers.

The study of the process of modernization in non-Western countries did not start until the early 1950s, when a number of American social scientists began to show interest in understanding the development of non-Western regions. Throughout the 1950s and 1960s, the interest in the study of non-Western areas, both independently and in comparison with Western societies, grew drastically. The study of non-Western modernization attracted many scholars, among the best and brightest, in the various fields of American social sciences, and the interest in this area quickly gave rise to a relatively homogeneous conceptual framework, i.e. modernization theory. However, the momentum generated in the fifties and sixties came to an abrupt halt when many of the analyses and assumptions about Middle Eastern development were shattered by what is known today as the Islamic resurgence. The resurgence of Islam in the Middle East appeared quite puzzling from the perspective of modernization theory. For as early as the mid-fifties, Islamic forms were declared non-existent by virtually all students of Middle East politics. Perhaps the most important pronouncement in this regard was made by Daniel Lerner, the author of *The Passing of Traditional Society,* whose work is considered a classic on Third World development.

Although the Middle East was not the only area which attracted the attention of modernization theorists, it certainly proved to be a very crucial area. For quickly Middle Eastern development became the 'anomaly' which undermined the basic premises of the paradigm outlined by modernization theorists. The unmistakable failure to explain events and trends in the Middle East was a shattering experience, especially to the American students of non-Western modernity, an experience which put the field of comparative politics in disarray throughout the better part of the eighties, and continues today to perplex and bewilder many leading theorists in this field. The impact of this failure is felt today in the almost complete lack of understanding of changes and developments currently underway in the Middle Eastern region. It is not uncommon to hear today many commentators and experts on the Middle East using the catch phrase "this is after all the Middle East" to disguise their ignorance and to justify their inability to explain trends and events in this vital region of the world. What is implied in the phrase "this is after all the Middle East" is that if Middle Eastern events appear unintelligible, this is due to the very nature of Middle Eastern society and personality. That is to say, the inability of Middle East commentators and specialists to give us a coherent explanation of what goes on in the region is not attributed to conceptual inadequacy, but is rather dispensed with by subsuming all action in that area of the world under the rubric of "everything goes."

But is it true that action and behavior in the Middle East are beyond the pale of rational explanation? I do not wish to quarrel with the assertion that the Middle East is experiencing a violent change, and that the drastic change which the Middle East is undergoing has given rise to chaos and disorder. In fact the disordered reality of the Middle East is acknowledged in Part II of this dissertation, and reflected in its title as well. I only object to the suggestion that social disorder is an enigmatic phenomenon admitting of no explanation. The French Revolution was among the most violent experiences that a society could undergo, creating almost a complete chaos and utter disorder. But the disorder of the French revolution did not prevent able thinkers, such as Kant, Hegel, Burke, Tocqueville, Marx, and others, from explaining and analyzing its effects and implications, and providing a detailed account of the factors leading to it. These theorists were able to demonstrate to us that what may appear to the untrained eye to be the most irrational behavior could be quite intelligible if one is willing to see the chaotic and disordered world from the vantage point of those who are trapped in it.

Disorder and irrationalism, repugnant and distasteful though they may be, need not imply a world of mystery, i.e. a world in which reason and purpose are absent. The most one can claim about such a world is that using 'conventional' ideas and concepts, one is incapable of giving an explanation to events and activities taking place in that world. Therefore, the possibility remains open that one could gain insight into a disordered and irrational world (it is irrational after all because it does not conform to the standards of the rational) by discovering the reasons and purposes influencing the actions of those who constitute it.

Why is it then that modernization theory fails to provide a consistent and coherent explanation of the Middle East in particular, and Third World in general? The question is addressed in some detail throughout this dissertation, especially in Part I. Suffice it here to say that modernization theorists have attempted to understand Middle Eastern society, not by deriving concepts and theories through a systematic analysis of the Middle Eastern society, nor by identifying indigenous forces and processes in the course of their study of the cultural and structural trends of the Middle East. Rather, modernization theorists developed their model of modernization by contemplating the Western historical experience. These theorists, then, went on to employ the Western-based conceptual framework to study non-Western areas. But how could this be possible? Why were not the students of non-Western modernity confronted with the task of justifying their extrapolation from one cultural milieu to another? The answer to this important question lies in the long-standing claim of the *universality* of Western civilization. Modernization theorists did not feel the urge to validate their generalization of the Western experience because they could always fall back on a long-held tradition in Western literature which insists that Western modernity would inevitably encompass the entire globe. The *universality assumption* was further reinforced in the late nineteenth and throughout the better part of this century when Western hegemony was expanded to Third World societies, effecting structural changes therein. On the surface, many non-Western societies appear to have been more or less modernized. Doubtlessly, Western technologies and institutions could be traced to every corner of the globe. What is less appreciated is that below the façade of modernity larks a great deal of discontent, resistance, and distrust. Those who fail to penetrate beneath the surface mistake the pragmatic acceptance of the forms of Western modernity by non-Westerners for a genuine commitment to its ideas and ideals, and confuse the desire to enjoy the material fruits of Western civilization with a true conviction in the validity of the project of modernity.

The universality of Western experience cannot be taken as a given, i.e. as a self-evident phenomenon. For the claim of universality is not simply an assertion that Western modernity has universal implications for non-Western societies. If this was the claim, I do not think anyone could object to it, for obviously Western modernity has already made a profound and lasting impact on world history. The contributions of Western civilization will always be part of the evolution of human consciousness, and an important one for that. What is being questioned here is whether the cultural forms of Western modernity are destined to replace the traditional forms of non-Western societies as they did with regard to Western traditional forms. What is questioned is whether non-Western societies are bound to grow in the image of the West, as modernization school contends. This latter conception could be validated only if it can be shown that the basic historical trends leading to Western modernity have not been influenced by the historical specificities of Western experience, but by factors common to all cultures.

At the center of modernization theory's failure to explain changes taking place in the Middle Eastern society lies the functionalist approach currently predominant in the comparative politics subfield of American political science. The functionalist approach was introduced to the study of political organization as an alternative to the structural approach which was earlier predominant in the field. The functionalist approach was developed primarily by appropriating the system-theoretical aspects of the Parsonian social theory, while completely neglecting its action-theoretical aspects. Talcott Parsons used the concept of "system" to define the environment in which human action takes place. According to the schematic conceptualization advanced by Parsons, social reality may be divided along three perpendicularly interrelated axes: (1) *vertically*, into cultural, social, and personality systems; (2) *horizontally*, into community, economy, and polity; and (3) *temporally*, into industrial and preindustrial societies, organized around the the concept of "pattern variables." Yet Parsons realized that the concept of system is important only insofar as it represents the structural limitation on individual action. But social behavior has, ultimately, to be explained through the concept of action, i.e., by analyzing the agent's orientation, motive, and goal. The determination of these three elements requires that one has to view the various systems of action as intermediary links between two environments: the empirical and the metaphysical. The former takes the form of physical and biological existence, the latter that of a symbolic reality. Parsons termed his conceptual framework the "Theory of Action," and continued to stress the need to understand the symbolically constituted environment of action as a necessary step for determining the direction of social movement. Unfortunately, the functionalists, though conceding the significance of the concept of culture for analyzing social structure, were quick to drop the action-theoretical component of Parsons' social theory.

In short, this study purports, in the main, to do two things. First, it aspires to gain insight into the central aspects of modernity and the underlying factors at work in the process of modernization, both in Western and non-Western societies. It begins by examining Western modernity and then uses the insight gained from this examination to study the implications of Western modernity for non-Western societies. Secondly, this study attempts to demonstrate the inadequacy of the functionalist approach for understanding the process of modernization in non-Western regions.

An Overview

The study is divided into two parts. Part I is devoted to understanding the meaning of modernity and the unfolding of the process of modernization in the West. The objective here is to gain insight to the psychological, cognitive, and social conditions associated with the idea of modernity, and to examine the possibility of duplicating the project of Western modernity in Third World regions. After delineating the conceptual framework of modernization processes in Part I, we turn in Part II to study the modernization of the Middle East. The object now is to explore the extent to which the modernization of the Arab World has advanced over the last century, and to examine the validity of the conceptual framework delineated in Part I, to ascertain its ability, or the lack of it, and to explain and elucidate the nature and direction of intellectual debate and ideological struggle already underway in the Arab society.

Chapter 1 is devoted to reviewing the literature on the question of modernization and development. I discuss in this chapter the various concepts connected with the idea of modernization, and delineate the basic assumptions concerning the prospect for the modernization of non-Western areas. I argue that by embracing the functionalist approach, modernization theorists have come to believe that the modernization of non-Western societies is in essence a process of Westernization. I then point to the deficiencies of the functionalist approach and its inadequacy for studying developmental trends in non-Western regions.

In Chapter 2, I examine the Marxian model of development, first, as it was introduced by Karl Marx himself, and later as it was advanced and refined by some twentieth-century Marxists. I try to underscore the internal and external inconsistencies of the Marxian conception of societal change, by arguing that the notion of the primacy of the economic base is untenable. I then go on to analyze the efforts, began by Engels and latter advanced by Lukacs and Althusser, which aimed at balancing the notion of the primacy of the economy by putting more emphasis on the role played by the superstructure in determining social trends. I conclude that the Marxist revisionists have unwittingly undermined the basis of the theory of historical materialism by underscoring the decisiveness of the role played by cultural forms in determining the direction of political change.

Chapter 3 discusses an alternative approach to understanding historical change. The Weberian model of development provides us with a drastically different conception of societal change than that of Marx. The Weberian Model depicts modernization as a process of rationalization, whereby change begins in the efforts to rid social life from its irrational and superstitious elements. Weber perceives the process of modernization (rationalization) as a phased progression from a traditional to a modern state. In studying modernization as it is described by Weber, I endeavor to specify the most intrinsic features of the various stages of Western modernization, and to underline the inadequacy of the categories of "tradition" and "modernity" for reflecting the motivational basis for the inception of this process. I conclude by outlining what I termed the Weberian Paradox, according to which the more modern society advances in the process of rationalization, the more irrational it becomes.

The increased irrationalism of modern life results from the social and cultural fragmentation, whereby consciousness and reality are divided into autonomous value spheres. But the fragmentation itself results from the expansion of formal rationality at the expensive of substantive rationality. In Chapter 4, I attempt to trace this trend to its historical roots, and argue that the erosion of objective rationality need not be considered as an intrinsic aspect of development. The erosion of objective reason (or the subjectivization of reason) has been, rather, the result of an ill-fated strategy which attempted to move the grounding of 'truth' from the rational to the sensible. The important implication of the fragmentation of Western modernity is that Third World modernists are incapable of regenerating Western modernity in their societies because they have no access to the cultural totality of Western experience which lies at the roots of Western modernity.

In Chapter 5, I turn to analyze the cognitive and intellectual preconditions of modernity. Drawing partly on Weber's conception of intellectualism, and partly on Foucault's idea of the 'universal intellectual,' I portray the intellectual as a catalyst for development and change. The intellectual's contribution to the process of modernization is twofold. On the one hand, the intellectual defines the new direction of society by reinterpreting cultural symbols. This reinterpretation of the whole (e.g., the cosmos, the sacred, the beyond, etc.) brings new meaning to society by gradually pushing aside the old interpretation, and finally by assuming the status of the dominant discourse. The replacement of the old ideology with a new discourse is by no means a smooth occurrence, but, more often than not, takes the form of a fierce struggle between two groups of intellectuals: the *particular intellectual* who stands in support of the power that be, and the *universal intellectual* who is motivated by a profound commitment to bringing about a just order.

Yet although the struggle is essentially ideological, it can be resolved only by assuming a political form, i.e. by being reduced to group struggle. However, I reject the Marxist contention that the intellectual's ideas are shaped by the interests of the class to which he organically belongs. I rather contend that at the time when society makes the transition from a state of disorder (i.e., cultural distortion and social deformation) to an ordered state, such a transition can be made only when the intellectual is able to identify the underlying structure of reality (the ultimate reality), whose distortion and deformation has created the state of disorder. Such a discovery cannot be attained by a consciousness who is solely motivated by particular interests, but by one anchored in universality. It follows that the affinity between the universal intellectual and the oppressed and alienated classes (proletariat) results from the latter's recognition of the truth embodied in the discourse articulated by the former.

Having delineated a conceptual framework of modernity, I turn in Chapters 6 through 9 (Part II) to apply this framework to the Middle Eastern society. Reviewing the ideas advanced by a number of Arab intellectuals, representing three major movements (Marxist, Liberal, and Islamic), I argue that economic and political stagnation in the region should be attributed primarily to the absence of an authentic discourse. That is, the Middle East has failed to modernize because Arab leaders have attempted to bring about modernity by introducing Western social forms to Arab society, while completely ignoring the need for initiating a project of modernity from within the cultural milieu of society. In other words, Arab political and intellectual leaders, in congruence with the Marxist socialist model, assumed that by modernizing the social structures (infrastructure), cultural forms would automatically follow suit. It was not until the mid-seventies that many Arab leaders began to realize, under the pressure of Islamic extremism, the fiasco they have produced. Arab intellectuals, regardless of their ideological persuasion, have come to appreciate the primacy of the cultural over the structural, and the need for embarking on a project of cultural emancipation, as the first step to a true project of modernity.

A Caveat

Finally, before concluding this introduction, two points are in order. First, throughout this study I made references to, and employed the ideas of, numerous thinkers. In so doing, my concern was not to provide the reader with a complete account of the views of these thinkers, but to clarify and elucidate the various aspects of the model I endeavored to construct. That is to say, by bringing these thinkers into the discussion, my primary purpose was not to introduce the reader to the totality of the intellectual systems they ably produced, but to enrich the discussion on points relevant to the task at hand.

Secondly, I make no claim that the model of modernization I outlined in this study amounts to a comprehensive theory of non-Western modernity, or, for that matter, a systematic approach for understanding modernization processes in non-Western areas. I view this study as an effort to bring to the spotlight certain aspects of the process of modernization that have been, thus far, neglected or overlooked. By the same token, I do not wish that my critical reading of the functionalist approach be understood as a repudiation of the system-theoretical analysis, but rather as an attempt to point to its inadequacy and the need to combine it with an action-theoretical analysis. To put it in positive terms, I contend that understanding Third World development requires that the study of social structures and functions be combined with an analysis of the actions (i.e., purposes, motives, and commitments) of Third World people, as they are reflected in their intellectual discourses. The benefits derived from such an undertaking are not limited, however, only to gaining better insight to non-Western modernity, but they promise to enhance our understanding of Western modernity as well.

PART I

Understanding Modernization

Chapter 1

Modernization Theory

The Parsonian Legacy and The Functionalist Approach

Since the interest in studying the process of development in Third World countries was generated in the United States shortly after World War II, numerous studies have been made to isolate the principal determinants of this phenomenon. From the beginning, the Committee on Comparative Politics of the Social Science Research Council (SSRC) assumed, under the chairmanship of Gabriel Almond and later Lucian Pye, a Leading role in setting the agenda for research in this area, and continued to be very influential throughout the sixties and seventies.[1]

Although the SSRC Committee was greatly influenced by the evolutionary school, sharing many of its assumptions, it relied primarily on, and borrowed extensively from, the functionalist approach of the Parsonian social theory. In a book published in 1960, under the joint sponsorship of the SSRC Committee and the Center of International Studies of Princeton University, Almond outlined an analytical approach for studying developing areas in which the Parsonian "pattern variables" played a central role.[2]

Almond criticized the Parsonian schema for its "theoretical polarization," whereby premodern and modern societies were perceived to stand on diametrically opposing sides, and called for a "dualistic" conception of society in which premodern or traditional cultures and structures are seen to coexist alongside modern ones.[3] The *dualistic* model suggested by Almond permits us to view political development not as a singular moment at which all traditional aspects of society are replaced instantaneously by modern ones, but as a process in which development occurs gradually and with varying degrees of success across society. Yet Almond's substitution of the *dichotomous* model presented by Parsons with a *dualistic* model does not reflect any significant departure from the Parsonian schema. After all, Parsons himself, borrowing from the Weberian methodology, viewed his "pattern variables" as ideal types, rather than an accurate reflection of actual social structures. Parsons' developed a markedly elaborate and complex theory in which the cultural, structural, and personality aspects of society are interrelated and interconnected. Although he attempted to combine action theory and system theory perspectives, the system-theoretical components of his theory (which tend to reduce action to behavior) seem to have influenced modernization theorists the most.[4] The Parsonian concept of "pattern variables" has been the cornerstone in studying modernization processes in Third World countries. Talcott Parsons elaborated his "pattern variables" model in *The Social System* and in a book appeared nearly simultaneously in 1951, with the collaboration of Edward Shils entitled *Toward a General Theory of Action*. Parsons developed the concept of "pattern variables" to distinguish five pairs of social behavior. The first set of variables describe social behavior in premodern or traditional society. In such a society, behavior is described as "affective," "collectivity-oriented," "particularistic," "ascriptive," and "diffuse." The other alternative set of variables determine social behavior in modern society. Modern society is characterized as being "affective neutral," "self-oriented," "universalistic," "achievement-oriented," and "specific."[5]

The first pair of variables, distinguishing between social relations in traditional and modern societies, is the affective versus affective-neutral relationship. Social relationships are based, in traditional societies, on personal and emotional ties. Relationships between individuals interacting in economic and political institutions resembles those found in the family. Society itself may be viewed as a large family, whereby personal connections and affinities take precedence over other criteria. Employees, for example, are hired and promoted on the basis of their lineal proximity to their employers. Likewise, public officials are appointed from within the ranks of the ruling family or clan. As society moves towards modernity, social relations begin to acquire impersonal, detached, and rational forms.

The second pair of pattern variables, self-orientation versus collective-orientation, deals with the question of whether the goals pursued by the individual contribute to the advancement of the individual self-interest, or to the common interest of the collectivity. In premodern societies, the individual tends to be committed to the collective interests of his family, tribe, or community. In modern societies, on the other hand, the emphasis is placed on self-interest; the individual is encouraged to set, and then pursue, his personal goals which may or may not coincide with those of the collectivity to which he belongs.

The third pair of pattern variables, universalistic versus particularistic standards, addresses the question of the nature of the norms governing the lives of the members of a specific society. In traditional societies, people adopt parochial norms designed to respond to the particular needs of the social group to which they belong. In modern societies, people subscribe to general norms with universal implications. Such universalistic standards are needed to regulate social behavior in densely populated urban centers where individuals interact, more often than not, as strangers.

The fourth pair of pattern variables, the achievement versus the ascriptive, is concerned with the basis for the evaluation of individual status. In traditional societies, individuals are evaluated by the social status ascribed to them on the basis of the qualities they inherit from their families or classes. Whereas in modern societies people are evaluated by their performance and the qualities they achieve through their individual endeavors.

Finally, the fifth pair of pattern variables, the functionally specific versus the functionally diffused, relates to the question of whether social tasks are broadly or narrowly defined. In traditional societies, social tasks require little training and, hence, have low level of differentiation. In modern societies, on the other hand, social tasks require high level of specialization and extensive training; consequently, social structures are characterized by a high degree of differentiation and an elaborate scheme of division of labor.

In short, the Parsonian concept of pattern variables is designed to contrast two models of society: the traditional and the modern. The former is characterized by monolithic worldviews, collectivism, customary code of conduct, rigid social stratification, and little specialization. The latter is distinguished by pluralistic worldviews, individualism, rule of law, social mobility, and extensive specialization.[6] As we will see below, Parsons' conceptual schema lies at the heart of the analytical approach of functionalist theorists who have employed the Parsonian model to study political development in Third World countries.

The Parsonian schematic approach has been employed by many sociologists, economists, and political scientists to study the process of development or modernization in developing countries. Although functionalist theorists have brought diverse insights into the study of modernization and enhanced our understanding of some of the factors associated with political underdevelopment and economic backwardness, they all seem to uphold the notion that the transformation from preindustrial and premodern to industrial and modern society has to proceed along the lines suggested by the "pattern variables" schema.

In *Industrialism and Industrial Man,* Carl Kerr et. al. argued that the development of traditional societies is contingent on their transformation into industrial societies through the process of industrialization. Kerr et. al. stressed early on in their work that the course of industrialization *need not follow any specific pattern,* and that "underdeveloped countries need not grow in all important respects in 'the image' of any particular advanced country."[7] They went on to note that bringing about an advanced industrial society presupposes scientific and technological advancement, and, hence, a high degree of specialization and differentiation. Kerr saw Western elite playing a crucial role in effecting *global* industrialization by introducing social and institutional changes. Changes in the West are brought about peacefully through the historical struggle between the bourgeois elite and the workers, while changes in Third World countries are achieved through colonialism. Kerr insisted that the course of industrialization in Third World countries need not be identical with that of the West. He, nevertheless, contended that as traditional societies gradually progress toward the industrial model, normative differences disappear, and ideological commitments are replaced with a realistic and pragmatic outlook.

> When man first entered the irreversible journey into industrialization there were innumerable views about the best way to organize the society. Some of them have almost completely disappeared from the scene: anarchism, syndicalism, communalism, cooperativism. Others of them have been blunted and revised from their original form, particularly capitalism and socialism. The age of utopias is past. An age of realism has taken its place; an age in which there is little expectation of either utter perfection or complete doom.[8]

The *convergence* of industrial societies is not confined, Kerr tells us, to cultural worldviews, but to social arrangements as well. "Social arrangements," Kerr proclaims, "will be most uniform from one society to another when they are most closely tied to technology, they can be more diverse the farther removed they are from technology."[9]

Like Kerr, W.W. Rostow perceives development as the movement from tradition to modernity. Unlike Kerr, he sees this movement progressing through the *same path* that the Western society has traversed, following a definitive course, and taking specific steps. The journey from traditional to modern society passes through three stages: precondition for takeoff, takeoff, and the drive to technological maturity.[10] Rostow perceives the takeoff stage as a dramatic moment in the life of a nation, during which traditional ways of doing things are replaced by scientific methods and the preindustrial economy gives way to industrialization. The takeoff does not occur instantaneously throughout society. Rather, it starts in relatively few sectors, and spread gradually to others. The takeoff stage is followed by a longer stage in which the modernizing centers continue to expand, while science and technology keep improving. Rostow gives the label "the drive to technological maturity" to the latter stage. Yet the second and third stages are, according to Rostow, contingent on a more fundamental stage, a stage he terms the "pre-condition for takeoff." This stage signifies an event causing both *social* and *psychological* changes, such as an industrial or political revolution, and forcing people to rethink and reevaluate their old ideas and practices. Rostow contends that Third World societies must give up their traditional outlook and adopt "the Newtonian outlook" before they can experience the "takeoff."

> Men must transform or adapt the old culture in ways which make it compatible with modern activities and institutions. The face-to-face relations and warm, powerful family ties of a traditional society must give way, in degree, to new, more impersonal systems of evaluation in which men are judged by the way they perform specialized functions in the society.[11]

There seems to be an agreement among functionalist theorists on the need to replace traditional outlook with a "Newtonian" or secular outlook before the process of development or modernization can take place. In *Comparative Politics*, Almond and Powell argue that the secularization of culture is a *necessary* prelude for effecting structural change. People's orientations and attitudes should become increasingly *empirical* and *pragmatic*. Such a change is important because it helps replacing the rigidly structured decisions, characteristic of traditional system, with a dynamic decision-making process, allowing thereby more flexibility in the selection of possible alternative courses of action.[12] Almond and Powell perceive development as a movement from a less advanced political order, characterized by a *simplistic* structure, to a more *sophisticated* political order, distinguished by a markedly differentiated structure. The structural change presupposes, however, a more fundamental change in the political culture of traditional society.[13]

It is important to note that Almond, and functionalist theorists in general, sees the emerging modern culture in Third World countries as part of a *universal* trend. The new culture is a global culture, patterned after the Western model. In *The Civic Culture,* Almond and Verba portray the emerging global culture as "a pluralistic culture based on communication and persuasion."[14] The emerging "civic" culture permits diversity of beliefs and practices within a general framework of value consensus. Almond and Verba argue that the civic culture is the *outcome of a process of secularization,* whereby "rigid, ascribed, and diffuse customs" are replaced by "a set of codified, specifically political, and universalistic rules."[15] They further remark that the civic culture and the open polity associated with it are "the great problematic gifts of the West." They were both developed in Britain as the result of a protracted struggle between tradition and modernity.[16] Almond does not see the progress of non-Western areas to be inevitable. For, he argues, history shows us that it is quite possible that the progress of a political system can at any time be reversed. The Roman Empire, for example, went through such an experience. Almond, however, contends that the transfer of technology to Third World countries has already destroyed traditional cultures, and that cultural secularization and structural differentiation, which go hand in hand with modern technology, are likely to bring about a *global civic culture.*

In a book sponsored by SSRC Committee, published in 1971 under the title *Crises and Sequences in Political Development,* Leonard Binder reexamines the question of modernization and political development. Binder contends that even if we were to regard the combination of circumstances leading to the demise of traditional society and the emergence of modern society in the West to have been brought about by accidental historical changes, the recurrence of these circumstances in other areas will necessarily lead to similar changes from tradition to modernity. Binder insists that modernization must be viewed as a "singular event," occured first in Western Europe, and then spread throughout the glob.

> Whether Europe preempted the history of the world or even caused it, modernity appears to most of us as a great singular event, as an historical threshold. . . . The central point is that things are different after some point in history than they were before. This point can be called a threshold, and it may be thought as a singular event or a broad band of history through which different countries pass at different times, some more rapidly, some more slowly, some even slipping back, and some seemingly hopelessly bogged down. . . . If the Threshold is itself an historical period, then it affords us three principles of understanding; the traditional, the modernizing, and the modern.[17]

Binder perceives modernization, and its corollary concept of political development, as a dialectical process whereby the cultural and structural elements of society are constantly shaped and reshaped as the result of the encounters between tradition and modernity.[18] Binder's analysis leads to an important conclusion shared by many modernization theorists, namely, cultural and structural diversity among modernizing societies should be attributed to the plurality of traditional cultures. As these societies approach the *ideal* of modernity, and continue to resemble the model embedded in it, they begin to *converge into a global culture* and fairly identical structures. The idea of modernity itself, it is assumed, though originating through a specific historical experience, has universal implication and global application.

Discrepancy and Ambiguity

The foregoing discussion reveals certain inconsistencies and ambiguities which obscure the theoretical framework of modernization theory and render it unable to account for crucial aspects of developmental processes in Third World countries. The first difficulty connected with modernization theory lies in its dichotomous approach whereby tradition is seen to stand at the opposite side of modernity. Although leading modernization theorists recognize the difficulty posed by the tradition-modernity polarity, and go out of their way to emphasize that the two ideal types tend to overlap and intermingle in real cases,[19] they continue, nevertheless, to view the categories of tradition and modernity as *static* and *homogeneous*. E. N. Eisenstadt, for example, admits that the ascriptive, diffused, and particularistic criteria associated with traditional society do, more often than not, exist alongside the criteria of universalism, achievement, and specialization, usually connected with modern society, in most societies that have progressed beyond tribal organization.[20] Likewise, James Coleman notes that "many historically 'traditional' polities had typologically 'modern' structures and orientation, and visa versa."[21] Both, however, continue to treat modernization and political development as a progressive movement between two opposing poles--modernity and tradition. Although some modernization theorists are willing to concede the diversity of the traditional forms of society, they all support the notion that modern society must have definitive cognitive, normative, and structural forms, analogous to those developed in the West.

Secondly, modernization theory suffers from an ethnocentric bias. Modernization theorists abstract and then generalize from the sociocultural experience of Western society. Non-Western development is evaluated and examined against the background of *Western* modernity. The result, therefore, is that Western standards are elevated to the status of absoluteness. As Henry Bernstein puts it: "The question of ethnocentrism becomes central when it is asked from which historical source the paradigm of modernization is abstracted and universalized."[22] The ethnocentric bias may partially be attributed to the fact that many of the concepts employed by modernization theory originate with European evolutionary theory, associated with such eminent thinkers as Hegel, Marx, Spencer, Weber, and Durkheim. It has also been suggested that the ethnocentrism of modernization theory is only natural since "most modernization researchers are Americans and Europeans."[23]

Thirdly, modernization theory seems to have been more interested in policy matters than in understanding actual political changes in Third World countries. That is to say, modernization theorists may be accused of being interested in guiding policy and inducing change, instead of observing social changes or describing political trends within the sociocultural framework of Third World societies. Eisenstadt, a leading modernization theorists, observes:

It was only in the 1940s and 1950s that questions about the nature and quality of modern life again came into the forefront of the social science. . . . the major focus of interest of these concerns was how to bring about changes in the underdeveloped societies, how to "develop" them.[24]

The policy interest of modernization theorists has transformed modernization school into, more or less, an ideological movement whose primary interest is to advance and propagate Western liberalism in Third World countries. This tendency on the part of modernization theorists has been registered by several students of development. Peter Berger, for example, notes that W. W. Rostow presented his basic work, *Politics and the Stages of Growth*, as "a viable capitalist alternative to the Marxist versions of development."[25] Published in 1959 the work was originally subtitled "A Non-Communist Manifesto." Berger's remarks have been echoed by Alvin So, who sees an agreement between Rostow's recommendations for promoting Third World modernization and U.S. policy toward Third World regions.[26] Richard Higgott points out that modernization aims discussed in the works published by the SSRC Committee have changed between 1950s and 1970s from an emphasis on participation and democracy to an emphasis on mobilization and order.[27] By the early 1970s, maintaining order in Third World countries and ensuring the stability of Third world regimes became the primary concern of the SSRC Committee. *Crises and Consequences,* the seventh volume published in 1971 by the Committee reflected this new preoccupation. The book suggested strategies which Third World elites could use to deal with destabilizing factors in their countries.[28]

The Meaning of Modernization

The question of modernization and development has been tackled on various levels and by researchers with varying disciplinary backgrounds. These researchers have used a multiplicity of criteria to measure progress in developing areas. In this section we will examine some of the important concepts associated with the study of development in an attempt to gain more understanding of the phenomenon of modernity and the process of modernization.

Theorists and researchers specialized in the study of modernization and development are in disagreement over the meaning and use of the two concepts. In fact, a broader array of terms have been used to denote the phenomenon of social change. This list includes the terms: industrialization, modernization, political development, progress, growth, and rationalization. David Apter, for instance, observes that the concepts of development, modernization, and industrialization denote interrelated phenomena. Placed in a descending order of generality, development comes at the top as the most general concept of the three, followed by modernization and then by industrialization.[29] According to Apter, development refers to the increased differentiation of social structures, while modernization denotes a special case of development whereby the ideas of innovation and advanced technology become integral parts of the social order. Industrialization is yet a more specific case of modernization in which "the strategic functional roles are related to manufacturing."[30]

Unlike Apter who sees development in terms of structural differentiation or "proliferation of roles," Peter Berger links it to economic growth; "development refers," he writes, "to the process by which poor countries get richer, or try to do so."[31] Modernization, on the other hand, is seen as the institutional and cultural changes associated with economic growth.[32] Berger observes that although the correlation between economic and social change is recognized by virtually all students of development, an agreement over which takes precedence in the causal sequence is far from being attained.[33]

Yet whether a theorist decides to use different terms (e.g., industrialization, development, or modernization) to denote various aspects of the process of societal change, or use a single term to indicate such a change, should be of secondary concern. What is important is to gain an insight into the nature of the end states of the transformation process. How is modernity distinguished from tradition? Under what circumstances does the process of modernization originate? And how does it proceed? These are the questions which will command our attention in the remainder of this section.

Modernity, and the process of modernization leading to it, mean different things to different people. Almond and Verba associate it with structural differentiation and cultural

secularization.[34] Leonard Binder connects it with the growth in
economic capacity, social differentiation, and political equality.[35]
David Apter links it to the expansion of individual choice.[36]
Manning Nash sees modernization in the application of science to
production, and modernity in the social, cultural, and
psychological conditions facilitating this application.[37] S. N.
Eisenstadt associates modernity with the rise of *rational* culture
and the secularization of worldviews, with the emergence of
efficient economies and specialized roles, and with political
freedom and the creation of the system of nation-states.[38]
Frederique and Stephan Marglin succinctly summarize the
various views on the meaning of modernization:

> . . . there still remains a diversity of views about what
> development and modernization mean. However we probably
> shall not go far wrong if we place the following at the core; on
> the economic side, industrialization and urbanization, as well as
> the technological transformation of agriculture; on the political
> side, rationalization of authority and the growth of a
> rationalizing bureaucracy; on the social side, the weakening of
> ascriptive ties and the rise of achievement as the basis for
> personal advancement; culturally, the 'disenchantment' of the
> world (to use Max Weber's terminology), the growth of science
> and secularization based on increasing literacy and numeracy.[39]

Perhaps the most obvious, and less controversial, aspect of
modernity is the application of science and technology to
economic production. The use of advanced technology for
producing goods and services makes industrial economies much
superior in terms of total economic output when compared with
agricultural economies. Industrialization has, therefore, become
one of the most desired goals of societies with agriculturally
based economies.

Yet the creation of industrial economies *presupposes* scientific
and technological advancements, which are, in turn, *contingent*
on certain social and cultural changes. Socially, industrial tasks
require a high level of specialization and training and a complex
network of communication. Culturally, certain attitudes and
outlooks should prevail so that *innovation* and *cooperation,*
essential for creating an industrial economy, can be maintained.

This leads us to a third important question to be considered in
our endeavor to understand the idea of modernity and the process
of modernization, the question of political development. Political

development is by far the most difficult and most controversial aspect of modernization. For political development appears, at once, as the cause and consequence of modernization. On the one hand, cultural modernization presupposes the emergence of rational authority willing and capable of guiding the reconstruction of social and economic order. On the other hand, political development is contingent on the occurrence of some significant economic and social changes, forcing society, or at least some sectors in it, to rethink their old ideas and practices, and motivating them to introduce changes into the political order.

The word 'modernity' is usually used in Western literature to denote certain cognitive, normative, and structural changes that emerged in modern history in contrast with those that existed in classic and medieval world. These changes took place initially in Western Europe, before they were introduced to other areas during the expansion of major European powers. *Modernity may be perceived, therefore, as an ideal or goal that has been partially or completely approximated in some parts of the world* (e.g., Western Europe and North America) *or is still to be realized in other areas* (e.g., Latin America, Africa, and South Asia). As such modernization may be conceived as the process leading toward the ideal of modernity.

The ideal of modernity itself consists of two distinctive aspects. The first is technical, relating to production and organization skills and techniques. Modern skills and techniques are the result of a cumulative knowledge, based on the experience and contribution of different civilizations and cultures throughout human history, and has been constantly passed on from one *civilized culture* to another.[40] The other aspect of modernity is normative, associated with the values and beliefs of a specific culture. These values and beliefs, ultimately rooted in the metaphysical subsoil of cultural worldviews, are peculiar to the historically developed and transmitted *heritage* of a specific society. Modernization theory insists that non-Western cultures can modernize by appropriating not only the technical aspects of Western modernity, but its normative aspects as well. In a word, for non-Western cultures to be able to modernize, they have to be recreated in the image of the West. In fact, there is sufficient evidence to suggest that the non-Western world has *already* been Westernized in many significant ways. It is still, however, an open question whether this *Westernization* signifies fundamental cultural changes, or is merely a reflection of the structural *expansion* of Western modernity. In the next section, I will address the latter aspect of this question. I will come back to deal with the former in the following chapters.

Expansion of Western Centers

The confusion over the intrinsic aspects of modernity notwithstanding, one thing is clear: The historical and social *locus* of modernity lies in Western society. Historically, the idea of modernity and the process of modernization can be traced back to the recent experiences of Western European society. Socially, the intellectual and structural forms shaping the lives and influencing the minds of the bulk of humanity bear the unmistakable imprints of *Western civilization.* What is not so clear, however, is whether Western modernity, despite its *historical specificity,* represents a global trend. The question of the *universality* of Western modernity has been the focus of many studies, and is one of the major concerns of this study. Simply stated, the question may be phrased: Are non-Western societies destined to evolve towards the Western model of modernity?

The concept of modernization as a universal process was influenced by both evolutionary theory and the "philosophy of history" school. The idea received its early expression in the writings of Marquis de Condorcet, in the eighteenth century, and was further developed in the nineteenth century by such eminent thinkers as Comte and Hegel, and later by Marx and Spencer. Condorcet, for example, postulated the unity of human history and the *inevitability* and *irreversibility* of the progress of human rationality. He was convinced that all nations were bound to converge into one universal civilization and global culture.[41] August Comte, likewise, saw history as the evolution of human understanding from the realm of *theological* knowledge through the *metaphysical,* and ultimately to the *positive.* The normative divisions characteristic of the theological life, he contended, are bound to disappear when society is transformed into the positive stage in which human conduct is governed by universal reason.[42] Similarly, Hegel and Marx, despite the profound differences that separate the *metaphysical* underpinning of their thoughts, saw human history through evolutionary lens. The former conceived history as the universalization of rational freedom, and anticipated its culmination in the Germanic state, while the latter saw history as the universalization of property, and predicted its near end in the communist society. In fact the belief in the universalistic claims of modern Western experience were so much entrenched in nineteenth-century Western thought that Max Weber, though rejecting the premises of evolutionism and the philosophy of history, accepted readily their conclusion by postulating the universality of "Occident" rationalism.[43]

Central to the universalistic claim is the assumption that despite the historical specificity of modern Western experience, modernity project developed in the West has *global applications*. In Chapter 4, I will examine the theoretical underpinning of this claim. For now I would like to consider some of the circumstances surrounding the project of modernization. To begin with, it should be noted that it would be misleading to regard modernity as a concept that stands in complete opposition to the concept of tradition. Not only are the two concepts not mutually exclusive, but modernity itself should be regarded as a *tradition,* emerged to challenge, and ultimately replace, the medieval tradition which was earlier dominant in Western Europe.[44] The "tradition" of modernity grew in response to the normative and social configurations peculiar to medieval society. *Modernity project* continued to be confined to Western society for several centuries before it was introduced to non-Western areas by the turn of the nineteenth century, *mainly* through the agency of colonialism. In other words, the introduction of modernity to non-Western regions was, by and large, the result of the *expansion of Western centers.* The expansion itself marked the triumph of the "tradition" of Western modernity over the local traditions of non-Western areas.

The expansion of Western centers has been attained through various means, including economic and political. But it was the military conquest of non-Western areas, especially Africa and Asia, that was decisive in globalizing the "tradition" of modernity. The military triumph of Western powers, which was based on superior *scientific* and *organizational* foundations, weakened drastically the local traditions of the conquered areas. The colonization of non-Western countries has had far-reaching cultural and structural consequences. Culturally, the *confidence* of the people of the conquered areas in their local traditions was profoundly shaken after they were exposed to a superior civilization. structurally, the colonial powers managed to restructure the societies of the areas which came under their dominion. Political boundaries were redrawn, new political ideas and institutions were introduced, and education and communication systems were established.

Modernization trends in Third World countries continued, even intensified, long after these countries achieved their independence from European powers. Even in the Middle East, where the expansion of Western modernity encountered a fierce resistance, the process of modernization seemed by the mid-twentieth century to have come close to achieving its goals. In *The Passing of traditional Society,* Daniel Lerner observed in the fifties the profound changes which were underway in Middle Eastern society under the impact of Western modernity.

Whether from East or West, modernization poses the same basic challenge--the infusion of "a rationalist and positivist spirit" against which, scholars seem agreed, "Islam is absolutely defenseless." The phasing and modality of the process have changed, however, in the past decade. Where Europeanization once penetrated only the upper level of Middle East society, affecting mainly leisure-class fashions, modernization today diffuses among a wider population and touches public institutions as well as private aspirations with its disquieting "positivist spirit."[45]

Lerner cited in his work two principal reasons for choosing the Western model of modernization to study development in the Middle East. The first reason was that Western model appeared "in virtually all modernizing societies on all continents of the world, regardless of variations in race, color, creed . . ."[46] The second reason had to do with the developmental agents of the Middle Eastern society. Lerner explained:

Taking the Western model of modernization as a baseline is forced upon us, moreover, by the tacit assumptions and proclaimed goals which prevail among Middle East spokesmen. That some of these leaders, when convenient for diplomatic maneuver, denounce the West is politically important and explains why we have chosen to speak of "modernization" rather than "Westernization." Rather more important, Western society still provides the most developed model of societal attributes (power, wealth, skill, rationality) which Middle Eastern spokesmen continue to advocate as their own goal.[47]

Looking with hindsight on Lerner's remarks, it is clear that he had underestimated the deep roots of Islam in Middle Eastern consciousness, and mistook cultural *confusion* and structural *imbalance* created by *outside* pressure, for internally induced development. The temptation offered by Western modernity was so great to be ignored by Middle Easterners, and the confusion resulting from the triumph of modernity "tradition" over local traditions was overwhelming. Nevertheless, Lerner was able to detect at this early stage the *uneasiness* experienced by Middle Eastern modernists in presenting measures borrowed from the modern West, and pointed to the effort made by these modernists to *disguise* the process of *Westernization* under the rubric of *modernization*. Lerner further charged Middle Eastern modernists with ethnocentrism for attempting to appropriate the *technical* aspects of Western modernity while rejecting its *normative* aspects. He observed:

> The hatred sown by anticolonialism is harvested in the rejection of every appearance of foreign tutelage. Wanted are modern institutions but not modern ideologies, modern power but not modern purposes, modern wealth but not modern wisdom, modern commodities but not modern cant. It is not clear, however, that modern ways and words can so easily and so totally be sundered.[48]

Like all early adherents of modernization theory, Lerner fails to recognize the profound difference between the process of modernization in advanced societies and the one taking place in Third World countries. For while changes in advanced societies are generated by ethos *internal* to the local cultures of these societies, changes in Third World societies, on the other hand, are the consequence of *external* pressure brought to bear as a result of the expansion of Western centers.[49] In Middle Eastern societies, for instance, the desire to match the technical power and economic wealth of advanced Western countries is associated with intense rejection of, and fierce resistance to, Western values and symbols.

By late 1970s and early 1980s the notion of a universal modernization process began to lose its certainty and became the subject of serious doubts, expressed in the writings of leading students of development, including modernization theorists. The new doubts reflected the increased contradictions between the theoretical postulates of modernization theory and the reality of social change in developing areas, most notably the Middle East. Samuel Huntington, for example, questions the usefulness of employing Western standards to judge and assess modernization processes in non-Western countries. "May be the time has come," he writes, "to stop trying to change these societies and to change the model, to develop models of modern Islamic, Confucian, or Hindu society that would be more relevant to countries where those cultures prevail."[50] Similarly, Eisenstadt, a leading modernization theorist, observes that the Western model of modernity "is violently rejected by most non-Westerners."[51] It is not the technological and scientific aspects of Western modernity which are the object of the fierce resistance, Eisenstadt cautions, but rather the normative and cultural.[52]

The resistance to Western modernization has two dimensions: structural and cultural. Structurally, the resistance is directed against the *incorporation* of developing areas into an international system whose center is located in Western capitals. It is true that as a result of the expansion of the West, some periphery regions have experienced economic growth (e.g., Turkey, Egypt, and others). But this is a "growth without development," to use Peter Berger's phrase, for it is based on the *penetration* of Third World economies by foreign capital and technology. Consequently, a state of *economic dependency* is created in developing nations, where important economic and, hence, political decisions are made in foreign metropolis.[53] Culturally, the introduction of new forms of behavior based on foreign norms and values is being met with a strong opposition on the part of increasing segments of non-Western societies. Nowhere is the opposition more evident than in the Middle East. Since the early seventies, Middle Eastern countries have been witnessing Islamic resurgence.

The resurgence of Islam appears quite *puzzling* from the perspective of modernization theory. It is not clear, for instance, whether the strong influence of Islamic values and ideas on an increasing sectors of Middle Eastern society, including a significant portion of the intelligentsia, should be viewed as simply a reactionary movement against modernity, or whether it should be read as a sign of an *Islamic modernity*. Some modernization theorists have been quick to dismiss the new development in the Middle East under the rubric of "Islamic fundamentalism." As will be shown in Part II, the phenomenon of Islamic resurgence is quite *complicated* to be reduced to the simple category of "fundamentalism."

The concepts associated with modernization theory seem incapable of giving us an access to Middle Eastern consciousness. Being abstracted from the recent experience of Western society, these concepts have all the prejudices connected with the cultural outlook of Western societies. For example, modernization theory insists that cultural secularization, considered as a prerequisite for modernity, is a *global* phenomenon, and moves on to conclude that the secularization of Middle Eastern society should follow the same patterns experienced by Western society in modern times. Yet this conclusion can be granted only by assuming that the features of the traditional European society and traditional Middle Eastern society are identical; such an assumption clearly belies sociological evidence and historical records.[54]

From Modern Culture to Cultural Modernization

Modernization theory seems to advance at once two contradictory theses. On the one hand, modernization theorists accept the Weberian proposition that structural modernization presupposes cultural modernization, i.e., the rationalization of worldviews. On the other hand, these theorists appear to endorse the Marxian postulate, according to which changes in the material conditions of a society inevitably result in altering the ideas and values of its members. Modernization theorists tend to apply the Weberian thesis to explain changes in advanced societies, while employing the Marxist thesis to interpret developmental processes in Third World countries. This inconsistency is reflected in the almost complete *lack* of interest on the part of modernization theorists to understand the ideas and thoughts of Third World intellectuals, or to study the processes of *cultural rationalization* which have been taking place in developing areas.

Almond and Powell, for example, remind us of the need to identify the "underlying propensities" of any political system if we are to make sense of it at all. By "propensities" they understand the *psychological* dimension of the political system, as it is embodied in its political culture. The importance of the political culture comes from the fact that it provides us with an access to understanding the *structures of consciousness* associated with a specific normative system. As such, culture is "a valuable conceptual tool by means of which we can bridge the 'micro-macro' gap in political theory."[55] Similarly, W.W. Rostow posits a number of conditions which, he claims, are required for transforming society from the preindustrial to the industrial level of development, and regards *psychological* change to be the most fundamental condition. "It was the acceptance of the view," Rostow points to the attitudinal change that made scientific revolution possible, "that the physical world is capable of being understood and manipulated in terms of a relatively few stable rules which man could master."[56]

Yet rather than examining cultural changes taking place in Third World countries to infer the likely shape that structural changes may resemble, both Almond and Rostow assume the universality of Western culture and proceed to use Western standards to evaluate the development and modernization of non-Western areas. The analytical approach of modernization theory appears to be in direct contradiction with some important elements of its theoretical premises. If the motivational forces are embedded in the cultural and religious subsoil of society, the study of cultural rationalization should be our point of departure for monitoring developmental trends in developing areas.

Modernization theory assumed all along that introducing modern forms is sufficient for reshaping the structures of consciousness in developing areas, thereby failing to recognize that developmental purposes and goals may command the commitment of individual members of society only when they are located within a broader frame of meaning. As Soed Jakmoko puts it: "In order to be sufficiently persuasive, it is necessary to relate the purposes of the development process to other worthwhile purposes of human endeavor and of society."[57]

In Chapter 4, I will discuss the historical process which resulted in the transformation of the structures of Western consciousness and society from those which were dominant in medieval times to the structures characteristic of modern life. In Chapter 5, I outline a conceptual framework which, I propose, can provide more insight into, and better explanation of, the process of modernization in non-Western societies. I then employ the outlined conceptual framework to examine the possibilities of modernization in the Middle East. But first, I delineate in the next two chapters two drastically different approaches to understanding social change, the Marxian and the Weberian models of development. The former locates the motor of change

in the economic realm of society, while the latter assigns the
locus of modernization process to the cultural.

Notes

1. The Committee was active throughout the sixties and seventies.
It consisted of a number of leading modernization theorists including
Myron Weiner, James Coleman, Leonard Binder, Sidney Verba, and
others. For more detailed discussion of the work of the Committee see
the concluding chapter of Myron Weiner and Samuel Hantington (eds.)
Understanding Political Development. See also Richard A. Higgott,
Political Development Theory: The Contemporary Debate (London:
Groom Helm, 1983), pp. 15-8; and Gabriel A. Almond and James S.
Coleman (eds.), The Politics of Developing Areas (N.J.: Princeton
University Press, 1960), p. v.

2. Almond and Coleman, *The Politics of Developing Areas*, pp.
3-64.

3. Ibid., pp. 22-4.

4. For an analysis of Talcott Parsons' impact on the behavioral
school of social sciences see Jurgen Habermas, *The Theory of
Communicative Action*, Vol. 2 , trans. Thomas McCarthy (Boston;
Beacon Press, 1984), pp. 199-235.

5. Talcott Parsons, *The Social System* (Glencoe, Ill.: The Free
Press, 1951), pp. 62-7.

6. Almond and Coleman, *The Politics of Developing Areas*, pp.
22-3.

7. Carl Kerr et al., *Industrialism and Industrial Man* (Cambridge,
Mass.: Harvard University Press,1960), p. 31.

8. Ibid., p. 282.

9. Carl Kerr et. al., p. 285.

10. W.W. Rostow, *Politics and the Stages of Growth* (Cambridge
University Press,1971), pp. 98-101.

11. Ibid., pp. 58-9.

12. Gabriel A. Almond and G. Binghanm Powell, Jr., *Comparative
Politics: A Development Approach* (Boston: Little, Brown and Co.,
1966), p. 24.

13. Ibid., pp. 21-3.

14. Gabrial A. Almond and Sidney Verba, *The Civic Culture:
Political Attitudes and   Democracy in Five Nations* (Princeton, N.J.:
Princeton University Press, 1963), p. 6.

15. Ibid., p. 60.

16. Ibid., p. 5-7.

17. Leonard Binder et. al., *Crises and Sequences in Political Development* (Princeton University Press,1971), p. 12.

18. Ibid., p. 21.

19. See Almond and Coleman; also Binder et. al.

20. S. N. Eisenstadt, *Tradition, Change, and Modernity* (N.J.: John Wiley & Sons,1973), p. 162.

21. Binder et. al., p. 74.

22. Henry Bernstein, "Modernization Theory and the Sociological Study of Development," in *Journal of Development Studies*, (October 1971) 7:147.

23. Alvin Y. So, *Social Change and Development* (Newbury Park, CA.: Sage Publications, 1990), p. 54.

24. Eisenstadt, *Tradition, Change, and Modernity*, p. 11.

25. Peter L. Berger, *Pyramids of Sacrifice* (N.Y.: Basic Books, Inc., 1974), p. 38.

26. So, p. 30.

27. Higgott, pp. 19-20.

28. See Leonard Binder el al.

29. David E. Apter, *The Politics of Modernization* (The University of Chicago Press, 1965), p. 67.

30. Ibid.

31. Berger, p. 34.

32. Ibid.

33. Ibid., p. 37.

34. Almond and Verba, p. 34.

35. Binder et al., p. 24.

36. Apter, p. 10.

37. Manning Nash, *Unified Agenda: The Dynamics of Modernization in Developing Nations* (London: Westview Press, 1984), p. 6.

38. S. N. Eisenstadt, *Patterns of Modernity, Vol. I* (London: Frances Pinter, 1987), pp. 2-7.

39. Frederique Apffel Marglin and Stephan A. Maglin (eds.), *Dominating Knowledge* (Oxford: Claredon, 1990), p. 2.

40. The idea of "civilized culture" will be discussed in some detail in chapter 3.

41. Habermas, *Communicative Action, Vol. 1*, p. 149; also The Encyclopedia of Philosophy, Paul Edward (ed.), Vol. 2, p. 184.

42. Raymond Aron, *Main Currents in Sociological Thought, Vol. 2* trans. Richard Howard & Helen Weaver (N.Y.: Basic Books, 1965),

pp. 59-95; *Encyclopedia of Philosophy*, Paul Edwards (ed.), vol. 2, pp. 173-5.

43. Max Weber, *The Protestant Ethic and The Spirit of capitalism*, trans. Talcott Parsons (London: George Allen and Unwin, 1976) P. 32.

44. Edward Shils, *Tradition*, (The University of Chicago Press, 1981), pp. 12-22.

45. Daniel Lerner, *The Passing of Traditional Society* (Glencoe, Ill: The Free Press, 1958), p. 45.

46. Ibid., p. 46.

47. Ibid., pp. 46-7.

48. Ibid., p. 47.

49. H. T. Wilson, *Tradition and Innovation: The Idea of Civilization as Culture and its Significance* (Boston, Mass.: Routledge & Kegan Paul, 1984), p. 63; see also S. N. Eisenstadt, *Modernization: Protest and Change* (N.J.: Prentice-Hall, 1966), p. 55.

50. Samuel Huntington, "Goals of Developmental" in *Understanding Political Development*, Myron Wiener and Samuel Huntington, eds. (Boston: Little, Brown & Co., 1987), p. 25.

51. Eisenstadt , *Patterns of Modernity*, p. 13.

52. Ibid.

53. Berger, pp. 48-9.

54. See Bryan S. Turner, *Weber and Islam* (Boston: Routledge & Kegan Paul, 1974), p. 160.

55. Almond and Powell, pp. 21-3; also Almond and Verba, p.51.

56. Rostow, p. 26.

57. Soed Jatmoko, "Cultural Movements to Progress," in *Religion and Progress in Modern Asia*, Robert N. Bellah, ed. (N.Y.: The Free Press, 1965), p. 2.

Chapter 2

The Marxian Model of Development

I have argued in the previous chapter that the functionalist approach, which lies at the heart of modernization school, confuses two markedly distinct approaches to understanding development, the Marxian and the Weberian. This confusion results from the lack of a rigorous and systematic conceptualization of the phenomenon of social and political change. Modernization theorists borrow, in an ad hoc fashion, concepts and theorems developed within the confines of drastically different frames of reference, and use them eclectically to analyze developmental trends in Third World areas. While accepting Weber's version of development, which perceives modern social and political structures as the outcome of a long process of cultural rationalization, modernization theory embraces, at the same time, the Marxian postulate, according to which changes in the material substratum of Third World societies are bound to reshape the values and ideas of Third World people, and ultimately transform life in Third World societies from tradition to modernity. This materialistic perception of social and political change in the Third World was first envisaged by Marx, and explicitly articulated in one of his commentaries on Britain's colonial adventures in South Asia. In an Article published in the *New York Daily Tribune* in 1853, under the title "On Imperialism in India," Marx commented on Britain's formal colonization of India: "England has to fulfill a double mission in India: one destructive, the other generating-- the annihilation of old Asiatic society, and the laying of the material foundations of Western society in Asia."[1] Although Marx blamed the backwardness of the Indian society on the religious ethics of Hinduism, he predicted the near Westernization of India, not through cultural contacts, but rather through structural and technological changes.

In this chapter, I probe into the Marxist conception of development and examine the extent to which economic and technological changes can effect a true structural and cultural modernization. I argue that historical materialism cannot, by itself, provide us with a coherent account of historical change, and that we are therefore bound to study the historical evolution of consciousness if we are to understand the forces behind the structural development of modern (bourgeois) society.

Historical Materialism

Marx developed his theory of history, or historical materialism, in the wake of his criticism of what he saw as idealistic tendencies in German philosophy. In *The German Ideology,* written in collaboration with Friedrick Engels in 1845-46, Marx repudiated the highly abstract conception of history expounded by Hegel. Hegel depicted human history as the unfolding of the "Idea," i.e. as the evolution of the forms of consciousness, and their materialization in an increasingly more rational social forms.

Praising Hegel for discovering the dialectical method which depicted man not as a *given*, but as a *process*,[2] he, nevertheless, rejected the content of the Hegelian philosophy for failing to ground its categories in actual-life forms. He accused German philosophy, as it was exemplified in Hegel's thought, of mystifying history and life by relying exclusively on metaphysical categories that lack any grounding in empirical reality. Marx argued that history and society are more intelligible when viewed from a materialistic viewpoint, that is, when social forms are seen not as the manifestation of moral or ideological forms, but as their basis. As Marx put it:

> In direct contrast to German philosophy which descends form heaven to earth, here [from the materialistic perspective] we ascend from earth to heaven. . . . Morality, religion, metaphysics, all the rest of ideology and their corresponding forms of consciousness, thus no longer retain the semblance of independence. They have no history, no development, but men, developing their material production and their material intercourse, alter, along with this, their real existence, their thinking and the products of their thinking. Life is not determined by consciousness, but consciousness by life.[3]

The movement from the idealistic to the materialistic mode of thinking represents, for Marx, a shift in focus from the realm of consciousness, ideas, or religion, to the process of material production. Viewed from this perspective, Marx maintained, history appears not as the unfolding of the "Idea," but rather as the process of producing the means of subsistence, and therefore, as the process of preserving and refining the "material life itself."[4] To survive both as individuals and as a species, people have to produce their means of subsistence in labor and their species in reproduction. It follows that the process of production is, at once, natural and social. The production of the material means necessary for the perpetuation and refinement of life is contingent on people's ability to cooperate by entering into certain forms of social relationships, whereby the task of production is divided among the members of the social unit. It is this very act of division of labor, Marx insisted, is what precipitated historical development in the first place.[5]

The duality of the production process is, therefore, the key concept which Marx employed to explain historical development. The act of production of the material life of a specific society is conditioned by two components. First, the physical elements available for reproducing the material life itself, which Marx termed "productive forces." Secondly, the social relations which make the social cooperation needed for facilitating production possible, which Marx called "relations of production." Relations of production are essentially property relations, defining the conditions that allow people to have access to the means of production, and, consequently, the method of distributing the socially produced wealth.[6] Viewed from the bottom up, history appears as the evolution of the productive forces of society, both the human   and material, and the social intercourses corresponding to them.

Marx identified five essential historical stages corresponding to five different *modes of production* (i. e., five distinct forms of *productive forces* and the *property relations* associated with them): tribal, communal, feudalist, capitalist, and socialist. Social transformation from one historical stage to another is precipitated by internal contradictions which appear in each production mode, and gradually develop until they reach an epoch-making proportion, resulting thereby in the dissolution of one mode of production   and   the   creation   of   another.[7]   The   task   of understanding social development is reduced, from the Marxist point of view, to studying the "laws of motion" which govern the development of the internal contradictions generated within each of the five modes of production.[8]

Marx taught that the forces of production of an epoch, both the human and material, are created in the womb of the previous epoch.[9] The continuous growth of these forces creates an increasing tension between them and the predominant relations of production. Eventually, the tension culminates in a major crisis when the contradiction between the forces and relations of production becomes so severe that the latter have to give way to new forms of productive relations, more compatible with the emerging productive forces.[10] Yet the transformation from one epoch to another, Marx argued, is not automatic; nor is it smooth or peaceful. On the contrary, more often than not, this transition is carried out through a violent revolution, for the relations of production, predominant in a specific historical epoch, are promoted and perpetuated by the major social and political institutions. This means that the tensions and contradictions between the forces and relations of production manifest themselves in social antagonism between two distinct social classes, the beneficiaries of the current social organization, who have complete control over the major political and economic institutions of society on the one hand, and those who are part of the emerging productive forces, who see in the predominant institutions, and hence the relations of production created and maintained through them, an obstacle preventing them from realizing their potentials.

With the introduction of the concepts of "social class" and "class struggle," the process of development assumes a new, and more complicated, dimension. For, on the one hand, social development appears as a technological, and hence apolitical process, resulting from the gradual, but constant, evolution of man's technical ability to manipulate nature. On the other hand, development is contingent on the outcome of the political struggle between social classes. We cannot, therefore, devote our full attention to economic and technical activities if we are to fully comprehend the process of development. We have to pay equal attention to social and political activities, which, according to Marx, reflect the continuous struggle and tension between major social groups, and which occasionally assume the form of violent clashes and collisions. Clearly, the concept of class struggle brings additional complications to our endeavor to understand the root causes of historical change, especially when Marx attributes to the struggle between classes a central role in historical development, so much so that he could proclaim that "[t]he history of all hitherto existing society is the history of class struggle."[11] To undermine the sociopolitical structure, or superstructure, hindering the progress of the economic base, a class has to arise, and enter into political struggle with the ruling class.

The difficulty confronting us in this three-story model of society (i.e., the division of society into *superstructure* and *economic base*, and the subsequent division of the economic base into *relations of production* and *forces of production*) expounded by Marx lies in understanding the essence of historical change. Is social development a natural process, subject to "natural" forces outside the control and influence of conscious individuals? Or, alternatively, is it a social phenomenon inspired by the purposive actions of meaningful human beings, who actively contemplate and cooperate for achieving social change?

The difficulty inherent in the Marxian account of historical change may be appreciated when it is realized that Marx does not see the struggle between the classes as an attempt on the part of the oppressed class, motivated by some ideals, to assert certain rights (e.g. justice, equality, freedom, fair share, etc.), but regards it as simply the consequence of economic 'facts,' working independently of the intentions and purposive actions of the social classes who are engaged in a political struggle. "Communism is for us not a *state of affairs* which is to be established, an *ideal* to which reality [will] have to adjust itself." Marx wrote in *The German Ideology*. "We call communism the real movement which abolishes the present state of things."[12]

Marx, therefore, does not perceive the deformation of structural forms, reflected in the oppressive nature of the relations of production, to be the manifestation of distorted forms of consciousness, but sees it as a consequence of forces which lie in the economic and technological substructures. This already complicated conception of historical change becomes even more equivocal when it is realized that Marx does not perceive historical development to be 'natural' in the positivist sense, i.e. a process effected by universal laws similar to those advocated by classic political economists. In the *Economic and Philosophic Manuscripts of 1844,* Marx rebuked the political economists for predicating their conception of the market on conditions created by the very economic structure they were supposed to explain.

Do not let us go back to a fictitious primordial condition as the political economist does, when he tries to explain such a primordial conditions explains nothing. He merely pushes the question away into a grey nebulous distance. He assumes in the form of fact, of an event, what he is supposed to decide.[13]

Marx's polemical writings have made the task of Marxists who endeavored to expound his ideas all more difficult, and gave rise to numerous interpretations and explications of his theory of history. One can identify, nonetheless, *two main interpretations* of historical materialism among Marxists writers: The *reductionist* interpretation espoused by Lenin and orthodox Marxists, which advances *economic determinist* views of history; and the *revisionist* interpretation adopted by Engels after the death of Marx, and later expounded and refined by Gramsci, Lukacs, Althusser, and, most recently, by Habermas.

The Reductionist Interpretation

The reductionist interpretation of historical materialism assigns the locus of change to the economic base of society. According to this view, changes take place mainly in the economy, and more specifically in the forces of production, thereby prompting a conflict between the forces and relations of production. Technological development in the means of production transforms the essential composition of the productive forces, thereby forcing a change in the relations of production; the latter have to change so as to become compatible with the new forces. With the creation of new relations of production, the whole superstructure would have to change so as to reflect the new order. Viewed from this perspective, historical materialism is reduced to a "technological determinism" theory, whereby the economic base assumes a one-sided causal relationship with the superstructure, in which the latter appears to reflect changes occuring in the former. Changes in the forces of production leads to changes in the relations of production, which in turn result in changes in the superstructure. The reductionist version of historical materialism is succinctly epitomized in a frequently quoted passage in the Preface of Marx's *Contribution to the Critique of Political economy*.

In the social production of their life, men enter into definite relations that are indispensable and *independent of their will,* these relations of production which correspond to a definite stage of development of their material productive forces. The sum total of these relations of production constitutes *the economic structure of society, the real foundation, on which rises a legal and political superstructure* and to which correspond a definite forms of social consciousness. The mode of production in material life *conditions* the social, political, and intellectual life process in general. It is not the consciousness of men that determines their being, but, on the contrary, their social being that determine their consciousness. At a certain stage of their development, the material productive forces in society come in conflict with the existing relations of production, or–what is but a legal expression for the same thing–with the property relations within which they have been at work hitherto. From forms of development of the forces of production these relations turn into their fetters. Then begins an epoch of social revolution. *With the change of the economic foundation the entire immense superstructure is more or less rapidly transformed.*[14]

This passage, which was quoted approvingly by Lenin[15] as representing the core of the Marxist theory of history, has all the ingredients of economic reductionism, and even technological determinism. For here we find Marx unequivocally (a) attributing social relations to the level of development of the "material forces of production"; (b) establishing one-sided causal relationship between the "mode of production" and the "social, political and intellectual life processes" in which, he proclaims, the latter are "determined" by the former; and (c) concluding that the change in the "economic foundation" inevitably precipitates the total transformation of society's "superstructure."

The reductionist account of historical materialism is not confined to the Preface, but could be found elsewhere in the writings of Marx. In a letter addressed to P. V. Annekov, Marx forcefully attacked the notion of universal reason, which Pierre-Joseph Proudhon posited, in his book *The Philosophy of Poverty* (1846). The notion of universal reason was introduced by Proudhon in an attempt to explain the discrepancy between historical development and the lack of an overall awareness of this development among the bulk of individuals who contribute to historical progress. Marx later expounded his critique of Proudhon's views in a book he published in 1847 under the title

The Poverty of Philosophy. In unequivocal terms, Marx insisted that changes in social relations, or the relations of production as he put it, is the immediate and direct result of the "change and growth of the productive forces."[16] The level of development of the technological skills that society possesses determine the nature of production relations, and consequently the structure and culture of society in general. "Assume particular stage of development in production, commerce and consumption," Marx wrote, "and you will have a corresponding civil society."[17]

The mechanisms which facilitate the transformation of society from one historical stage to another involve increased contradictions between the forces of production (i.e., the new means of production and technological skills) and the prevailing relations of production. The technology and the means of production associated with a particular historical stage do not come to existence simultaneously with this stage, but they rather emerge in the previous stage. According to Marx, The means of production and exchange of the capitalist stage of history were generated in the feudal society. The bourgeois revolution which took place in European countries was precipitated by the increased incompatibility between production relations and productive forces. That is, as the forces of production grow, the relation of production are turned into fetters, preventing the further development of the productive forces, thereby prompting those who are suppressed by the ossified ruling institutions to revolt and overthrow the established political order. The bourgeois revolution was able, therefore, to abolish the feudal relations of production by establishing new property relations more conducive to advancing the interests of the bourgeoisie. In many respects, however, the bourgeois revolution is not over yet, for it is still working today, Marx contended, to complete its mission of destroying the reminisces of the old superstructure, including the forms of consciousness which existed under the old regime. Marx clearly realized the far-reaching implications of the changes brought about by the bourgeois revolution. He realized that all ideas, values, and beliefs which once existed and gave meaning and structure to the old society have come under devastating and unsparing attacks.

> The bourgeoisie cannot exist without constantly revolutionizing the instruments of production, and thereby the relations of production, and with them the whole relations of society. . . . Constant revolutionising of production, uninterrupted

disturbance of all social conditions, everlasting uncertainty and agitation distinguish the bourgeois epoch from all earlier ones. *All fixed, fast-frozen relations, with their train of ancient and venerable prejudices and opinions, are swept away, all new-formed ones become antiquated before they can ossify.* All that is solid melts into air, all that is holy is profaned, and man is at last compelled to face with sober senses, his real conditions of life, and his relations with his kind.[18]

According to Marx, the bourgeois forces were actively working to destroy all social and cultural forms associated with human existence up until now. The destructive activities of the bourgeoisie were a welcome news to Marx, for the dismantling of the old order and the disappearance of premodern personality was a necessary step for setting the ground for the emergence of new forms of life, a new human species unlike anything known before.

Although Marx was clearly uncertain as to the exact structure future life would resemble, he asserted in the strongest possible terms, and with great optimism, that regardless of the shape or form life would take under communism, it was going to be much freer, and significantly more superior. By no means did he argue that communism was an ideal to be realized by the people. Rather it was the culmination of all the historical evolution of society from times immemorial, and a happy ending to a long history of pain and suffering. Marx saw communism as the fulfillment of social needs, not the realization of moral ideals. He, therefore, insisted that his mission was not one of a moralist philosopher preaching equality, advocating human rights, or defending the interests of the dispossessed and the have-nots. Rather, he saw himself as a scientific researcher whose job was to understand the "laws of motion" of history in general, and capitalism in particular.[19] Marx condemned all forms of consciousness which transpired in the past, for they were all grounded in religion. To him, religion was "the sigh of the oppressed," an attempt to find some sort of condolence for the earthly suffering of man—an illusory happiness of man that is. Religion, Marx once wrote, is "the sentiment of a heartless world, and the soul of soulless conditions."[20] Although he recognized the revolutionary role played by the Protestant Reformation in changing society and transforming life forms, he saw the revolution led by Martin Luther as incomplete one. For while Luther was able to undermine the authority of the Church, he endeavored to strengthen the authority of faith and conviction. As Marx put it:

> Luther, without question, overcomes servitude through devotion but only by substituting servitude through *conviction*. He shattered the faith in authority by restoring the authority of faith. He transformed the priests into laymen by turning laymen into priests. He liberated man from external religiosity by making religiosity the innermost essence of man. He liberated the body from its chains because he fettered the heart with chains.[21]

In addition to his deterministic views regarding social development, which he expressed in very unequivocal terms as I tried to illustrate above, Marx's writings espouse another, albeit less prominent, view where the purposive actions of individuals are depicted to have exerted some significant influence over historical development. In the opening of "The Eighteenth Brumaire of Louis Bonaparte" (1851), Marx put forth a milder version of his theory of history in which he struck a delicate balance between social structures and individual actions. "Men make their own history," he wrote, "but they do no make it just as they please, they do not make it under circumstances chosen by themselves, but under circumstances directly found, given and transmitted from the past. The tradition of all the dead generations weigh like a nightmare on the brain of the living."[22] This statement seems to lend some credibility to the notion that the purposive actions of people play a positive role in shaping history, while recognizing, at the same time, the limits imposed by social institutions and culture on individual choice. That is to say, Marx seems to argue that although social institutions limit individual choice and action, this limitation could be overcome when the will needed for transforming these institutions is generated among the members of society. And so it is under the control of men to change their "circumstances" if people's attachment to the old institutions could be undermined. Marx, however, categorically rejected the notion that institutions are ultimately grounded in individual commitment to a set of values or ideals, insisting that institutions are grounded in the economic base of society. Marx's account of social change raises an important question regarding the nature of the interrelationship between *structure* and *agency*. Are social institutions and norms grounded in a historical patterns of primarily technological nature, or are they anchored in social beliefs and values?

The question of how historical change relates to the conscious actions of people became the major concern of Marxist revolutionaries who attempted to realize Marx's vision of a communist state. In *What Is To Be Done?*, Lenin, the leading spokesman of orthodox Marxism, grappled with this question. He realized that the proletariat are not capable by themselves of developing a socialist consciousness. The most they can hope for, he insisted, is a trade-union consciousness. As he put it:

> We have said that there could not have been social-democratic consciousness among the workers. It could only have been brought to them from without. The history of all countries shows that *the working class exclusively by its own efforts is able to develop only trade-union consciousness*, i.e., the conviction that it is necessary to combine in unions, fight the employer. . . . *The teaching of socialism, however, grew out of the philosophic, historic, and economic theories, elaborated by educated representatives of the propertied classes, by the intelligentsia.*[23]

In short, the socialist worldview is developed first in the consciousness of the bourgeois intellectual, and later introduced to the worker's. Lenin concluded therefore that the proletarian revolution has to be led by bourgeois-turned-socialist intellectuals, who have acquired, by studying historical materialism, an insight to the nature of historical change.

Yet Lenin himself did not seem to have fully realized the far-reaching theoretical implications of the practical problem he grappled with. For while emphasizing the crucial role played by theory and consciousness in effecting practical changes in society, and attacking vulgar Marxists who naively believed that "politics always obediently follows economics,"[24] he continued to vigorously support the orthodox (reductionist) version of historical materialism, insisting that the economic system is "the foundation on which the political superstructure is erected."[25] However, while Lenin remained oblivious to the theoretical ramifications of the inconsistencies he uncovered in the orthodox interpretation of historical materialism, later Marxist philosophers (e.g. Lukacs, Gramsci, Althusser, etc.) had to deal with the aftermath of Lenin's important discovery, and tried to repair the damage he did to the theoretical basis of historical materialism, by offering a new interpretation which took into account the significant role the ideological superstructure of society plays in social development, i.e. the revisionist interpretation.

The Revisionist Interpretation

The first attempt to restore the role of individual wills and social purposes to the process of social change, and to repudiate economic determinism was made by Marx's lifelong intellectual partner, Friedrick Engels. In a letter to J. Bloch, dated 21 September 1890, Engels noted that young Marxists have exaggerated the significance of the economic base in the evolution of history. He admitted that he and Marx were partially responsible for misleading young Marxists, but denied that he and Marx had ever intended to advocate an economic reductionist conception of history. "Marx and I," he wrote, "are ourselves partly to blame for the fact that the younger people sometimes lay more stress on the economic side than is due to it."[26] In his argument, Engels recognized the relevant role played by superstructural elements in effecting social change, but insisted nonetheless that ultimately the *locus of change* resides in the economy.

> Thus past history proceeds in *the manner of a natural process* and is essentially subject to the same laws of motion. But from the fact that individual wills–of which each desires what he is impelled to by his physical constitution and external, *in the last resort economic,* circumstances . . . – do not attain what they want, but are merged into a collective mean, a common resultant, it must not be concluded that their value is equal to zero.[27]

The theme advanced by Engels was picked up by a number of leading twentieth-century Marxists,[28] who came to appreciate the significant role played by cultural spheres in determining developmental trends. In *History and Class Consciousness*, George Lukacs rejected the deterministic and one-sided interpretation of historical change advocated by orthodox Marxism. He contended that the process of development leading to communism is far from being the direct and spontaneous consequence of economic or technological change.

It could easily appear at this point that the whole process is nothing more than the 'inevitable' consequence of concentrating masses of workers in large factories, of mechanising and standardising the processes of work and levelling down the standard of living. It is therefore of vital importance to see the truth concealed behind this deceptively one-sided picture. . . . It is self-evident that immediacy must be abandoned at this point. If the attempt is made to attribute an immediate form of existence to class consciousness, it is not possible to avoid lapsing into mythology: the result will be a mysterious species-consciousness (as enigmatic as the 'spirits of the nation' in Hegel).[29]

Lukacs, likewise, cautioned that the goal of the proletarian movement does not exist in "a 'state of the future' awaiting the proletariat somewhere independent of the movement and the path leading up to it."[30] The goal of the proletariat, he remarked, *cannot be realized as part of a natural process* that may proceed regardless of the willful intents and the purposive actions of the working class. Nor is the ultimate goal an ideal, arbitrarily chosen by the proletariat in isolation of actual social processes. The ultimate goal of the proletariat is rather realized as a result of the interaction among the various cultural and social spheres of society.[31] "Only in this context which sees the isolated facts of social life as aspects of the historical process and *integrates them in a totality,* can knowledge of the facts hope to become knowledge of reality."[32] In essence, Lukacs contends in this passage that social change presupposes two factors. First, the presence of social or factual conditions, which warrant and call for such change. In the case of the bourgeois society, these conditions present themselves in the inequitable distribution of societal wealth among social classes. Second, social change does not automatically result from the inequity experienced by the working class, but is contingent on the awareness of the source of social inequity on the part of the proletariat. Only when the working classes realize that their misery is the outcome of the internal contradictions of the bourgeois society that the restructuring of social relations become possible.

Lukacs's interpretation of the theory of historical materialism represents a significant departure from the original statement of the theory by Marx. For here we are not faced with a question of historical determinism in which certain changes seem inevitable as a result of mechanical processes taking place apart from the purposive actions of the people involved. Social forms peculiar to capitalism, despite their inadequacy, can be, and are indeed, reified, Lukacs contended, and may continue to exist indefinitely until the proletariat develop a "class consciousness" and decides to do something about them.

> Reification is, then, the necessary immediate reality of every person living in capitalist society. It can be overcome only by constant and constantly renewed efforts to disrupt the reified structure of existence by concretely relating to the concretely manifested contradictions of the total development, by becoming conscious of the immanent meanings of these contradictions for the total development.[33]

The significance of Lukacs's reinterpretation of historical materialism is that it underscores the important role the superstructure plays in sustaining the economic structure.

The emphasis on the *totality* of human experience and the *integrity* of social life brings to the fore the question of the impact cultural forms have on social structures. That is to say, the introduction of the concept of totality brings Hegel back to the theoretical debate, and makes Hegelian categories relevant to the study of history. For if politics does not "obediently follows economics,"[34] and if class consciousness (i.e. "the ideological maturity of the proletariat"[35]) is an essential determinant of historical change, one can hardly dismiss Hegel (culture) as irrelevant. Hegelian ideas would have to be resuscitated and married to Marxian ideas so that the one-sidedness of orthodox Marxism can be counterbalanced by the one-sidedness of Hegelianism. In short, orthodox Marxism had to be replaced by Hegelian Marxism. Marx, therefore, had to be presented not as the theorist who repudiated and rejected Hegel's philosophy, but rather as the one who perfected and brought it to its logical conclusion. Lukacs remarked:

> In this sense Marx's critique of Hegel is the direct continuation and extension of the criticism that Hegel himself levelled at Kant and Fichte. So it came about that Marx's dialectical method continued what Hegel had striven for but had failed to achieve in a concrete form.[36]

The theme of the totality of social experience and the interdependence of the various aspects of social life, alluded to by Lukacs, was further advanced by the French Marxist Louis Althusser. In a book published in 1965, under the title *For Marx*, Althusser embraced the revisionist interpretation of historical materialism, introduced early on by Engels, and further refined by Gramsci and Lukacs. In his book, Althusser pointed to the intricate web of reciprocal relations existing among the various levels and segments of society. Given the intricate nature of social interrelations, one cannot, Althusser proclaimed, reduce historical development to a single factor, or explain social change on the basis of a single determinant. Economic contradictions between social classes cannot, and should not, be assessed in isolation of the cultural forms Marx assigned to the superstructure. For, after all, while the economic base is a determinant of social and cultural forms, it is itself determined by these forms. Law, politics, and ideology are not simply the reflection of economic contradictions, for they themselves are presupposed by economic relations. Economic activities, capitalist or otherwise, do not exist in a vacuum, but presuppose the emergence of certain ideas and values which are embedded in law and played out in politics.[37]

Yet while Althusser appropriated Lukacs's conception of *totality* he rejected the latter's efforts to study Marx through Hegel. Evidently, Althusser wrote *For Marx*, in part to purge Western Marxism of Hegel, after Lukacs and Gramsci integrated his ideas into Marxist thought. "Why do many Marxist philosophers," Althusser exclaimed, "seem to feel the need to appeal to the pre-Marxist ideological concept of alienation in order supposedly to think and resolve these concrete historical problems?"[38] To extricate Marx from Hegel, Althusser contended that beginning with *The German Ideology*, Marx experienced an "epistomological break" with his Hegelian past. Althusser wrote:

In 1845, Marx broke radically with every theory that based history and politics on an essence of man. This unique rupture contained three indissociable elements. (1) The formation of a theory of history and politics based on radically new concepts: the concepts of social formation, productive forces . . . (2) A radical critique of the theoretical pretensions of every philosophical humanism. (3) The definition of humanism as an ideology.[39]

Althusser contended, moreover, that the mature Marx did repudiate his early reductionist views in which historical changes were attributed to economic and technological changes. Reducing the dialectic of history to successive modes of production, he proclaimed, amounts to "economism or even technologism."[40] The economy should be seen only as *one factor in a comprehensive totality* combining, in addition to economic, social and political elements. However, he joined Engels and Lukacs in declaring that the economy is "in the last instance" the determinant of historical change.[41]

But how is it possible for Althusser to completely separate Marx from Hegel while continuing to embrace the concept of totality? And why is he, in the first place, so anxious to cleanse Marxism of all traces of Hegelian thought? To answer the latter question first, I propose that, as an astute thinker, Althusser reasoned that with the restoration of Hegel, Marxism would inevitably be transformed into a critical theory, used primarily for refining and bettering the moral, political, and economic practices of Western liberalism. He, therefore, feared that if this trend was allowed to continue, Marxists would soon be reduced to mere critics of bourgeois philosophy. He thus insisted that the Marxist and Hegelian conceptions of totality are markedly distinct. The Hegelian totality sees historical change as the evolution of a simple unified principle, i.e. the Hegelian Idea.

> The Hegelian totality is the alienated development of a simple unity, of a simple principle, itself a moment of the development of the Idea: so, strictly speaking, it is the phenomenon, the self-manifestation of this simple principle which persists in all its manifestations, and therefore even in the alienation which prepares its restoration.[42]

The Marxist totality, on the other hand, is complex and multifaceted, or, to use Althusser's terminology, *overdetermined*, for it takes into account the various superstructural determinants of historical development, without losing sight of the crucially important factor, the determinant of historical change 'in the last instance,' i.e. the economy.[43]

One cannot help but notice that Althusser's characterization of the difference between the Hegelian and Marxian totality as one of *simplicity* versus *overdetermination* is arbitrary, and itself an oversimplification. For one thing, the Marxist totality, like the

Hegelian, can also be reduced to one simple principle, viz. production. As I tried to show earlier, the reductionist (orthodox) interpretation of historical materialism does just that, it insists that the history of mankind can be explained by making reference to one basic and simple principle of production. But Althusser's interpretation of Hegel is an oversimplification because it ignores the fact that Hegel managed to show that within the simple unity of the Idea lies a world of infinite complexity. Indeed, one of Hegel's major intellectual contributions was to illustrate how human reason is continuously perfecting itself through its successive encounters with reality. It is fair, therefore, to say that the difference between the Hegelian and Marxist totality is not one of simplicity versus overdetermination, but rather one of *inversion*. The former revolves around the ideal or the spiritual, the latter around the economic or the material.

Indeed the "inversion" metaphor was used by the *mature* Marx himself to characterize the difference between his dialectical method and that of Hegel. In the Preface to the second edition of *Capital*, Marx remarked:

> The mystification which the dialectic suffers in Hegel's hands by no means prevents him from being the first to present its general forms of motion in a comprehensive and conscious manner. With him it is standing on its head. It must be inverted, in order to discover the rational Kernel within the mystical shell.[44]

And so if one is permitted to claim that the Marxist totality is only economic "in the last instance," one should also be permitted to argue that the Hegelian totality is spiritual (cultural) only in *the last instance*.

But is Althusser's, and Lukacs's for that matter, revision of the Marxian theory of history a real solution to our problem, or is it merely an equivocation of the meaning of the materialistic interpretation of history advanced by Marx? By recognizing that the superstructural elements of society do not merely stand at the receiving end of historical change, but are themselves active determinants of history, Lukacs and Althusser helped in bringing more balance, and hence more credibility, to the Marxist theory of history. The former managed to do so by restoring Hegel to the Marxist dialectic, the latter by injecting an intrinsically Hegelian conception, i.e. the totality or the whole, to Marxism while denying the relevance of its theoretical roots. Ultimately, however, both thinkers remained faithful to the materialistic perception of history, by insisting that, at bottom, the economy is the final determinant of historical development. Yet having acknowledged that the restructuring of society would have ultimately to await the emergence of class consciousness and that social transformation was the result of the purposive actions of the working class, their assertion of the primacy of the economic was dogmatic. For how it could be otherwise when it is stated that the collapse of one order and the creation of another is *dependent* on the reorientation of people's perception of reality, and the alteration of their ideas and thoughts. How could it be otherwise when it is admitted that the rise and fall of the social order is contingent on the restructuring of consciousness forms, which are, after all, located in the cultural, not economic, spheres of social existence.

If it is admitted that social structures cannot rise and fall on their own, but only in correspondence to changes that take place on the cultural plane, i.e. changes in the social consciousness of the relevant actors, one can in vain talk about the primacy of the economic, or defend a model of society in which economic forms are placed at the center of historical evolution. In fact, long before Althusser observed the impact the superstructure has on the development of the economic base, Marx himself noted, without dwelling on the question, the significant role the Protestant Reformation played in setting the tone for the emancipation of the German people. Marx admitted that the ongoing struggle for the emancipation of the German society, in which he was an active participant, became possible only because it was preceded by a "theoretical revolution," signified in the Protestant Reformation. As he put it:

> Even from the historical standpoint theoretical emancipation has a specific practical importance for Germany. In fact Germany's *revolutionary* past is theoretical–it is the *Reformation*. In that period the revolution originated in the brain of a monk, today in the brain of the philosopher.[45]

In this passage, Marx touched upon an important trend in the evolution of the modern West, a trend which has far-reaching implications for the study of non-Western modernization. For here one can see that Western society experienced two distinct types of revolutions: *theoretical* and *practical*. The Reformation signaled the beginning of the theoretical revolution, the restructuring of Western consciousness. By the time Marx wrote this passage, Europe was undergoing the practical revolution, which manifested itself in *production* (the Industrial Revolution) as well as in *social relations* (The Puritan and French Revolutions). Marx, along with other socialist thinkers, was preoccupied with the question of restructuring society, devoting himself primarily to uncovering the flaws of capitalist distribution. However, the significance of the theoretical development for the subsequent changes in Western society was, apparently of little interest to him. The question of the relationship between the Protestant Reformation and subsequent changes in the German society in particular, and in Western Europe in general, a question which Marx touched upon without given it serious thought, had to await for Max Weber. As we will see in the next chapter, Weber took up the task of analyzing the impact the Reformation had on the development of the Occident. Not only did Weber propose an alternative way of thinking about historical development and change, but he presented a diametrically opposed explanation to that of Marx by arguing that it was not the bourgeois superstructure that was grounded in the capitalist economic base, but rather that It was capitalism which was anchored in the Protestant morality.

Notes

1. Karl Marx, "On Imperialism in India," in The Marx-Engels Reader, Robert C.Tucker (ed.) (N.Y.: Norton, 1978), p. 659.

2. Marx, *The Philosophic and Economic Manuscripts of 1944* in Robert C.Tucker, The Marx-Engels Reader (ed.), 2nd ed. (N.Y.: W. W. Norton & Company, 1978), p.112

3. Marx in Tucker, p. 155.

4. Karl Marx and Frederick Engels, *The German Ideology* in Tucker, pp. 156-64.

5. Ibid., p. 156.

6. Ibid., p. 157, 164.

7. Marx, *The German Ideology* in Tucker, pp. 150-7.

8. Marx, *Preface to the Critique of Political Economy* in *Karl Marx Selected Writings*, ed. David McLellan (Oxford University Press, 1077).

9. Marx and Engels, *The Communist Manifesto* in Tucker, p. 478.

10. Marx and Engels, T*he German Ideology*, p. 198.

11. Ibid., p. 473.

12. Ibid., p. 162.

13. Marx, *The Economic and Philosophic Manuscript of 1844* in Tucker p.71.

14. Karl Marx, *The Preface to A Contribution to the Critique of Political Economy* in David McLellan, ed., *Karl Marx Selected Writings* (Oxford University Press, 1977), P. 389.

15. Quoted in Lenin, *Introduction to Marx, Engels, Marxism* (N.Y.: International Publishers, 1987), p.65.

16. Marx in Tucker, p. 140.

17. Ibid., p. 136.

18 Marx, *The Communist Manifesto* in Tucker, p. 476.

19. See The Preface to the second edition of *Capital: A Critique of Political Economy, Vol. 1*, 2nd ed. trans. Ben Fowkes (N.Y.: Vintage Books, 1977), p. 90.

20. Marx, *Contribution to the Critique of Political Economy* in Tucker, p. 54.

21. Ibid., p.60.

22. Marx in Tucker, p. 594.

23. Lenin, *What Is To Be Done?*, p. 98.

24. Ibid., p. 109.

25. Lenin, *Marx, Engels, and Marxism*, p. 43.

26. Quoted in Althusser, *For Marx*, trans. Ben Brewster (N.Y.: Pantheon Books, 1069) p. 120.

27. Quoted in Althusser, *For Marx*, p. 120. Stress in mine.

28. Gramsci, Lukacs, Althusser, and Habermas to count a few.

29. George Lukacs, *History and Class Consciousness*, trans. Rodney Livingstone (Cambridge, Mass.: The MIT Press, 1971), p. 173.

30. Ibid., p. 22.

31. Ibid.

32. Ibid., p.9.

33. Ibid., p. 197

34. Lenin, *What Is To Be Done?*, p. 109.

35. Lukacs, *History and Class Consciousness* , p. 70.

36. Ibid., p. 17.

37. Althusser, *For Marx*, pp. 95-101.

38. Ibid., p. 239.

39. Althusser, *For Marx*, p. 227.

40. Ibid., p. 108.

41. Ibid., p. 112. Quoting Engels, Lukacs wrote in *History and Class Consciousness* : "By recognizing that 'the production and

reproduction of real life (is) in the last resort the decisive factor in history', Marx and Engels gained a vantage point from which they could settle accounts with all methodologies." (p. 18).

42.Althusser, *For Marx*, p. 203.
43. Ibid., pp. 204-6.
44. Marx, *Capital*, p. 103.
45. Marx, *Contribution*, p. 60.

Chapter 3

The Weberian Model
of Development

Modernization as Rationalization

Marx neglected, we noted in the previous chapter, to account for
the theoretical revolution which took place at the dawn of modern
(bourgeois) society, i. e. the Reformation. To assess the
significance of the Reformation and its implications for Western
modernity we have to turn to Max Weber, who devoted much of
his writings to analyzing the nature of the theoretical revolution
which lay at the root of Western civilization.

In this chapter, I discuss in general terms Weber's account of
Western modernity. My objective here is twofold. First, to locate
the essential determinants which gave rise to the phenomenon we
call modernity. Secondly, to identify the *patterns* according to
which the process of modernization has been unfolding in
Western society. Such an analysis is necessary and crucial for
studying the process of modernization in Third World regions.
We will see in Chapter 4 that the patterns of change taking place
in Western society have far-reaching implications for the
possibilities of non-Western modernization.

Weber set out to examine the process of modernization in
Western society and isolate the "combination of circumstances"
leading to the rise of Western civilization. More specifically,
Weber was interested in revealing the social and cultural
underpinnings of Western capitalism. In *The Protestant Ethic and
The Spirit of Capitalism,* Weber rejected the notion advanced
earlier by Marx, according to which capitalism was attributed to
the development of new technological possibilities. Weber
conceded that "modern Western form of capitalism" was
distinguished by "the technical utilization of scientific
knowledge." He contended however that the drive to
technological and scientific advancement, though encouraged by
economic considerations, was rooted in the "particularities of the

social structure of the Occident."[1] Among the particularities of Western society which made the rise of "rational" capitalism possible Weber cited the "rational structures of law and administration." For "rational capitalism" presupposes a legal and administrative systems which permit the "calculability" of economic action. Yet Weber still attributed the emergence of rational law and administration to more fundamental basis, namely cultural values and beliefs. "For though the development of economic rationalism is partly dependent on rational technique and law," he observed, "it is at the same time determined by the ability and disposition of men to adopt certain types of practical rational conduct."[2]

Weber perceived *rationalism* to be the essence of Western modernity, and used the term *rationalization,* therefore, to refer to the process of Western modernization. In *The Protestant Ethic,* Weber, though taking every opportunity to remind us of the complexity of the process of rationalization, advanced a relatively simple thesis. Weber attributed the new capitalistic impulses to ethical emancipation effected by the emerging Protestant worldviews. Weber succinctly summarized his views at the end of *The Protestant Ethic*:

> This worldly Protestant asceticism, as we may recapitulate up to this point, acted powerfully against the spontaneous enjoyment of possessions; it restricted consumption, especially of luxuries. On the other hand, it had the psychological effect of freeing the acquisition of goods from the inhibitions of traditionalistic ethics. It broke the bonds of the impulse of acquisition in that it not only legalized it, but (in the sense discussed) looked upon it as directly willed by God.[3]

The peculiarity of the modern system of Western capitalism was, according to Weber, revealed in its emphasis on the "calculability" of economic action. First, economic action is *calculable* because it is anchored in a cultural worldview which sees natural phenomena operating in accordance with rational, and hence scientifically discoverable, laws. Second, action is calculable because it is based on a system of production and exchange where transactions are legitimized not by emotional appeals, but are made pursuant to the rational principle of self-interest. Third, economic action is calculable because the legal and administrative systems are based on a set of rational principles, which enable individual actors to fairly anticipate and predict short and long term consequences of their actions.[4] Clearly, the calculability of economic action is linked, in the mind of Weber, directly to the rationality of its cultural and social environment. Yet for Weber, the concept of rational action is not limited to economic activities, but permeates virtually all aspects of human existence. We are still, therefore, confronted with the question: what does Weber mean by the term rationality, and what are the principal characteristics of rationalism?

It would be worthwhile to note, before we attempt to examine the meaning of the term rationality, that the Weberian conception of rationalism is exceedingly complex. It takes a multiplicity of meanings pursuant to the context in which it is employed, and to the sphere of life to which it refers. Similarly, the process of rationalization is multidimensional, proceeding on different levels of human consciousness, and taking place within various spheres of social life. Furthermore, the process of rationalization does not necessarily proceed in the various spheres of life toward an integral set of goals, but may progress in different directions, and pursue diverse sets of objectives.

> Now by this term [rationalism] very different things may be understood, as the following discussion will repeatedly show. There is, for example, rationalization of mystical contemplation, that is of an attitude which viewed from other department of life, is specifically irrational, just as much as there are rationalizations of economic life, of technique, of scientific research, of military training, of law and administration. Furthermore, each one of these fields may be rationalized in terms of very different ultimate values and ends, and what is rational from one point of view may well be irrational from another.[5]

The many possible meanings of the concept of rationalization can be reduced, however, to two basic levels of meaning: rationalization of belief, or *cultural rationalization,* and rationalization of action, or *structural rationalization.* By rationalization of belief, Max Weber refers to the process of reexamining cultural worldviews, whereby all ideas and values inconsistent with a core set of beliefs are systematically eliminated through a program of cultural *self-criticism.* Rationalization of action, on the other hand, refers to the ordering of social activities in accordance with an underlying principle or criterion. That is, social actions should be systematized so as to bring about the realization of some well-defined ends.

> We have to remind ourselves in advance that 'rationalism' may mean very different things. It means one thing if we think of the kind of rationalization the systematic thinker performs on the image of the world: an increasing theoretical mastery of reality by means of increasingly precise and abstract concepts. Rationalism means another thing if we think of the methodical attainment of a definitely given and practical end by means of an increasingly precise articulation of adequate means. These types of rationalization are very different, in spite of the fact that ultimately they belong inseparable together.[6]

In this passage, Weber points to the interconnectedness of culture and structure, of thinking and acting. Structural rationalization cannot proceeds on its own, but has to be associated and guided by cultural rationalization, a pattern attested to even by Marx, as we saw in the previous chapter, in his discussion of the Protestant Reformation. As it will be shown below, Weber goes on to advocate the primacy of cultural over structural modernization, and the dependency of the latter on the former.

The Orientation Of Action

Weber understands the rationalization (or modernization) of Western society as a comprehensive process, whereby the orientation of social action is gradually transformed. Weber posits that social change is contingent on intellectual and psychological changes, and therefore, he maintains all along that the reconfiguration of social structures is the result of a more fundamental reconfiguration, that of the structures of consciousness. Social change, therefore, reflects a change in the orientation of action, i.e., change in the meaning the actor associates with his action. To explain this transformation he introduces a fourfold typology. According to Weber, actions may be subsumed under four basic types of orientation: (1) instrumentally (or purposive) rational, (2) value rational, (3) affectual, and (4) traditional. Instrumentally rational is defined in terms of the *means* necessary for the attainment of certain given ends. The rationality of the action here pertains to the selection of *efficient means* for attaining desired ends. The ends themselves are not selected pursuant to any preconceived methods or standards, but discretely chosen by the actor himself. Value rational is determined by a *conscious* belief in an *absolute* value. The action is undertaken regardless of its prospects for success, and is justified on the basis of the actor's commitment to ethical, aesthetic, or religious principles. The affectual involves an *emotional* and impulsive reaction. The action is not based on deliberate or rational decision, but is rather induced by the actor's passions and feelings. Finally, the traditional is determined by "ingrained habituation," and hence, reflects the tendency of an actor to conform to customs and traditions.[7]

Weber conceives modernization as the movement from the least rationalized, i.e., traditional orientation, to the most rationalized, i.e., purposive orientation. The latter represents for Weber rationality *par excellence*, and hence is the richest in meaning. Traditional action is, on the other hand, devoid of meaning because it cannot be related to an intended purpose. Weber's classification, and consequently his conception of the process of modernization, is problematic. For he fails to distinguish between the meaning of an action and its motive. He considers the value-rational action to be less meaningful than the purposive rational because the intended purpose of the former is not directly related to the self-interest of the actor. In the case of value-rational action, both the purpose and the means of its realization are restricted by the actor's commitment to certain principles, such as duty or morality. These limitations on the individual freedom to act are absent in the case of purposive-rational action, for here both the ends and the means are directly chosen by the actor on the basis of their utility and effectiveness respectively. It is important to note that the first three types of action (purposive rational, value rational, and affectual) differ essentially in terms of their motives. They are respectively motivated by utility, value, and sentiment. The fourth type, the traditional, is a residual category. For traditional action seems to lack any motivational basis, except perhaps the desire to conform to prevailing rules. But even here the motivational basis of the traditional action could be reduced to one of three basic motivations: utility, morality, or sentiment.[8]

Yet the *motive* of an action is by no means identical with its *meaning*. For an action can be meaningful only when it is placed within the broader *purposes of life*. Any discrete action is meaningless unless it is viewed in the context of the cultural purposes of individual life. For example, the execution of a murderer is meaningless when we view the act of killing apart from its broader purposes. Only when the act of killing is linked to the concept of justice do we begin to apprehend the meaning associated with the act. The motive of the executor may or may not coincide with the real purpose of the act. The question of meaning or orientation of an action has to be looked at in two interrelated contexts: individual and social. Individually, the action should be understood in the context of the *life plan* of the individual. In the case of purposive orientation, the purpose of the action is supposedly not given, but chosen by the discrete judgment of the individual. Here the action is meaningful only insofar as it contributes to the fulfillment of the individual life project. Socially (or collectively), an action is meaningful when it advances the *common purposes* of the collectivity. In this regard, it is quite possible that a purposive-rational action may be meaningless, while an affectual action could be meaningful when it is evaluated from the standpoint of the collective purpose. An act of self-sacrifice in defense of national independence, induced by patriotism (affectual), or an absolute commitment to freedom (value rational), is far from being meaningless, and is certainly much richer in meaning than a shrewdly calculated act of betrayal of one's social obligations, motivated by the actor's self-interest (purposive rational).

Yet the ambiguity of the Weberian classification of action is not confined to the motive of the action, but extends to its goals. Weber's typology assumes that goals or purposes selected under the three basic orientations of action (purposive rational, value rational, and affectual) are determined respectively by the actor's ad hoc evaluation of the situation at hand, his moral commitment, and his emotional disposition. At first glance, the three classes of orientation appear to refer to separate systems of action. However, on closer examination it becomes clear that these classes reflect varying levels of meaning in an *integral* system of action. The affectual type is indicative of emotional and cultural dispositions to certain goals and purposes; purposive rational involves technical activities aimed at the realization of individual and social ends. These two types of orientation are governed by value rationality which constitutes the normative basis of action. Value rationality furnishes ethical justification for, and imposes social constraint on, individual action. The difference between purposive and value rationality resembles the difference between judgments on the desired ends of action, and the means required for attaining those ends. As Karl Mannheim puts it:

> The mechanistic mode of thought is of assistance only as long as the goal or the value is given from another source and the "means" alone are to be treated. The most important role of thought in life consists, however, in providing guidance for conduct when decisions must be made. Every real decision (such as one's evaluation of other persons or how society should be organized) implies a judgment concerning good and evil, concerning the meaning of life and mind.[9]

Weber himself came close to espousing the foregoing schematic interpretation of the interrelation between value-rational and purposive-rational action. In chapter II of *Economy and Society* (entitled "Sociological Categories of Economic Action"), Weber differentiates between technical and economic "rationality." "Rational" technique involves the selection of technical means for the attainment of a given end. The actor at this level is not concerned with the value judgment of the end, but takes it as a given. The rationality of the action at this level consists in the conscious and systematic efforts to improve and refine the instruments and methods, required for the realization of the goal, through the employment of technical knowledge. Rational economic action, on the other hand, involves decisions on the desirability of the ends.[10] Weber recognizes that the decision concerning the "economic" ends has to be made by employing some criteria. He chooses the economic self-interest of individual dealers as the only "rational" criterion for the purpose of regulating economic activities. (Clearly economic actions are subject to a variety of normative constraints, e.g., proscription of fraud, "fair" competition, faithful observation of the terms of contract, etc.) Weber writes:

> Economic action is primarily orientated to the problem of choosing the end to which a thing shall be applied; technology, to the problem, given the end, of choosing the appropriate means. For purposes of theoretical (not, of course, practical) definition of technical rationality it is wholly indifferent whether the product of a technical process is in any sense useful. In the present terminology . . . it would be possible . . . to apply the most modern methods to the production of atmospheric air. . . . Economically, on the other hand, the procedure would under

normal circumstances be clearly irrational because there would
be no demand for the product.[11]

Although Weber treats in this chapter utility maximization and
capital accumulation as non-normative criteria, he is fully aware
that these criteria are neither neutral nor universal, but are partial
to the cultural outlook of the Occident, and are ultimately rooted
in the religious subsoil of the Protestant ethics. Purposive
rationality can never exist apart from value rationality, for it has
to be anchored in the personality system as well as in the system
of institutions, both are organized around values and norms. In
short, value rationality constitutes the normative framework
which regulate purposive rationality.[12]

In light of the foregoing discussion, the process of
modernization may now be understood as the transformation of
society from one normative order to another, or from one
"tradition" to another. The change in attitudes and values is the
consequence of the reorientation of the individual, and it, in turn,
leads to social reorganization. If the new social order appears to
have abandoned traditionalism for rationalism, this is simply
because the normative order has gradually shifted from an order
that emphasizes collectivity, obligation, and communal interest,
to another placing emphasis on individuality, utility, and self-
interest. (the process which moved the human subject to the
center of the modern world is discussed at some length in
Chapter 4.)

The Disenchantment of The World

Historically, the transformation from tradition to modernity did
not happen suddenly, but occurred gradually over a relatively
long period of time. Moreover, the rationalization of Western
society was a *phased* process. We can identify, in the writings of
Weber, three distinct phases of Western rationalization:
intellectualization, differentiation, and formalization.

Intellectualization -- intellectualization of worldviews involves
the *systematization* of religious beliefs and the repudiation of
myth and superstition. The systematization was carried out
through a program of *self-criticism* aiming at overcoming
inconsistencies, and reorienting action towards worldly activities.
Weber credited the Reformation, and more specifically
Calvinism, for restructuring the theoretical doctrines of the

Occident, thereby effecting ethical-psychological change in the form of the Protestant ethic of "calling." The emergence of a Protestant ethics slanted toward worldly asceticism provided the "motivational basis for purposive action in the sphere of social labor."[13] At this phase, purposive-rational action continued to be confined to the framework of an *integral value-rational* system. That is to say, economic, political, and social purposes continued to be influenced by the doctrinal and ethical demands of religious worldviews.

The process of intellectualization, initially prompted by the Protestant Reformation, was furthered by the establishment of scientific methods and the advancement of technology.[14] One important aspect of intellectualism was what Weber, using Schiller's terminology, occasionally referred to as the "disenchantment of the world." By disenchantment Weber meant the gradual displacement of religious views and magical means with scientific views and technical means.[15] The world is no more governed by mysterious incalculable forces, but rather operates in accordance with discoverable laws

> . . . Intellectualist rationalization, created by science and by scientifically orientated technology . . . means that principally there are no mysterious incalculable forces that come into play, but rather that one can, in principle, master all things by calculation. This means that the world is disenchanted. One need no longer have recourse to magical means in order to master or implore the spirit, as did the savage, for whom such mysterious powers existed. Technical means and calculations perform the service. This above all is what intellectualism means.[16]

Rationalization of life spheres -- The process of intellectualization is a prelude for further rationalization. Once the conception of the mysterious incalculable old world is replaced by a new worldview, whereby the world is seen as a rational and calculable place, the ground is set for the processes of cultural and structural rationalization. According to Weber, cultural rationalization is set in motion when cultural worldviews, once unified and integrated by religion, are *differentiated into independent spheres,* detached from one another, and systematically developed according to their own inner purposes and logics. Cognitive, expressive, and moral aspects of the traditional culture grow into independent spheres of science, art, and morality. Social rationalization, on the other hand, reflects the institutional embodiment of modern structures of consciousness.[17] Societal rationalization is, therefore, a multidimensional phenomenon, combining psychological and social elements; the emerging purposive-rational orientations are anchored in both the personality system and the system of social institutions.[18] While Weber sees cultural rationalization in the scientific basis of knowledge, in autonomous art, and in professional ethics, he perceives structural rationalization to stem from the establishment of subsystems of purposive-rational action, including the political, the economic, the legal, and the administrative. Weber considers the *capitalist enterprise* and the *modern state* as the most developed spheres of modern society, and, therefore, the *cornerstone* of capitalist civilization. He associates the rationality of modern society with the *centralization* of economic production and political decision-making, both of which depend on specialization of tasks and application of scientific knowledge to production and administration, i.e. on bureaucratic administration.[19]

Weber is aware of the partial and imbalanced rationalization of the capitalist civilization. Like Marx, he recognizes that the highly rationalized economic organization, based on specialized knowledge and efficient techniques, is subordinated to "outside" interests, which take the form of "wealth" and "gambling" interests.[20] Under capitalism, the control over managerial positions is maintained not by the economic organization itself, but by stock holders. The partial rationalization of society is further reflected in the subordination of economic organization to the interests of the "capitalist entrepreneur."

> Superior to bureaucracy in the knowledge of techniques and facts is only the capitalist entrepreneur, within his own sphere of interest. He is the only type who has been able to maintain at least relative immunity from subjection to the control of rational bureaucratic knowledge.[21]

Weber is ambivalent when it comes to assessing the capitalist system. On the one hand, he recognizes the partial rationalization of modern capitalist system by pointing out to the subordination of the rational economic organization to outside, and therefore irrational, interests. On the other hand, he seems to take comfort in this partiality because it permits a zone of freedom in modern society and allows certain spheres of society to escape the "iron cage" of bureaucratic control.

Formalization -- Formalization is the most advanced stage in the process of rationalization. It is also the most problematic stage. For here, the differentiation of society and culture into autonomous spheres gradually assumes the form of *structural fragmentation of society and consciousness.* This fragmentation results from the increased tension between social and cultural spheres, on the one hand, and the absence of a unifying principle capable of integrating these spheres, on the other. As the various spheres of life grow under the influence of their own self-selected values and logics, their values become increasingly incompatible with one another. Eventually each particular sphere of life appears irrational when it is viewed from the perspective of others, and hence life loses its meaning.

To explain this seemingly paradoxical conclusion of the process of rationalization, Weber employs the concepts of *formal* and *substantive* rationality. By *formal rationality* Weber refers to technical adequacy and available means for achieving certain goals. The more efficient the techniques are the more formally rational the action is. By *substantive rationality* Weber means whether the action is consistent with a particular set of values and beliefs.[22] The rationalization of autonomous spheres of life poses a dilemma for modern man. This is because modern social subsystems (e.g., capitalist economy, technology, the legal and administrative systems, etc.) are rational only when they are viewed from the formal point of view. Substantively, however, social subsystems appear irrational when viewed from a particular substantive end or value. For example, capitalism is seen rational when it is judged from the point of view of utility maximization. It will be judged irrational when it is viewed from the perspective, say, of human solidarity. Likewise, bureaucratic administration may be deemed rational from the technical point of view (e.g., from the point of view of controlled and coordinated collective action.) But it would be seen completely irrational from the normative perspective of human dignity. "Bureaucracy develops the more perfectly," Weber observes, "the more completely it succeeds in eliminating from official business love, hatred, and all purely personal . . . and emotional which escape calculation."[23]

The formal rationalism of modern civilization is the direct cause of the fragmentation of consciousness and society. Weber shows that rationalization is not a single process, but a multiplicity of diverse and autonomous processes. Rationalization in the spheres of economy, law, administration, and religious ethics progresses in different directions and pursuant to different principles. Consequently, one can hardly find any unifying principle, or a set of principles, which may confer an overall meaning on modern experience. In modern society, one can talk only of *meaningful action,* but not *meaningful life.*

The loss of meaning, experienced by modern man, is the outcome of the historical process of cultural rationalization, which in the West took the form of *secularization* whereby the Enlightenment's effort to undermine the authority of organized religion culminated in undermining objective rationality as well. The modern dilemma caused by the *loss of meaning* is compounded by another, equally troubling, problem, viz. the problem of the *loss of freedom.* The loss of freedom results from the process of societal rationalization, which assumes, in the Western experience, the form of bureaucratic control. Although bureaucracy, which Weber considers to be the cornerstone of capitalist civilization, brings superior form of organization to society, it, at the same time, transforms society into an enormous human machine in which everyone has to fill in a socially predetermined niche, and perform a socially predesigned role. Clearly this mechanical environment, though resulting in a tremendously increased efficiency, undermines individual freedom, and turns society into an "iron cage."

The Weberian Paradox

In "Science as a Vocation," Weber agreed with Leo Tolstoy that science is "meaningless" because it fails to give an answer to "the only question important to us: 'what shall we do and how shall we live?'"[24] But despite the more modest tone adopted by science in the twentieth century, and its open admission of its inability to clarify questions which fall outside the area of technological mastery of life, religion is in no position today to reclaim its lost empire. For as the result of the fierce confrontation between science and religion, which lasted for centuries, the latter has been pushed into the *realm of irrationalism.*[25] Weber believed that the historical process of secularization which led to the divorce of life and religion had gone beyond the point of no return. One has to accept the fate of his time with courage, and prepare himself to live in a meaningless world if he is to maintain his rational integrity intact. One still has the choice, however, to search for a meaningful life if he is willing to undertake the horrible sacrifice which this choice entails. Weber explains:

> To the person who cannot bear the fate of the times like a man, one must say: may he rather return silently, without the usual publicity build-up of renegades, but simply and plainly. The arms of the old churches are opened widely an compassionately for him. . . . one way or another he has to bring his 'intellectual sacrifice'--that is inevitable.[26]

Weber further argued that science would have to content itself with the task of understanding and interpreting "facts." The science's *vocation* is to understand the world as it *is,* and not as it *ought* to be. The mission of changing the world and giving it meaning should be left to prophets and sages. As to the question "what shall we do, and how shall we arrange our lives?," Weber suggested that, with the demise of objective reason, modern man would have to decide *privately and quietly* which of the "warring gods" he ought to serve.[27] Lacking the benefit of an *objectively acknowledged truth,* modern man has to choose for himself what values and beliefs, if any, should guide his life.

Weber recognizes that the concern over the meaning of the world does not disappear by adopting a positivistic outlook toward life. "The conflict between empirical reality and this conception of the world as a meaningful totality," he remarks, "which is based on religious postulate, produces the strongest tensions in man's inner life as well as in his external relationship to the world."[28] The question of meaning, he notes, has been the central question not only in prophecy but in philosophy as well. He insists, however, that as a result of the ascendance of scientific outlook and empirical research, the question has to be *relegated to the privacy* of one's inner life.

What Weber fails to recognize is that positivism itself, despite its anti-metaphysical prejudices, *presupposes* certain meta-empirical, ontological, and metaphysical judgments. Positivism *abstracts* and *generalizes* from a reality that has been historically brought about by *contrasting the real with the ideal, the actual with the transcendent.* By refusing to recognize that modern society and culture have been historically shaped by the ideas and ideals of the Enlightenment, *positivism serves to idealize modern society,* taking the values and principles embodied in its culture as *absolute standards* to be used to evaluate human experience. As Max Horkheimer remarks:

> The merit of positivism consists in having carried the fight of Enlightenment against mythologies into the sacred realm of traditional logic. However, like modern mythologists, the positivists may be accused of serving a purpose instead of abandoning purpose for truth. The idealists glorified commercial culture by attributing a higher meaning to it. The positivists glorify it by adopting the principles of this culture as the measure of truth, in a manner not unlike that in which modern popular art and literature glorify life as it is--not by idealization or lofty interpretation, but by simply repeating it on canvas, stage, and screen.[29]

Weber provides a powerful counter-arguments to the Marxian theory of history, by sheding light on the period in Western history when Western society made the transition from the ancient to the modern order. He brilliantly brings home the point that material progress, in the absence of socially institutionalized behavior, can not be inspired simply by materialistic motives, or by pure self-interest. Civilization, at least in its initial stages, presupposes a commitment to values and principles that transcend a sheer desire for material gratification. Further, he demonstrates that the capitalist system would have never matured had not the Western culture produced the legal and administrative systems which made economic and material progress possible.

Weber's account also shows us the unsettling aspects of Western modernity, and the disturbing trend whereby objective rationality, which brings cohesiveness and integrity to social life, has been suffering of a slow, but constant, erosion. *Weber provides us with a paradox in which the more the process of ratoinalization progresses the more modern society becomes irrational.*

Weber's insight to the process of Western modernization raises an important question, having direct implications for the study of Third World development: Is it inevitable that non-Western cultures have to follow the same path traversed by Western rationalization? That is to say, is the separation between formal and substantive, and the ultimate demise of objective reason, the only alternative open to other cultures? Granted that the underlying values and principles which make civilization possible (e.g., respecting human dignity, appreciating the value of social solidarity and cooperation, etc.) have universal implications, *one can accept the universality of the Western modern experience only if it can be shown that the basic trends of Western modernity have not been influenced by the historical specificities of Western society, but are the outcome of forces and processes embodied in all human societies.* But if it can be shown, as I intend to do in the next chapter, that some of the essential trends of Western modernity are the result of circumstances peculiar to Western experience, and rise out of historical events and accidents which may not be described as imminent or inevitable, then the claim of universality would be rendered arbitrary.

Notes

1. Max Weber, The Protestant Ethic and the Spirit of Capitalism, Tran. Talcott Parsons (London: George Allen & Unwin, 1976), pp. 24-5.
2. Ibid. p. 26.
3. Ibid., pp.170-171.
4. Max Weber, *Economy and Society,* trans. Guenther Roth and Glaus Wittich (N.Y.: Bedminister Press, 1968), pp. 635-6; Rogers Brubaker, *The Limits of Rationality* (London: George Allen & Unwin, 1984), pp. 10-12.
5. Max Weber, *The Protestant Ethic,* p. 26.
6. Max Weber, *From Max Weber,* trans. H.H. Gerth and C. Wright Mills (N.Y.: Oxford University Press, 1946), p. 295.
7. Weber, *Economy and Society,* pp. 24-5.
8. For further discussion of this point see Alfred Shutz, *The Phenomenology of the Social World,* trans. George Walsh (N.Y.: Northeastern University Press, 1967), p. 19; and Habermas, *Communicative Action,* Val.1, p. 281.
9. Mannheim, *Ideology and Utopia* (N.Y.: Harcourt, Brace & Co., 1940), p. 17.
10. Weber, *Economy and Society,* pp. 65-7.
11. Weber, *Economy and Society,* p. 67.
12. For further discussion of this point see Habermas, *Communicative Action, Vol. 1,* p. 219.
13. Habermas, *Communicative Action, Vol. 1,* p. 228; see also Rogers Brubaker, *The Limits of Rationality: An Essay on the Social*

and Moral Thought of Max Weber (London: George Allen and Unwin, 1984), pp. 24-5.

14. Weber, *From Max Weber*, p. 139.

15. For further discussion of the concept of disenchantment see Brubaker, p. 31; also Bryan S.Turner, *Weber and Islam* (Boston: Routledge & Kegan Paul, 1974), p. 153; and Habermas, *Communicative Action, Vol. 1*, p. 216.

16. Weber, *From Max Weber*, p. 139.

17. Habermas, *Communicative Action, Vol. 1*, pp. 168, 182-86, 220.

18. Ibid., p. 219.

19. Weber, *Economy and Society*, p. 225.

20. Ibid., p. 140.

21. Ibid., p. 225.

22. Ibid., pp. 85-6.

23. Weber, *Economy and Society*, p. 975, quoted in Brubaker, p.22.

24. Weber, *From Max Weber*, p. 143.

25. Ibid., pp. 153-55, 181.

26. Ibid., p. 155.

27. Ibid., p. 153.

28. Weber, *Economy and Society, Vol. 2*, p. 451.

29. Horkheimer, p. 86.

Chapter 4

The Eclipse of Substantive Rationality

The Weberian model, it was argued in Chapter 3, locates the beginning of the process of modernization in the Protestant Reformation. The Reformation effected a theoretical revolution by introducing a new outlook which provided the individual with a practical incentive to work hard toward the betterment of social conditions, and freed his creative energies from superstition and irrationalism. Yet we saw also that the same model which depicts modernization as a process of cultural and social rationalization uncovers a disturbing trend in Western modernity whereby the rationalized structures of consciousness and society are gradually fragmented. With the fragmentation of society, the ability to interrelate activities taking place in different value spheres is increasingly lost. In short, with the advance of the project of modernization, the objective reason which once permeated and united the various spheres of life is permanently vanished. We referred to this phenomenon by the phrase "the Weberian paradox."

In this chapter, I would like to examine two interrelated questions stemming directly from the Weberian paradox. First, what is the nature of the factors leading to the erosion of objective reason? More specifically, are those factors universal, and hence common to all societies undergoing modernization, or are they specific to Western society? Secondly, regardless of whether Western modernity is universal or specific, can it be exported to, and regenerated in, non-Western countries? In addressing these questions I will focus on the intellectual contribution of two leading Enlightenment thinkers, Rene Descartes and Immanuel Kant, whose ideas have by far made the most profound impact on the process of modern intellectualization. In analyzing the work of these two eminent thinkers, I am interested primarily in showing that the fragmentation of modern consciousness and reality has been the outcome of a specific methodical approach, markedly influenced by the historical specificity of Western society, and hence is not, and need not be considered as, an example of a general process of rationalization.

The Emancipatory Project of Enlightenment

The absence of an overarching development of substantive rationality cannot be explained merely by a reference to the process of rationalization itself. For one has to explain why Western modernization has developed a clear bias toward the formal type of rationality at the expense of the substantive . Such an explanation can be found in the antagonism which historically existed between Enlightenment philosophy and Christian theology, predominant in traditional European society. Enlightenment philosophers embarked on a *project* aiming at discrediting the then predominant outlook, which was based on traditional beliefs, and replacing it with modern outlook, predicated on reason and science. The Enlightenment thinker was *not solely* motivated by intellectual concerns, but by political and existential ones as well. Animosity toward the authority of the Catholic Church, and the tight control it maintained for centuries over moral and political life, molded the intellectual and moral environment, and consequently shaped the psychological and social developments of modern life. Anticlericalism, which permeated Europe at the eve of the Enlightenment, fueled the attack on the *ancien regime* on both the political and intellectual levels. The successes of the Enlightenment were not, however, merely the result of the persuasiveness of the criticism it levelled against the historical accounts contained in the sacred text, but also grew from the distrust the public had towards priests and bishops, many of whom were seen to have led a luxurious and unscrupulous life, in complete contradiction to the Christian teachings they espoused.[1] The strategy the Enlightenment developed in its struggle to unseat the Church from its authoritative position was a simple one, consisting of two interrelated thrusts. On the one hand, the Enlightenment philosophers attempted to replace the objective interpretation of the world, derived from Christian theology and substantiated by divine revelation, with one derived from nature and validated by scientific method. On the other hand, Enlightenment intellectuals managed to shift the locus of moral authority from the Church to secular institutions, guided and supported by the nation-state.

The Enlightenment major thinkers, from Bacon and Descartes to Hume and Kant, through Locke and Rousseau had all endeavored to undermine the authority of the Church. The Enlightenment project was at heart an "emancipatory" project, aiming at freeing the human being from the absolute standards, established by theological authority and manipulated by the Church.[2] As Nietzsche observed in *Beyond Good and Evil*, the emancipatory tendencies of the Enlightenment were not initially directed against religion *per se,* but were definitely against organized religion and religious institutions.

> What is the whole of modern philosophy doing at bottom? Since Descartes--actually more despite him than because of his precedent--all the philosophers seek to assassinate the old soul concept, under the guise of a critique of the subject-and-predicate concept--which means an attempt on the life of the basic presupposition of the Christian doctrine. Modern philosophy, being an epistemological skepticism, is, covertly or overtly, anti-Chirstian--although, to say this for the benefit of more refined ears, by no means anti-religious.[3]

One trend, however, was clear from the beginning: The superhumanly sanctioned order, in which individual purposes and conducts were made subservient to an *objective* "truth," was being gradually replaced by a humanly sanctioned order, whereby social organization was subordinated to *subjective* purposes. The human being was moved to the center of the universe, and social life was, slowly but surely, acquiring an individualistic color and taste.

The historical process of subjectivization of reason, i.e. the predominance of the subjective over the objective aspect of reason, is the product of the Enlightenment project. We are indebted to Max Horkheimer for uncovering the historical patterns leading to the subjectivization of reason. In *The Eclipse of Reason,* Horkheimer noted that although both the subjective and objective aspects of reason concomitantly existed at the outset of this process, the latter was systematically undermined, and was ultimately trivialized by the turn of the twentieth century.[4] Originally, Enlightenment philosophers aspired to replace objective "truth" embodied in traditional religion with objective reason based on methodical and philosophical thought. They, evidently, did not desire to eradicate "objective truth," but rather to "give it a new rational foundation."[5] The contention was initially whether revelation (religion) or reason (philosophy) should be the *ultimate authority* in determining the nature of *the absolute*. Although philosophy failed, after a fierce and protracted struggle, to replace religion as the sole source of objective truth, it succeeded in neutralizing it. Religion was reduced to a cultural category among others, competing with them for the purpose of imputing meaning to life. In the aftermath of the clash between religion and the philosophy of Enlightenment, the concept of objective reason was rendered unworkable, and the idea of the absoluteness of religious revelation was reduced to nonexistence.

Horkheimer's critical reading of the Enlightenment as the catalyst of subjective rationalism has been shared by a host of twentieth-century philosophers, who, though approaching the question from different perspectives, have came to the same conclusion. Hans Reiss, for example, contended that the Enlightenment had successfully reduced religion into a cultural sphere alongside science, politics, art, ethics, and law. The latter spheres were isolated from religion and organized in accordance with their own separate "universal" laws.[6] Hans-Georg Gadamer, likewise, argued that the validation of knowledge and experience was ensured by appealing to methodical approach. In their search for truth, Enlightenment philosophers, rejecting traditional appeal to divine *authority*, turned inside to find in the formal self the most fundamental basis of *certainty*. The Cartesian model, in which the formally defined self was perceived as the point of departure, and the methodological basis as the only means for validating acquired knowledge, was embraced by Enlightenment scholars.[7] *It was this particular development that marked the subordination of substantive rationality to formal rationality, and paved the way for the supremacy of purposive rationality.*

I would like, in the remainder of this chapter, to focus on the work of two influential Enlightenment philosophers, Descartes and Kant. I would like, first, to examine how, and in what ways, have these thinkers contributed to the erosion of substantive rationality, alluded to by Weber, and then assess the implications of modern subjectivism for the modernization of non-Western societies.

Transcendental Subjectivism

Rene Descartes introduced his new method of ascertaining the truth in *Discourse on Method,* which he later refined in *Meditations on the First Philosophy.* In *Discourse on Method,* Descartes outlines his method in four rules:

> The first was never to accept anything for true which I did not clearly know to be such; that is to say, carefully to avoid precipitancy and prejudice, and to comprise nothing more in my judgment than what was presented to my mind so clearly and distinctly as to exclude all ground of doubt.
> The second, to divide each of the difficulties under examination into as many parts as possible, and as might be necessary for its adequate solution.
> The third, to conduct my thoughts in such order that, by commencing with objects the simplest and easiest to know, I might ascend by little and little, and, as it were, step by step, to the knowledge of the more complex; assigning in thought a certain order even to those objects which in their own nature do not stand in a relation of antecedence and sequence.
> And the last, in every case to make enumerations so complete, and reviews so general, that I might be assured that nothing was omitted.[8]

Descartes begins his search for truth with *hyperbolic doubt,* whereby all the ideas and thoughts he received through education or based on trust in authority were declared doubtful and suspended in a state of negation until such time that they could be grounded in certainty.[9] He justifies his *wholesale* rejection of his ideas by arguing that it would be an "endless task" to run though all of them individually. He then proceeds to argue that even after we have doubted the existence of all objects we are capable of perceiving that one thing can never be doubted, namely, that we, the subjects who undertake the task of doubting, do exist. The conscious self, which is capable of thinking and doubting, is therefore the most fundamental basis of certainty. Hence the famous Cartesian axiom: "I think, therefore I exist."[10]

It should be pointed out here that Descartes' conclusion of the certainty of his existence is in itself problematic, because this certainty is not based on the immediate and self-evident awareness of the conscious self of its existence, but rather on the mediated process of thinking. In the latter case the statement "I think, I am" can be true only when we accept the truth of the principle of non-contradiction. Yet Descartes makes no attempt to establish the principle of non-contradiction which says that something can never exist and not exist at the same time, a principle whose validity is presupposed by the notion "I think, I am." At any rate, *Descartes has now a bedrock foundation on which he can reconstruct his ideas, viz. the certainty of a thinking existence.* The second step is to establish a connection between his thinking activities and an outer reality. Descartes finds this connection in judgment. For among all the mental forms that the individual may possess, only judgments refer to external objects, and are therefore susceptible to error and deception. Wants, desires, and imaginations cannot be declared to be true or false, since they make no claim of resembling or duplicating outer reality.[11]

Descartes accepts, without any further doubts, the principle of causality. He argues that the ideas, which he has, must be the effects of some objects. The problem is to decide whether the causes of his ideas reside in himself, and therefore are unreal, or exist outside him in the objective world. Descartes contends that although ideas such as heat, stone, earth, etc., cannot possibly be conceived by him unless they are the effects of some external causes, it would be difficult to ascertain that the conceived ideas have as much formal reality as there is objective reality in their causes.[12] That is to say, it is difficult for the perceiving self to establish an accurate correspondence between the mental representation of the ideas and there objective reality. Clearly, Descartes is confronted here with the problem of *correspondence* between ideas and objects, thought and reality, in its rudimentary form, a problem which, as we will see below, forces Kant to distinguish between *phenomena* and *noumena*. The difficulty of extending the subjective certainty to the objective world, stemming essentially from the finite and interdependent nature of external objects, is finally resolved when Descartes realizes that among the ideas he possesses is the idea of God, the independent and complete being. Unlike the other ideas the thinking individual has, the idea of an infinite and perfect being cannot originate in the mind of a finite imperfect being for the effect cannot be superior to the cause. By establishing the truth of the concept of God, Descartes argues, certainty can now be extended to outer reality. And he can now proceed to establish the existence of material things.

Descartes' method constituted a radical departure from all methods of ascertaining the truth known before it. To begin with, Descartes does not dissipate doubtful ideas by a means of evidence whereby only those ideas which are found to be lacking in objectivity are rejected after being subjected to a thorough investigation. Rather, he shows us the entire body of accumulated knowledge vanishing instantly before our eyes. According to the Cartesian skeptical approach, all things should be declared nonexistent until they are proven (with absolute certainty) otherwise. Doubt and uncertainty are the norm; truth and certainty are the exception. Things can be admitted back to reality only when "all ground of doubt" are excluded. *Descartes shifts the locus of certainty from the objective world into the subjective consciousness.* His philosophy inaugurates therefore the end of "naive objectivism" and the beginning of "transcendental subjectivism."[13]

Having divided reality into objects according to the second principle of his method, he proceeds in the third principle to create a new order on the ruin of the old. Although the new order is supposed to progress from "the simplest and easiest to know . . . to the more complex," Descartes seems to violate his own rules when he finds it necessary to establish the existence of God as the basic ground for objective reality. Perhaps the most troubling aspect of the Cartesian approach is that it fails to establish a comprehensive set of criteria for readmitting things back to the realm of truth. Hence, in the absence of a well-defined regime for inclusion and exclusion, the reconstructed order would inevitably embody a great deal of arbitrariness. The arbitrariness of the Cartesian approach was noted, early on by Leibniz, who remarked that Descartes' rules tell us: "Take what you need, and do what you should, and you will get what you want."[14]

Despite all the problems, ambiguities, and difficulties associated with the Cartesian method, it was celebrated and embraced by the Enlightenment philosophers and intellectuals.[15] For it embedded an ingenious mechanism which allowed these intellectuals to break with the past, and provided an easy way out of the traditional frame of reference. The Enlightenment possesses now a method of theorizing which it could use to start anew. The method was quickly embraced and employed for the purpose of revolutionizing both the intellectual and social life. Thomas Hobbes was among the first philosophers to make use of the new approach and to translate the Cartesian transcendental subjectivism, to political individualism.

The Demise of Transcendence

The onslaught on transcendental ideas took its sophisticated form in Kant's critical philosophy. While Descartes shifted the locus of certainty from the objective to the subjective world, Kant was able to move it from the transcendental to the sensible world. Descartes saw the idea of God as the fundamental basis for the establishment of the truth of objective reality, whereas Kant placed the same idea outside the sphere of ascertained knowledge, and endeavored to ground 'truth' in sensible objects. A child of the Enlightenment, Kant was intent on undermining all authority that lay outside reason, and ended up limiting the authority of reason itself. In an article entitled "An Answer to the Question: 'What is Enlightenment?'," Kant epitomized the true spirit of Enlightenment. "Enlightenment," he wrote, "is man's emergence from his self-incurred immaturity."[16] By immaturity Kant meant "the inability to use one's own understanding without the guidance of another."[17] Kant saw the Enlightenment as the beginning of a new age where man can finally stand on his own. Man, Kant believed, needed no guidance from without, and could rely on his own physical and mental strength for his own development. Kant was fully aware that human maturation was not simply an individual achievement, but a social process, requiring social cooperation. "In man . . .," Kant argued, "those natural capacities which are directed towards the use of his reason are such that they could be fully developed only in the species, but not in the individual."[18] He, further, understood maturation to be an historical process, a project that had to be advanced and refined by successive generations. He saw little benefit, if at all, in introducing radical and revolutionary measures to hasten social change.

> Thus a public can only achieve enlightenment slowly. A revolution may well put an end to autocratic despotism and to rapacious or power-seeking oppression, but it will never produce a true reform in ways of thinking. Instead, new prejudices, like the ones they replaced, will serve as a leash to control the great unthinking mass.[19]

Kant saw his mission as one of building the epistemological foundation for the emancipatory project of Enlightenment. He recognized that if reason were to replace revelation as the guiding principle of human thought and conduct, reason would have to be able to furnish not only the theoretical ground for thought and judgment, but also the moral ground for conduct. His three highly influential *Critiques* (*The Critique of Pure Reason, The Critique of Practical Reason,* and *the Critique of Judgment*) were written for the purpose of ensuring the autonomy of human reason, an to end its reliance and dependence on other sources.[20] His efforts led, however, to the further differentiation and formalization of reason, and ultimately undermined the authority of substantive reason. By dividing reason into the three separated areas of theoretical cognition, practical rationality, and aesthetic judgment, giving each a foundation unto itself, the Kantian critical philosophy differentiated what Weber referred to later as the "value spheres of culture."[21]

Kant set out, in *The Critique of Pure Reason*, to examine "whether such thing as metaphysics be even possible at all?"[22] That is, the main question which prompted Kant to write his *Critique* was to find out whether it is possible for the mind to acquire knowledge apart from experience. Kant terms the knowledge which precedes experience *a priori*. He observes that all judgments, in which two heterogeneous elements (the subject and the predicate) are united, may be divided into two types: analytic judgments, in which the predicate is already manifested in the subject, and synthetic judgments, in which the predicate lies outside the subject. Analytic judgments are, therefore, tautological, since the predicate adds nothing new which is not already included in the subject, while synthetic judgments add to our knowledge because the information brought to bear on the subject cannot be deduced by analyzing the latter. Kant further observers that synthetic judgements are of two types: *posteriori*, obtained through experience and is, therefore, part of the empirical world, and *a priori,* preceding all experience, and is part of the metaphysical world.

Having made this distinction, Kant can now reduce the initial question about the possibility of metaphysical knowledge into a more manageable question: "How are *a priori* synthetic judgments possible?"[23] Kant, obviously, has a practical interest in examining the possibility of *a priori* synthetic judgment. Since dogma and superstition could be ascertained only through this kind of judgments, establishing criteria which would exclude these two types of judgment would definitely contribute to human progress. Like Descartes, Kant recognizes that judgments are the only mental entities that connect mind with outer reality and link the realm of thinking with the realm of objective being. For judgments establish an absolute identity between the subject, which is "particular and in the form of being," and the predicate, which is "universal and in the form of thought."[24] Unlike Descartes, he is intent on discrediting metaphysical inquiry and limiting the scope of theoretical research.

Kant distinguishes among three levels of apprehension: intuition, understanding, and reason. *Intuition* is the faculty of sense-perception, whereby the representations effected by the sensible objects are apprehended. The received representations are then organized through the concepts of the *understanding*. The faculty of understanding furnishes the rules by which sense-data are subsumed under the various concepts, and hence imputing unity and order to the world of appearances. Finally, *reason* provides the principles which permit the unity of the concepts.[25] Kant maintains that this series of mental activities in which intuition is connected with pure reason through the understanding are interrelated, and that the validity of each can be ascertained only insofar as the connection between the three levels of apprehension is maintained. That is to say, the validity of the mental processes which take place at the level of reason could be ascertained only as long as reason is employed for the purpose of demarcating the principles of logic, whose functions are to regulate *posteriori* syntheses. Kant justifies the limitation he imposes on the use of pure reason by arguing that since sense-data is the only access the mind has to the objective world, the correspondence between thoughts and objects has to be substantiated by intuition.

Kant terms the system of principles which determines the proper use of understanding "transcendental analytic," and concludes that synthetical knowledge is possible only through the "faculty" of understanding:

> Since, properly, this transcendental analytic should be used only as a canon for passing judgment upon the empirical employment of the understanding, it is misapplied if appealed to as an organon of its general and unlimited application, and if consequently we venture, with the pure understanding alone, to judge synthetically, to affirm, and to decide regarding objects in general.[26]

Yet Kant does not dismiss *a priori* knowledge as a whole, for after all, the rules of understanding, he maintains, are *a priori*.[27] That is, the concepts which unite and order appearances are not themselves acquired through experience, as the empiricist would argue, but are innate to the human mind, and constitute the internal structure of understanding. But if we ask Kant how it is possible for him to ascertain the truth of the concepts of the understanding and the rules which guide their operation, even though these rules and concepts are not part of the sensible world and, hence, unrecognized by the intuition, he would respond by arguing that such knowledge is possible through pure reason. For "reason," Kant proclaims, "is the faculty which supplies the principles of *a priori* knowledge. Pure reason is, therefore, that "which claims the principles whereby we know anything absolutely *a priori*."[28] But if we now ask how it is possible that pure reason is capable of ascertaining the rules of understanding *a priori*, and at the same time fails to ascertain the truth of other transcendental concepts. Here we should expect no easy answer, for we find that any response derived from Kant's critical philosophy will inevitably run into difficulties and inconsistencies. Since the purpose of this analysis is not to attempt any detailed examination of Kant's *Critique*, but to underline Kant's vital impact on the process of subjectivization, I will briefly refer to Kant's basic argument in this regard.

Kant points out that the truth of transcendental ideas (or the reality of ostensible objects) cannot be affirmed in the absence of any formal conditions which permits us to subsume transcendental objects under concepts.[29] He writes:

> The pure categories, apart from formal conditions of sensibility, have only transcendental meaning; nevertheless they may not be employed transcendentally, such an employment being in itself impossible, inasmuch as all conditions of any employment in judgments are lacking to them, namely, the formal conditions of the subsumption of any ostensible object under these concepts.[30]

As to the truth of the formal conditions of the subsumption of sensible objects, Kant invokes the principle of necessity whereby the rules regulating the subsumption of objects (identity and difference) acquire their universality and objective validity by being borne concomitantly in the minds of rational beings in general, and *substantiated through general consensus.*

> . . . the business of the senses is to intuit, that of the understanding is to think. But thinking is uniting representations in one consciousness. This union originates either merely relative to the subject and is accidental and subjective, or takes place absolutely and is necessary or objective. The union of representations in the consciousness is judgment. Thinking, therefore, is the same as judging or referring representations to judgments in general. Hence judgments are either merely subjective when representations are referred to a consciousness in one subject only and united in it, or objective, when they are united in consciousness in general, that is, necessarily.[31]

Any concept whose object cannot be intuited through the senses is therefore an empty concept, "without meaning." Furthermore, Kant insists that the rules of understanding are the only "source of truth."[32] For since the formal definition of truth, Kant tells us, is "the agreement of knowledge and its object," and since such an agreement can be ascertained only between concepts and sensible objects, the certainty of transcendental objects can never be affirmed. It follows that we can in vain talk about truth beyond the empirical world.

Yet Kant recognizes that his refutation notwithstanding, metaphysics is indispensable because it addresses questions of great importance to man, namely, the questions of the freedom of the will, the immortality of the soul, and the existence of God.[33] He suggests that transcendental ideas, the object of metaphysical inquiries, will always be a primary concern of reason in its *speculative mode.* From now on, however, such an undertaking would have to be carried out on the level of *subjective* rationality.[34] Every person would have to address these questions and resolve them in the solitudes of his inner self. Kant contends that the three cardinal questions of metaphysics (i.e., God, Freedom, and the Soul) have insignificant implications, if at all, for theoretical knowledge. They are of primary interest, however, in relation to guiding human conduct, and have bearing mainly on questions of practical significance.

Kant distinguishes between theoretical (speculative) and practical reason. Unlike his earlier distinction between understanding and reason, which corresponded to the internal division of reason to two levels of apprehension, the latter distinction between the theoretical and practical corresponds to the application of reason to two, externally separate, realms, viz. the realm of necessity (nature) and the realm of freedom (society). That is to say, while reason *qua* understanding is employed by Kant for the purpose of bringing order to nature, reason *qua* practical reason is employed to bring order to social behavior.[35] The former relates to us what *is* happening, the latter tells us what *ought* to happen. Kant reduces all interests of reason to three principal questions: (1) What can I know?, (2) what ought I to do?, and (3) what may I hope? The first question, he argues, is merely speculative, and is the subject matter of the *Critique of Pure Reason.* The second is merely moral, and is dealt with in the *Critique of Practical Reason.* The third is both theoretical and practical: It is practical only insofar as it gives the individual an incentive to hope for if he is to follow the laws of freedom established by practical reason; however, it is purely theoretical in terms of ascertaining the possibility of hope. In fact it is this third question that underlines the problematic nature of the Kantian division of reason. Evidently Kant was quite aware of the interrelationship between pure and practical reason, between necessity and freedom, or between *is* and *ought*,[36] and was careful not to completely separate the two realms from one another. His very approach, however, resulted in confining pure reason to the realm of empirical reasoning and scientific research, thereby undermining the credibility of speculative reason and relegating transcendental ideas and interest to the realm of the absurd and irrational.

Kant contends that the practical rules of regulating individual behavior can be either pragmatic, derived from "the motive of happiness," or moral, effected by the motive of "worthiness of being happy."[37] He recognizes that the former rules are grounded in the empirical world, while the latter are anchored in the realm of transcendence. "Thus without a God and without a world invisible to us now but hoped for," Kant observes,"the glorious ideas of morality are indeed objects of approval and admiration, but not springs of purpose and action."[38]

Having denoted the necessary link between a moral system derived from "the motive of worthiness of happiness" and a belief in transcendental world, Kant turns, in *The Critique of Practical Reason,* to delineate a moral system based on a commitment to universal rules. To act morally, Kant asserted, one has to act in accordance with universal principles. Since particular interests are caused by personal desires, one has to purge oneself of all desires in order to arrive at universal rules, because, Kant tells us, one would then be left with mere reason-- i.e., the formal elements of rationality--which Kant termed the categorical imperative: "Act according to a maxim which can be adopted at the same time as a universal law."[39] Yet Kant's categorical imperative is a formal principle without any content or substance. For the categorical imperative is simply a principle of consistency or non-contradiction. It can only show us that our actions are consistent with our fundamental values, but cannot help us discover what values are most appropriate for guiding human action. Therefore, if we have no point to depart from, the principle of categorical imperative, or practical reasonableness, can get us nowhere. For example, if we do accept the validity of marital fidelity, extra-marital affairs are inconsistent, but if we do not, they are consistent.[40]

With Kant, transcendental subjectivism, inaugurated by Descartes, became a firmly established metatheory. Interestingly enough, Kant employed transcendental arguments to rescue empiricism, which came to a dead end with Hume, and then to undermine transcendental ideas. Kant distinguished between understanding and reason which he considered to be two separate "faculties" of the mind. The objects of the former are empirical beings, while the objects of the latter are transcendental entities. Kant employed reason to show that *a priori* synthetic judgment is possible through the unity of appearances in the concepts. The concepts, themselves, though are not part of the empirical world, cannot be doubted because their existence is necessary for giving meaning and order to the empirical world. Yet he refused to employ reason for the purpose of ascertaining, or even recognizing, the truth of other transcendental ideas even though their postulation is necessary for giving meaning and order to the moral world. Such ideas as infinity, freedom, dignity, equality, responsibility have no reality unless they are expressed in a mathematical or physical forms. That is to say, unless the idea can be reduced to number or matter, it can be stripped from its truth and turned into fiction. Clearly, the Kantian epistemology is a theory of empirical knowledge, not of knowledge in general. It takes mathematical reasoning as its prototype. Yet by insisting that all truth has to be firmly grounded in the empirical world, *Kant's transcendental subjectivism has postulated the absoluteness of finitude.*

The new method introduced by Descartes and elaborated and refined by Kant, marked a drastic, or to use Kuhnian phraseology, a paradigmatic shift in the way truth is ascertained. No longer is the researcher's and scholar's task to clarify, reinterpret, refute, or ascertain ideas which are part of the *cultural milieu* he inherited, but he has to declare all ideas untrue until they are substantiated through empirical evidence. Sings and ideas may no more "wait in silence for the coming of a man capable of recognizing" their truth: they "can be constituted only by an act of knowledge."[41]

By establishing scientific procedure as the only source of truth, Kant's transcendental analytic was able to destroy the theoretical basis of superstition. But along with it, it undermined the theoretical foundation of all transcendental ideas. Evidently, Kant himself recognized that empirical objects do not occupy the whole field of individual consciousness, and believed therefore that human reason would "not be satisfied save through the completion of its course in [the apprehension of] a self-subsistent systematic whole."[42] He singled out three transcendental ideas which he considered to be the primary concern of speculative reason: "the freedom of the will, the immortality of the soul, and the existence of God." [43] But he contended that these ideas have primarily practical significance. He thus concluded that reason has mainly practical employment: reason's primary role is to provide us with "laws which are imperative, that is, *objective laws* of freedom, which tell us *what ought to happen*--although perhaps it never does happen--therein differing from *laws of nature,* which relate only *to that which happens.*"[44]

The only task Kant was willing to allocate to reason was the determination of moral principles. He recognized that principles of morality receive their legitimacy by being anchored in transcendent ideas or values. He, nevertheless, insisted that the latter could not be a proper objects of reason and had to be postulated, and to be taken as self-evident. He believed that the infinite and the universal were the source of order the mind discovers or imposes upon nature and society through the medium of the concept and the categorical imperative respectively. Yet by refusing to grant any rational grounding to *ideas,* the Kantian philosophy facilitated the triumph of *logical positivism* (or scientism) over *dialectical rationalism,* and the ethics of *happiness* (or utilitarianism) over the ethics of the *worthiness of happiness* (or the ethics of duty), to which his own moral philosophy belonged.

Perhaps the most enduring legacy of Kant, and the one that has far-reaching consequences in terms of its contribution to the erosion of substantive rationality and the fragmentation of the structures of both consciousness and reality, has been the separation of truth from right. According to Kant, differentiating right and wrong and distinguishing truth from falsehood are two distinct types of mental activities. The former falls in the domain of pure-reason-turned-practical, while the latter is the prerogative of understanding. Clearly it is the Kantian philosophy which lay at the roots of secularization processes, whereby ethics is severed from science, truth from right, and the transcendental and infinite from the empirical and finite.

It may be argued with some plausibility that Kant would have never permitted the use of scientific methods designed for the investigation of natural phenomenon in social, or cultural, inquiries, for, after all, Kant assigned the sociocultural to the realm of freedom. In fact there is sufficient evidence in the writings of Kant to warrant this argument.[45] Yet the fact of the matter is that by separating truth from right, Kant paved the way for the fragmentation of culture (and consequently) social spheres. It was only a matter of time that the study of economic, political, or even legal issues was designed after the patterns of natural sciences, whereby the aim was to discover that which *is*, rather than that which *ought to be*.

The Crisis of Subjective Culture: Alienation and Nihilism

It is against this background that the Marxian and Nietzschean revolt against bourgeois civilization and modern culture should be understood.[46] Marx protested the exploitative nature of the structural forms developed under capitalism, and the *alienation* of the worker resulting from it. Nietzsche, on the other hand, objected to the *nihilistic* tendencies of modern culture and the loss of meaning in modern life. Both attributed what they perceived to be the crisis of modernity to the fragmentation of modern life.

In *Economic and Philosophic Manuscripts of 1844*, Marx attacked political economy for being insensitive toward the misery and suffering of the worker in the name of science. Describing how the political economist manages to ignore the plight of the laborer under the guise of specialized knowledge, he noted:

> If I ask the political economist: Do I obey economic laws if I exact money by offering my body for sale, by surrendering it to another's lust? . . . or am I not acting in keeping with political economy if I sell my friend to the Moroccans? Then the political economist replies to me: You do not transgress my laws; but see what Cousin Ethics and Cousin Religion have to say about it.[47]

The fragmentation of cultural spheres manifests itself directly in society in the form of the estrangement of the worker and the alienation of the structural forms from the forms of consciousness. Marx again:

> It stems from the very nature of estrangement that each sphere applies to me a different and opposite yardstick--ethics one and political economy another, for each is a specific estrangement of man and focuses attention on a particular round of estranged essential activity, and each stand in an estranged relation to the other.[48]

While the crisis of modernity presented itself to Marx in the form of *alienation* (loss of freedom), whereby the individual loses control over the fruits of his labor and work, it appeared to Nietzsche in the form of *nihilism* (loss of meaning), whereby the individual loses the meaning of his life and existence. For Nietzsche, nihilism represents a psychological state in which the individual experiences a loss of enthusiasm for life, growth, and progress. Such a state of mind is precipitated by the loss of direction and purpose.[49] He sees nihilistic tendencies as part of modern rationalism which has degraded all transcendental ideas and values, reducing them respectively into the categories of empirical knowledge and happiness. Nietzsche's critique of modern culture, with its nihilistic, empiricist, and utilitarian tendencies, permeates all of his writings. Perhaps no where his attitude toward modern culture is more revealing than in the section entitled "The Madman" in his work *The Gay Science*, where he appeals to the idea of *madness* to underscore the dilemma of modern rationality.

Have you not heard of the madman who lit a lantern in the bright morning hours, ran to the market place, and cried incessantly: 'I seek God! I see God!"--As many of those who did not believe in God were standing around just then, he provoked much laughter. Has he got lost? asked one. Did he lose his way like a child? asked another. Or is he hiding? Is he afraid of us? Has he gone on a voyage? emigrated?--Thus they yelled and laughed.

The madman jumped into their midst and pierced them with his eyes. "Whither is God?" he cried: "I will tell you. We *have killed him*--you and I. All of us are his murderers. But how did we do that? How could we drink up the sea? Who gave us the sponge to wipe away the entire horizon? What were we doing when we unchained this earth from its sun? Whither is it moving now? Whither are we moving? Backward, sideward, forward, in all directions? Is there still any up or down? Are we not staying as though on infinite nothing? . . . God is dead. God remains dead. And we have killed him.[50]

By the words "God is dead" Nietzsche referred to the historical process, elsewhere he termed nihilism, which rendered *the absolute* and the "ideals," "principles," and "values" associated with it irrelevant to societal norms and institutions. The death of God meant that transcendence had lost its power over the determination of human conduct. The death of God marked the loss of meaning, and the end of moral and intellectual certainty. No more could anyone evaluate actions by referring to absolute standards. Henceforth, everything is relative, subjective, and uncertain. Absoluteness, objectivity, and certainty are now things of the past.

Ironically, Nietzsche's own words were received by his contemporaries in the same spirit the madman's words were received by the crowd. His writings had to await for over half a century before they could be deciphered and employed by Martin Heidegger, Michel Foucault, and others, for the purpose of criticizing modernity and modern rationalism. Aside from his unorthodox use of linguistic terms, Nietzsche's irrationalism may be attributed primarily to his blunt criticism and untactful attack on modern philosophy, an attack which gave philosophy a devastating blow from which it has never recovered. At any rate, what is of interest to us in the context of understanding the process of subjectivization of reason is Nietzsche's insight to the consequences of the disappearance of objectively recognized transcendental ideas, namely, that in the absence of extra-empirical principles, human life can have neither an overall goal, nor an overarching connectedness, nor an intrinsic truth. "What has happened, at bottom?," he wrote. "The feeling of valuelessness was reached with the realization that overall character of existence may not be interpreted by means of the concept of 'aim,' the concept of 'unity,' or the concept of 'truth.'"[51] Nietzsche ultimately adopted a system of pure realism which recognized a single principle of 'truth': the will to power. His account of modernity is clearly an exaggerated and dramatized one, and is by no means reflective of the actual life as it was experienced by the majority of people around the turn of the twentieth century. His was more of a magnification, and projection to the future, of the essential trends of modern life.

Implications for Non-Western Development

The project of transcendental subjectivism, inaugurated by Descartes, and developed and refined by Kant, was originally designed to rid Western culture of its superstitious and irrational elements. The project, however, turned sour by the end of the nineteenth century. Despite Hegel's attempt (some would say because of it) to restore objective rationality, the process of subjectivization continued to unfold. Gradually transcendental subjectivism lost its transcendence and was finally reduced to subjectivism, pure and simple, by the turn of the twentieth century. The implications of this process for Western society, and the possibility of restoring objective reason to Western culture is the subject of an ongoing debate in Western literature, and has become the major concern of what is referred to today as Post-modernism. Here, our main interest with regard to the process of subjectivization of reason has to do with its possible implications for the development of the non-Western World. In this connection, I would like to make three interrelated remarks.

First, Modernization is an historical process originating in the efforts aiming at reordering and restructuring cultural worldviews, which are ultimately rooted in the religious ideals of society. The rationalization of the worldviews of traditional Western religion has taken the form of cultural secularization whereby religious values and beliefs have gradually lost their power over society and were ultimately reduced to one cultural sphere among others. This development has led to the demise of objective reason and the primacy of subjectivism. As we saw earlier, the subjectivization of reason was the result of a strategy aimed at undermining the authority of the Church. Those who employed this strategy had no desire to repudiate the basic beliefs and values associated with the sacred text. Descartes continued to insist that the concept of God was not only essential for human reasoning, but was also the idea without which no other concept could have validity or objectivity. Kant, likewise, reembraced the Christian ethic of duty even when he was undermining its metaphysical basis.

Modern/Western culture, while commanding the respect of non-Westerners for its technological and scientific accomplishment, continues to trouble non-Western intellectuals primarily because of its rational subjectivism and the lack of objective truth.[52] Indeed the absence of objective truth has become increasingly troubling to a significant number of Western thinkers. But while it is imperative for a person who is a product of modern culture to accept the loss of meaning as a matter of "fate," to use Weber's characterization, if he is to avoid committing intellectual suicide and falling into the realm of irrationalism, non-Westerners would found it increasingly difficult to voluntarily make a meaningless conception of the world their conscious choice. A point which I hope to be able to reflect in Part II of this study.

Secondly, Modern structures of consciousness and reality have emerged as a result of the dissolution of substantive rationality. They form what Weber calls "the autonomous value spheres of life," which have been developed in accordance with idiosyncratic principles. *This means that as Western rationality progresses, it loses its capacity to regenerate itself.* For as the various spheres of life grow in separate directions, it becomes increasingly difficult for anyone to reexamine and reassess overall social progress from within these independent, and almost completely isolated, spheres. In the absence of an overarching component that can bring purpose, unity, and meaning to the various value spheres which constitute modern experience, the integrity of modern society depends partly on the interlocking memberships which individual members have in various spheres, and partly on the momentum generated by past trends.

This reality puts non-Westerners who come in contact with Western civilization at a great disadvantage. For neither can they experience social life across the various value spheres of Western society, nor do they have access to the historical roots of Western culture, which, because of the increased subjectivization of reason in the West, have moved from the realm of articulated 'truth' to the realm of symbolic and latent communication. A significant area of Western culture is being transmitted non-discursively from one generation to another, albeit with increasingly diminishing effects. If it is true that Western society is gradually losing its ability to regenerate itself, it is unlikely that Western modernity could be regenerated by individuals who may come into brief and superficial contact with modern society

Thirdly, Modern personality, defined in terms of formal rationality, is incapable of effecting fundamental social changes. Purged of all substantive principles except that of happiness and self-gratification, and emptied of all purposes except that of survival and self-preservation, the modern self has the capacity only to *adapt* to social forces, and the freedom to choose among *available* options. The emancipation of man from the absolute standards of the traditional society, as Max Horkheimer observed, has not resulted in an increased autonomy, but, paradoxically, has made the individual more vulnerable to economic and social forces. The formal self, emptied of all substance, and deprived of all standards, except those which are relevant to means calculation, lacks the capacity to evaluate alternatives, to recognize distortions, or to change directions. The formal self would have therefore to succumb to social forces and adapt to social trends if it is to survive. In the absence of an overall meaning and universal standards, the individual falls prey to his impulses. The attainment of happiness, defined in terms of subjective needs and desires, has become the only empirically discernable purpose worthy of human endeavor.[53]

The absence of substantive principles that can internally guide individual choice and action is even more troubling in a society where the external environment is disordered and choatic. In developing countries, where the military and secrete police (state security organs) are the only institutions where structures and functions coincide, order can only be achieved through national consensus, i.e., through objective rationality.

Notes

1. For a more detailed discussion of the impact of anticlericalism sentiment of political and intellectual development see Edward Shils, *Tradition* (The University of Chicago, 1981), pp. 223-226.
2. See Richard L.Velkley, *Freedom and the End of Reason* (University of Chicago Press, 1989), p. 12; and Karl Mannheim, *Ideology and Utopia* (N.Y.: Harcourt, Brace & C., 1940), p. 31.
3. Friedrich Nietzsche, *Beyond Good and Evil* trans. Walter Kaufmann (N.Y.: Vintage Books, 1966), p. 66.
4. Max Horkheimer, *Eclipse of Reason* (N.Y.: continuum, 1947), p. 6.
5. Ibid., p. 16.
6. Hans Reiss (ed.), *Kant's Political Writings*, trans. H. B. Nisbet (Cambridge University Press, 1970), p. 6-7.
7. Hans-Georg Gadamer, *Truth and Method*, trans. Joel Weinsheimer and Donald G. Marshall (N.Y.: Crossroad, 1989), p. 271; see also David Kolb, *The Critique of Pure Modernity: Hegel, Heidegger and After* (University of Chicago Press, 1986), p. 138; and Mannheim, p. 65.
8. Rene Descartes, *Discourse on Method: A Discourse On Method*, trans. John Veitch (N.Y.: Everyman's Library, 1969), pp. 15-16.
9. Ibid., pp. 12-5.
10. Ibid., p. 18.
11. Ibid., p. 26.
12. Ibid., p. 28.
13. See Husserl, *Cartesian Meditations*, p. 4.
14. Quoted in The *Encyclopedia of Philosophy*, p. 345.
15. Hobbes, Locke, and Rousseau, to name just few, adopted the Cartesain method by completely rejecting the prevalent political structure, and positing a new one, based on logical premises.
16. Kant, "What is Enlightenment?" in Reiss, p. 54.
17. Ibid.
18. Kant, "Idea for a Universal History," in Reiss, p. 42.
19. Ibid., p. 55.
20. See Velkly, pp. 13-19.
21. See David M. Rasmussen, *Reading Habermas* (Cambridge, Mass.: Basil Blackwell, 1990), p. 21.
22. Kant, *Prolegomena to Any Future Metaphysics* (N.Y.: Macmillan Publishing Company, 1988), p. 3; also *Critique of Pure*

Reason, trans. Norman Kemp Smith (N.Y.: Martin's Press, 1965).p. 57.

23. Kant, *Critique of Pure Reason,* p. 55.

24. Hegel, *Faith and Knowledge,* trans. H. S. Baillie (N.Y.: Harper and Row, Publisher, 1967), p. 69.

25. Kant, *Critique of Pure Reason,* pp. 105, 303.

26. Ibid., p. 100.

27. Ibid., p. 258.

28. Ibid., p. 58.

29. See also Ibid., pp. 180-7.

30. Ibid., p. 265.

31. Kant, *Prolegomena,* p. 52; Also Ibid., pp. 46-52.

32. Ibid., p. 258.

33. Kant, *Critique of Pure Reason,* p. 631.

34. Kant, *Prolegomena,* pp. 101, 116.

35. Ibid., p. 67; see also Kant, *Critique of Pure Reason,* pp. 633-4;

36. See Kant, *Critique of Pure Reason,* p. 634.

37. Ibid., p. 636.

38. Ibid., p. 40.

39. Immanuel Kant, *Philosophy of Law* (Cligton, N.J.: Augustus M. Kelley Publishers, 1974), p.36.

40. See Peter Singer, *Hegel* (Oxford University Press, 1983), pp. 30-2.

41. Foucault, *Order of Things: An Archaeology of the Human Sciences* (N.Y.: Vintage Books, 1973), p. 59.

42. Kant, *Critique of Pure Reason,* p. 630.

43. Ibid., p. 631.

44. Ibid., p. 634.

45. See Kant's *Philosophy of Law.*

46. Against the same background one can understand the protest of contemporary writers who are classified within the radical paradigm, and studied today under the rubric of Post-modernism. Among whom we can include Heidegger, Max Horkheimer, Foucault, Derrida, and others.

47. in Tucker, p. 97.

48. Ibid.

49. Nietzsche, *Will to Power,* trans. Walter Kaufmann and R.J. Hollingdale (N.Y.: Vintage Books, 1967), p. 12.

50. Nietzsche, *The Gay Science* (N.Y.: Random House, 1974), p. 181.

51. Nietzsche, *Will to Power,* p. 13.

52. The ambivalent attitude Arab intellectuals have vis-a-vis modern culture will be discussed at some length in Part II.

53. See Shils, *Tradition*, pp. 287, 303; also Robert Bellah, *Habits of the Heart.*

Chapter 5

The Quest for Order

In chapters 2 and 3 we examined two models of development: the Marxian and the Weberian. We saw that the Marxian model attributes development to forces which either are solely economic in nature, or, as some of Marx's interpreters insisted, are economic only in the last instance or resort. The Weberian model, on the other hand, assigns the forces of change to the cultural realm, whereby the origin of development is located in the rationalization of worldviews.

The question I would like to address in this chapter is crucial for resolving some of the difficulties generated in the confines of both the Marxian and Weberian approaches to modernity. The question could be put as follows: Can the impasse created by the two drastically different accounts of modernity be surpassed or overcome? That is, is it possible to integrate the two accounts of Western modernization into one comprehensive model? Clearly, the task of achieving a general synthesis of the Marxian and Weberian models is beyond the scope of this work.[1] I will, therefore, attempt to achieve a limited synthesis and confine myself to developing a conceptual framework, consisting of a limited number of propositions, whereby certain aspects of the two models are affirmed, while others are eliminated. This conceptual framework will, then, be used as an analytical background for studying the process of modernization in the Arab world in Part II.

I contend first that, contrary to the Marxist assertion, historical change is not merely the outcome of economic laws, but is influenced and shaped by moral laws which have their roots in the symbolic and transcendental aspects of life. I argue, then, that reforming a full-fledged sociopolitical disorder cannot be attempted on the practical plane, but has to start on the theoretical, viz. by restructuring the worldviews which shape social consciousness. I stress, however, that ideas and thoughts are articulated historically by a socially bound consciousness, and that the articulated meaning is, hence, never absolute, but relative to a specific social and historical setting. I attempt, finally, to underscore the vital role played by the intellectual in determining future directions, and in bringing about social consensus for undertaking a project of modernity.

Intentionality and Spontaneity

To begin with, it is worth noting that the question of the nature of the interrelationship between consciousness and reality we are dealing with is rooted in the subject-object duality created by Descartes' efforts to predicate existence on thinking. It is in the Cartesian *cogito ergo sum* (I think, therefore I am) that we confront the sharp distinction between being and thinking, between the spiritual and the material. Therefore the ultimate solution of our dilemma can be realized only in transcending the dichotomy of body and soul, matter and mind. Our immediate concern in this study is, however, more limited, for we are primarily interested in determining the nature of the forces guiding and directing the unfolding of human history. Are these forces primarily cultural, or are they, in the last instance economic? To put the question more precisely, are the laws which control social development economic, or are they moral?

In addressing this question, let me emphasize at the outset that economic and cultural forces are by no means independent of each other, they are both interrelated and interconnected in a comprehensive whole we call society. This interconnectedness between the economic and the cultural has been acknowledged by both Marx and Weber, and was theoretically established by Lukacs and Althusser.[2] What is not clear, however, is whether historical change is guided by laws embodied in the economic structure of society, and are hence operating independently of human consciousness and intentionality, or whether change is brought about by the contemplation and conscious design of willful moral agents. Marx emphatically insisted that the laws that guide the movement of history, which he termed the "laws of motion" are economic in nature. He therefore set out in *Capital* to uncover these laws and to use them to demonstrate the inevitability of the socialist revolution. Marx discovered that the capitalist mode of production is subject to two fundamental tendencies, which he ultimately unified under one general law. With some oversimplification, Marx's analysis of the basic trends, or laws, governing the development of bourgeois society may be rendered as follows. Capitalism, he contended, is progressing along two parallel thrusts. Modern (bourgeois) society is experiencing, Marx argued, an increased concentration of wealth in fewer hands. He called this trend the "law of capitalist accumulation," and attributed it to the constant transformation of surplus value to capital.[3] This trend or "law" of increased concentration of wealth and consolidation of capital corresponds to another trend, viz. an increasing impoverishment (pauperism) of the working class. Marx called the latter trend which creates superfluous class of unemployed workers the law of "progressive production of surplus population," or "the industrial reserve army."[4] Marx unified these two "laws" in one "general law" he called "the general law of capitalist accumulation." "The greater the social wealth, the functioning capital," he observed, " the extent and energy of its growth, and therefore also the greater the absolute mass of the proletariat and the productivity of its labour, the greater is the industrial reserve army. . . . *This is the absolute general law of capitalist accumulation.*"[5] He predicted, therefore, that as capitalism progresses, society experiences an increased contradiction between capital and labor interests. The capitalist inability to manage the social consequences of these economic trends puts society in a permanent crisis, and set the tone for class struggle between the bourgeois and the proletariat, a struggle ultimately culminates in a socialist revolution when the internal contradictions of capitalism become acute.

But is the development of modern (bourgeois) society guided by the "general law of capitalist accumulation," or is this law itself precipitated by other laws of different nature? A clue to answering this question could be found at the conclusion of Volume One of *Capital.* In a chapter entitled "The Secret of Primitive Accumulation," Marx argues that primitive accumulation of capital was the result of a series of legislation intended to regulate economic activities, dating back to the fourteenth century, over three centuries before the Industrial Revolution became manifest. Marx remarks:

> Legislation on wage-labor, which aimed from the first at the exploitation of the worker and, as it progressed, remained equally hostile to him, begins in England with the Statute of Labourers issued by Edward III in 1349. The ordinance of 1350 in France, issued in the name of King John, corresponds to it.[6]

He then goes on to argue that the "Statute of Labourer," and other subsequent legislation, set the ground for the creation of a class of free laborers who were forced to sell their labor-power on the market, thereby marking the beginning of the primitive accumulation of capital possible.

Yet even if we were to accept Marx's interpretation of the origin of primitive accumulation, it would be logical to argue that if the roots of capital accumulation lie in the *de jure* misappropriation of labor-power and the exploitation of the worker, one can hardly conclude that social structures evolve pursuant to economic laws, for these laws (e.g. the general law of capitalist accumulation) are themselves controlled by legal laws rooted in the value commitments and ideological orientation of the dominant social groups. To put it differently, the "laws of motion" of modern society, i.e. economic laws, would have been completely different, had society been organized according to drastically different social norms, say in a society where social inequality was benign. That is, if the scientific and technological revolution took place in an egalitarian society, one can argue that capitalism, with its distinct economic laws, would have not been possible. Marx may protest that technological advancement would have not been possible under conditions of equality, since technological advancement, he may insist, requires capital accumulation, and hence extraction of surplus value. Such an objection could be sustained only if we accept the proposition that surplus value can be generated solely through the capitalist misappropriation of labor-power. But capitalist exploitation is by no means the only possible process for extracting surplus value. Capital accumulation may be realized whenever (a) total social production exceeds total social consumption, and (b) society is willing to reinvest the surplus-value generated in future production. These two conditions could possibly be met not only by individual capitalists, but also by corporate management, cooperative management, state bureaucracy, and numerous other possible forms of economic organization. However, what makes one form of organization effective in one society and ineffective in another is the nature of the prevailing social norms, i.e. whether social values and beliefs permit this or that type of economic organization.

But aside from the issue of the effects of cultural norms on economic organization, the question of the nature of the forces that guide historical change boils down to whether social development occurs pursuant to imminent laws beyond the intentional and conscious manipulation of social actors, or whether sociopolitical changes are the outcome of the contemplated actions of willful moral agents? Here we find the Marxist explanation of history at its weakest. The confusion over the nature of the interaction between *human agency* and *institutional limitation* could be detected not only in the system-theoretical orientation of orthodox Marxism, but also in the more rounded approach advocated by Lukacs and Althusser. Lukacs, for example, continued, even after acknowledging the active role played by the superstructure in controlling social development, to be equivocal in defining the relationship between consciousness (which after all is what the superstructure is about) and history. "The essence of scientific Marxism," he wrote in *History and Class Consciousness*, "consists, then, in the realisation that the real motor forces of history are *independent of man's (psychological) consciousness of them.*"[7] He therefore insisted that "[o]nly when the core of existence stands revealed as a social process can existence be seen as the product, *albeit the hitherto unconscious product*, of human activity."[8] Yet Lukacs acknowledges two chapters later that the social reality of the bourgeois society is instituted in such a way that the interests of the capitalist could be accommodated.

> We have already described the characteristic features of this situation several times: man in capitalist society confronts a reality 'made' by himself (as a class) which appears to him to be a natural phenomenon alien to himself; he is wholly at the mercy of its 'laws', his activity is confined to the exploitation of the inexorable fulfillment of certain individual laws for his own (egoistic) interests.[9]

The apparent contradiction between the latter passage in which Lukacs affirms human agency on the one hand, and the two earlier quotations in which he denies it on the other, could be resolved by distinguishing man the individual from man the class, as the above quoted statement by Lukacs seems to suggest. But this resolution of the conceptual problem we are dealing with would reveal much deeper difficulty, namely, the difficulty of explaining how individual members of social groups can pursue the collective interests of their class while remaining incognizant of their nature and scope. Implicit in this assumption is the notion that individual ideas and interests are not part of the same action system, but do belong to separate and independent systems. In other words, by affirming intentionality to the class and denying it to the individual it is assumed that social classes can non-discursively advance their class interests, or better that social cooperation among individuals who share similar interests can proceed apart from their articulated ideas and goals. We, thus, turn now to examine whether the claim of separate and independent systems of ideas and interests can be sustained, and to explore, in general terms, how ideas and interests are interrelated.

Idea-Interest Interplay

Marx rejected, we saw earlier, the idealist assertion that man's social conditions and material production are determined by his consciousness. "Life is not determined by consciousness," he wrote, "but consciousness by life."[10] He insisted that people's consciousness, their ideas and conceptions, initially reflected, and was directly connected with, their material activities. "Consciousness can never be anything else than conscious of existence," he proclaimed, "and the existence of men is their actual life-process."[11] Marx contended that ideas began to develop in isolation of social processes and claim a power of their own at an advanced stage in the social evolution of mankind, when mental work was separated from physical work. Henceforth, ideas and thoughts lost their direct link with material life, and assumed, therefore, the form of ideology, i.e. a "false consciousness", a set of ideas whose net effect was to distort reality and obscure the exploitative "relations of production." With the emergence of a new group of professional theorists and philosophers, the coincidence between theoretical and practical consciousness disappeared, and the connection between theory and practice was severed. Henceforth, Intellectuals who arose from the ranks of the ruling class used their mental skills to advance and defend their class interests.[12] Marx maintained that in any social order, morality, law, religion, and political ideas are designed to protect the interests of the social classes which control the means of production. "The ideas of the ruling class," Marx wrote, "are in every epoch the ruling ideas."[13]

Marx's rejection of the primacy of ideas was echoed by Nietzsche. However, unlike Marx who conceived ideas as instruments employed for promoting the interests of the ruling class, Nietzsche saw them as means used by the intellectual to disguise his real motives. "[O]ne must follow the instinct," he proclaimed, "but persuade reason to assist them with good reasons."[14] For Nietzsche, the bottom line for all intellectual and philosophical endeavors was not the love of *truth* or wisdom, as philosophers would like us to believe, but the love of *power*, pure and simple. The philosopher's thinking, he asserted, was guided not by pure reason, but by practical interests.[15] He went so far as to ridicule the rationalists for failing to recognize the *instrumental* nature of reason. "The father of rationalism," he wrote referring to Descartes, "conceded authority to reason alone: but reason is an instrument, and Descartes was superficial."[16]

The notion of the *primacy* of interest over idea, and instinct over reason seems to have had adherents not only among materialists and realists, but also among eminent empiricists and rationalists. David Hume, for example, noted in *A Treatise of Human Nature* that "reason alone can never be a motive to any action of the will."[17] Kant, likewise, accepted the primacy of practical over theoretical reason. "The practical sciences," Kant wrote, "determine the worth of the theoretical. What has no such [practical] employment is indeed useless. The practical sciences are the first according to intention because ends must precede means. But in execution the theoretical sciences must be first."[18] In spite of the diversity of their theoretical backgrounds, Marx, Nietzsche, Hume, and Kant seem all to agree that the ultimate motivational basis for human action lies beyond the impassive and cold principles of reason. Yet this is a far cry from concluding that ideas are superfluous or that theoretical consciousness is unimportant. By no means does any of the foregoing philosophers argue that social action is possible solely on the basis of mere interest or instinct. Even Marx who contended that consciousness is determined by economic infrastructure, and that ideology serves to mask the exploitative relations of production, recognized that social interaction is contingent on the existence of shared perception and understanding among the members of social classes. Social cooperation presupposes the existence of social consciousness, culture, or ideology. "Consciousness is, therefore, from the very beginning," Marx noted, "a social product, and remains so as long as men exist at all."[19]

Since the realization of individual interest is only possible in social settings, individual action must be coordinated with, and adapted to, the actions of other social members. Consequently, a system of ideas (i.e., ideology or political culture) has to emerge first to justify and legitimize the existing, or desired, social order. That is to say, for the individual to be able to pursue a specific interest, his interest must be recognized and accepted by the prevailing normative and social structures. This recognition, based on shared ideas or ideology, is necessary not only for preventing collision of actions and regulating conflict of interests, but also for securing cooperation and ensuring support. Similarly, the development of an ideology is needed for the purpose of generating support for restructuring society so that new interests can be accommodated. Commenting on the intricate relationship that exists between ideas and interests, Jurgen Habermas notes:

> Interests have to be tied to ideas if the institutions in which they are expressed are to be lasting; for only through ideas can an order of life acquire legitimacy . . . an instrumental order based on self-interest rest only on the "purposive rational weighing of advantages and disadvantages" by strategically acting subjects, such that their complementary interest-oriented expectations are mutually stabilizing. However, an order that rest "only on such foundation" (as repression, custom or self-interest) would be "relatively unstable."[20]

Marx himself did not deny that social cooperation presupposes ideas. He only believed that ideas would inevitably be used, in any socially stratified system, for the purpose of promoting the interests of the ruling class, and manipulating the masses. Marx, however, committed the same mistake he attributed to idealist philosophers. For while idealists downplayed the impact of social forces and material interests on the development of thought and culture, Marx ignored the role the symbolic system of a culture plays in shaping ideas and inspiring actions.

It was the one-sided causal dependency which Marx assumed between thinking and being, or idea and interest, which led him to conclude that backward Asia and Africa were destined to grow in the image of industrial Europe. Marx insisted, as we noted in Chapter 2, that the restructuring of Indian society by the British colonial authorities would ultimately result in the creation of a modern (bourgeois) society patterned after the European model.[21]

Unlike Marx, Weber, though conceding the primacy of the emotional and the psychological over the rational, rejected the causal one-sidedness of the Marxian interpretation of development. In the introduction to his study "The Economic Ethics of World Religions," Weber argued that people's actions are governed by both their "material and ideal interests." But he attributed the directions these actions take and the forms through which they are revealed to "the world images which have been created by 'ideas'."[22] Weber admitted that cultural values and religious ethics have been historically used to safeguard the interests of the ruling elite, or to justify inequitable social stratification. Yet he pointed out that one can also find cases where society was restructured so that social institutions and practices were guided by religious ideas and values.

> These comments [concerning the autonomy of religious doctrine] presuppose that the nature of the desired sacred values has been strongly influenced by the nature of the external interest--situation and the corresponding way of life of the ruling strata and thus by the social stratification itself. But the reverse also holds. Wherever the direction of the whole way of life has been methodically rationalized, it has been profoundly determined by the ultimate values toward which this rationalization has been directed. These values and positions were thus religiously determined.[23]

And so one can consistently argue that while the economic interests of the bourgeoisie prevailed in determining the direction of socio-political change during the Industrial Revolution, moral (religious) ideals were predominant in determining the direction of change during the Reformation stage of Western civilization.

Truth and Order

Based on the above discussion, we are now in a better position to shed more light on the nature of the relationship between the normative and the economic, between ideas and interests. We saw that social integration can be achieved only as a result of normative consensus. This means that the general framework that guide individual and collective action is determined by the shared ideas and values of the people. But within this general framework, ideas and values can be, and are, manipulated, reinterpreted, and used for advancing special interests. However, the manipulation of ideas for serving particular purposes gradually distorts the very structure of consciousness which made civilized life and social organization possible in the first place, thereby leading to the deformation of the very structures once allowed people to enjoy meaningful cooperation. Social structures (the relations of production of Marx) therefore reflect the general attitude of a people, their beliefs and perceptions of the world, and their value commitments. This means that the *social order is shaped in accordance with some transcendental order embedded in the people's understanding of the nature of ultimate reality.* Since our understanding of reality is not immediate, but rather mediated by a set of ideas, the disorder experienced in society reflects deeper disorder in the people's consciousness of ultimate reality. consequently, a people experiencing social disorder have to seek the resolution of their existential problems on the theoretical plane, i.e. on the level of consciousness.

Historically, social disorder which gave rise to Western modernity was the result of the deformation of social structures. This deformation took a variety of forms: the exploitation of one social group by another, misappropriation and misuse of societal resources by a center (or centers) of power, the failure to use societal resources (both human and natural) efficiently to address the various problems and difficulties confronting society, the lack of cooperation and coordination among the various individuals and groups that comprise society, or even a constant "war of all against all," a condition which Thomas Hobbes identified, in his major work the *Leviathan,* and rightly recognized as a major hindrance of civilization and progress.

But regardless of the shape and form through which social deformation may manifest itself, the root causes of this deformation have to be sought in the structure of consciousness. More specifically, it has to be sought in the way social consciousness understands and perceives the world. Social deformation signifies, therefore, a distortion in the general perception of the 'truth.' The distortion of truth need not, however, be precipitated by an act of malicious intent. It could well be, and is frequently, the result of a confusion between the moral ideals and their existential embodiment in individual personalities and social institutions. Distortion results from the mystification of the relationship between the ideal and its historical embodiment, between the volatile and abstract ideal and the concrete institutions derived from it and captured in the historical experience of a specific social organization. The distortion of truth is the direct consequence of the idealization of historical interpretations (discourse) and institutions, an idealization which has to be blamed on a faulty epistemology that mistakenly asserts that the ideals which society aspires to realize can be captured, once and for all, in the discourses and institutions of a specific historical society, and that these discourses and institutions, despite the temporal nature of their bearers and signifiers, have attainted an absolute universality. Such a perception is evidently faulty, for it could be true only if we ignore the historical evolution of human experience, and the cultural specificity of social groups.

It should be pointed out that the relationship between the ideal and its articulation in historical moments is dialectical, and should be kept that way if it is to inspire social conduct. Because in order for the ideal to have positive effect, it must surrender its universality and objectivity by becoming embodied in a specific and concrete doctrine. Only when the universal (ideal) is reduced to particular rules and institutions can it begin to transform the human world. However, the embodiment of the ideal in a concrete rules or institutions should always be regarded as tentative, and the possibility for future reevaluation or modification should be kept open.[24]

The search for order is, therefore, at bottom a quest for truth, i. e. a quest for the transcendental principles whose embodiment in social reality would establish the conditions responsible for unleashing human creativity and energy, and bringing unity, integrity, and cooperation to society. This requires a fresh look at social institutions and practices so as to examine the extent to which institutions and practices continue to be the embodiment of universal ideals. The search for order also requires a fresh encounter with cultural symbols, a new discourse capable of revealing a new meaning which takes into account the existential possibilities connected with the evolving structures of consciousness. It is this attempt at reinterpreting cultural symbols is what Weber terms intellectualism, which he places at the threshold of the process of rationalization. Historically, the process of intellectualism was always associated with the efforts of the intellectual strata (most notably the stratum of priesthood) to reinterpret the sacred text, and to have a new insight into the nature of the cosmos.[25] This process was basically the essence of the Protestant Reformation which attempted to have a direct access to the sacred text, overlooking the huge corpus of church interpretations and doctrines. The Protestant reformers viewed the church's interpretation of sacred symbols as an attempt to distort reality and conceal the truth.

Likewise, the Enlightenment attempted to discover the structure of the cosmos anew. It managed this time to do so not by contemplating the symbols of the sacred text, but the signs of nature. The Enlightenment philosophers found in nature the source of not only the laws of necessity that govern the behavior of matter, but also the laws of freedom which guide social conduct. The Enlightenment discovered ideology, or "the science of ideas" as Destutt de Tracy once referred to, and used it as an instrument of social integration to replace religious doctrines which played similar role in Medieval Europe. Yet de Tracy's hope, shared by many philosophers of the Enlightenment, to articulate a comprehensive set of ideas that would reflect the true nature of the individual and society has been proven to be mere illusion. Over the last three centuries since de Tracy announced his discovery of a "science of ideas," it has become increasingly evident that all ideas articulated by historically situated consciousness are bound to reflect the peculiarities of the historical and cultural milieu from which these ideas are articulated, and that the quest for truth has to continue generation after another. As Karl Mannheim put it: "the main hope of discovering truth in a form which is independent of an historically and socially determined sets of meaning will have to be given up."[26] Mannheim noted, in his major work *Ideology and Utopia*, that the very term "ideology" became, by the early twentieth century, synonymous with distorted views and false claims. Following the lead of Gramsci, he recognized that in addition to the particular meaning of ideology as an attempt to deceive others and disguise the true intent of its proponents, it also represents, in its total sense, a genuine effort on the part of its proponents to describe the world as it appears to them from their particular historical-social vantage point. Ideology, in its total sense, plays a constructive role in the life of the political community in that it helps demystifying social relations and revealing social contradictions.[27]

It follows that all discourses, regardless of whether they are classified as political, philosophical, or religious are ideological because they express the historical-social situations of their proponents. Truly, discourse, being susceptible to ideological distortion, may be used to mystify reality when its proponents refuse to recognize the temporal nature of their ideas, and the

inadequacy of these ideas for the progressive articulation of
human ideals. Yet by the same token, discourse is essential for
the demystification of reality for it can reveal cultural and
structural contradictions, and attempt, at the same time, at
reconciling these contradictions by reinterpreting the cultural
symbols that gave rise to the prevailing cultural and structural
forms in the first place.

The Intellectual as a Catalyst

The quest for order cannot begin on the level of social structures
and social institutions, for as we saw in Chapter 3, social
structures are instituted by the actions of individual members of
society, and therefore reflect the orientation of these actions. The
quest has to begin first on the level of individual consciousness,
through the processes of self-criticism and rationalization. The
former aims at reinterpreting cultural symbols and using this new
reinterpretation to discover, and then resolve, cultural
contradictions. The latter attempts to extend the newly achieved
reconciliation and reorientation from individual to the social
consciousness. *The medium through which an extension may
become possible is discourse.*

Yet the quest seems overwhelming to ordinary consciousness.
For one thing, the three levels of meaning which constitute social
reality (i.e., institutions, discourse or ideology, and symbols) are
not easily differentiated from one another by ordinary
consciousness. From this point of view, ideas appear as the
discursive expression of cultural symbols, and institutions as the
practical embodiment of ideas. But because of the instrumentality
of ideas for linking cultural symbols with social institutions, and
vice versa, they could be used to justify structural deformation by
distorting the truth of the symbols on the one hand, or using the
deformed structures of social reality to disguise and obscure the
true meaning of cultural symbols. But for another, even if
ordinary consciousness is able to detect the deceptive role ideas
may play, such realization, though necessary for creating a need
and motive for change, does not suffice for undertaking the
quest. For the search of order to begin, the realization of
deformity and distortion has to be brought from the level of
institutions to the level of discourse, so that analytical and
synthetical activities, central to the quest, can be undertaken. In

other words, the consciousness which will lead the search for order has to experience the state of disorder (either in its cultural nihilistic or structural alienating forms), be eager to replace it with a meaningful order, and has the necessary skills to undertake the task of externalizing the internally achieved order. The consciousness which can lead the quest for order has to be yearning for meaning, and has to be desirous of "penetrating beyond the screen of immediate concrete experience."[28] As Weber put it:

> The intellectual seeks in various ways, the casuistry of which extends into infinity, to endow his life with a pervasive meaning, and thus to find unity with himself, with his fellow men, and with the cosmos. It is the intellectual who conceives of the "world" as a problem of meaning. . . . As a consequence, there is a growing demand that the world and the total pattern of life be subject to an order that is significant and meaningful.[29]

Weber notes that, historically, all conscious departures from tradition had been made possible by prophetic pronouncements presented in the form of revolutionary mission. By "prophet" Weber understands a charismatic leader who uses his charisma to advance a new perception of reality through religious doctrines. He makes no distinction between a "founder" of a religion and a religious reformer.[30] Although Weber seems to suggest that social change may be brought about by the revolutionary forces of "reason," he places a major emphasis on the role of charismatic leadership in effecting profound change. Charismatic leaders effect change by altering their followers attitudes toward life, through an integrated worldview.[31] The change in attitude does not result from a merely intellectual contemplation, but is shaped in the process of struggling to restructure the old order.

> Charisma . . . may effect a subjective or internal reorganization born out of suffering, conflict, or enthusiasm. It may then result in a radical alternation of the central attitudes and directions of action with a completely new orientation of the central attitudes and the different problems of the world.[32]

Historically, the charismatic appeal of the prophet lay in two things: his ability to bring a new comprehensive revelation that could endow the entire life with meaning, and his exemplary character manifesting itself in personal commitment and devotion to the ideals embedded in revelation. The intellectuals' mission, on the other hand, has manifested itself in the elaboration and systematization of the cultural symbols established by prophethood, or in their reinterpretation so as to reconnect these ideals with the structure of reality after they have been reified in the practices and institutions of a specific historical moment.

The intellectual's major task is to bring unity and order to the objects of the world, both the natural and cultural. He manages to do so by working on what he has received form the past, by attempting to systemize and rationalize the intellectual and cultural heritage. In his endeavor to bring order, the intellectual strive to identify intellectual and moral distortion and institutional deformation, to eliminate cultural and structural obstacles, and to resolve theoretical inconsistencies and structural contradictions. Yet the process of intellectualization is not purely intellectual, concerned only with theoretical activities designed to overcome conceptual ambiguities, but is also political, involving efforts aimed at surpassing structural limitations. This means that the transformation of social reality, which is the essence of intellectualization, cannot be achieved simply by articulating the parameters of the new order in a discourse, but is contingent on the development of a comprehensive strategy and the emergence of a political movement led by an intellectual stratum. As Michel Foucault remarks:

> The essential political problem for the intellectual is not to criticise, or to ensure that his own scientific practice is accompanied by a correct ideology, but that of ascertaining the possibility of constituting a new politics of truth. The problem is not changing people's consciousness—or what's in their heads— but the political economic, institutional regime of production of truth.[33]

It should be noted here that not all intellectual activities are part of the intellectualization process which lies at the core of the modernization process, nor are all intellectuals equally equipped to undertake a project of modernity. For in addition to possessing the necessary technical skills, the intellectuals who are destined to lead society into a new, more equitable and fulfilling, order should enjoy an authentic personality, a personality whose purpose and aspirations are anchored in the transcendental world. He should be of the kind that would find more satisfaction in fulfilling his intellectual (spiritual) need for meaning, than in fulfilling his physical needs for pleasure. He should be of the kind that places moral and intellectual integrity over material gratification. He should be of the kind that will be willing to undertake risks to see to it that the ideas and ideals he espouses are objectified and institutionalized in real life, rather than give up his beliefs and values and succumb to the power that be. Foucault uses the adjective 'universal' to refer to this category of intellectuals who in the eighteenth-century Europe undertook the responsibility of standing up "to power, despotism and the abuses and arrogance of wealth."[34] The universal intellectual is "the person who utilizes his knowledge, his competence and his relation to truth in the field of political struggle,"[35] to see to it that equity and justice are applied to all human beings, rather than being the prerogative of a small group of well-to-do individuals. Foucault sees in the person of the eighteenth-century French intellectual Voltaire the prototype of such intellectuals.[36]

The process of intellectualization owes its genesis to the burning desire to discover the truth that lies beyond the distortion of an ossified ideology, its outcome, however, is determined by the intra-intellectual struggle between the 'universal' intellectual who is committed to reorganizing society in accordance with the principles of truth, and the 'particular' intellectual who employs his knowledge and skills in the service of the established power. It follows that the quest for truth quickly develop into a political struggle between the 'universal' intellectual who finds himself standing on the side of the oppressed segment of society, the victims of distortion and deformation, on the one hand, and the ruling elite who are the direct beneficiaries of structural deformation and the perpetuators of cultural distortion.

Intergroup struggle can not be explained (as Marxist revolutionaries--beginning with Lenin--came to realize) apart from intellectual struggle. And so while we may agree with Marx that the struggle for political change has historically assumed the form of antagonism and conflict between an economically privileged classes and proletarian classes, we could still reject the notion of the primacy of the economic, and insist that economic choices are consequential to the moral choices of the individual. Because wealth and economic consideration serve, more often than not, as a corrupting economic factor for the intellectuals who side with power, those who pose as defendants and advocates of the political and economic interests of the dominant groups lack not only the incentive and sensitivity to look beyond their social specificity and recognize distortion and deformation, but the impartiality needed for identifying the underlying principles of truth as well. The universal intellectual who is detached from the class structure of society and dedicated to the principles of right and truth is, consequently, far more significant for the process of change in society. His refusal to succumb to the power that be and to be corrupted by wealth and sensuous happiness, derives from his moral anchoring in transcendental values, and his orientation toward the beyond and the sacred.[37] The alliance between the universal intellectual and the oppressed and alienated "proletarian" groups occurs because the latter, being detached from social convention and the corrupting effects of material consideration, are more likely to respond positively to new interpretation and display "an original attitude toward the meaning of the cosmos."[38]

This argument runs contrary to the Marxist assertion that the intellectual is organically connected to social classes. Marxists have contended all along that the intellectual's search for order is inspired by his immediate class interests. Marx postulated that the intellectual, a product of the bourgeois class, will turn against the bourgeoisie, and work to promote the interests of the proletariat only when he is stripped from his economic privileges and reduced to a member of the proletariat class as a result of the progressive concentration of capital in fewer hands, and the constant shrinking of the capitalist class. Lenin, likewise, assumed that the proletarian class would be led by intellectuals who, being alienated by the ruling class, share the class interests of the workers. The communist intellectuals, he asserted, constituted the revolutionary vanguard who would lead the workers to the new communist order. Gramsci went further in *The Prison Notebooks* to argue that every social class produces its own intelligentsia. "Every social group, coming into existence on the original terrain of an essential function in the world of economic production," Gramsci wrote, "creates together with itself, organically, one or more strata of intellectuals which give it homogeneity and an awareness of its own function not only in the economic but also in the social and political field."[39]

The Marxist contention that the intellectual's activities are inspired by his class affiliation is problematic, for this argument overlooks the fact that the class affiliation of the intellectual is, more often than not, voluntarily chosen. That is, the intellectual himself very often chooses his social position in the conflict between social groups. For all it takes in most cases for the intellectual to change his affiliation with social groups is to denounce his old ideological and value commitments and adopt new ones. If *pure self-interest* is the guiding principle of all intellectuals, as the Marxist would have it, the question of why the universal intellectual would choose to maintain his commitment to certain ideals and principles at the expense of undertaking a great deal of pain and suffering, when he could avoid such a sacrifice by placing his knowledge in the service of the power that be, cannot be answered

The position of the universal intellectual becomes clearer when we realize that the coincidence between the interests of the intellectual and those of the oppressed groups (the proletariat) occurs not because the intellectual has become an organic part of the proletariat, as Gramsci and other Marxists insist, but because of the fact that by opposing deformation, he stands to support the interests of those who have been affected adversely as a result of structural deformation. By the same token, by lacking any interest in disguising and distorting the truth, the proletariat are less inhibited and more supportive and receptive to the activities of the universal intellectual which aim at uncovering the true implications of cultural symbols and reinterpreting them in light of existential changes so as to take into account new cultural and social developments. It follows that while Marx was right when he argued that the transition from one social order to another results from the increased contradiction between social groups, he was wrong when he concluded that the direction of historical change is determined by the material conditions of society.

It should be noted that no claim has been made in the above argument as to the intellectual's ability to maintain complete autonomy from all interest and power structures inherit in social organization. Such a claim would be too simplistic to reflect the complications and subtleties of intellectual activities. *The argument rather points to the need to recognize the intellectual's capacity to rise above his historical determinedness and transcend particular interests in his quest for meaning and order.* It is this longing for truth and order which makes social reformation possible. Clearly the intellectual has to find actual support among social groups and has to be able to relate social transformation to the material interests of those who will undertake the risky task of standing up against the established power. In addition, the intellectual's ability to disclose the "facts" and articulate the truth is conditioned by the structural (e.g., power structure) and conventional (e.g., social beliefs and values); such inhibition, however, has primarily a strategic significance. Doubtless, the necessity of recognizing the structural and cognitive obstacles that stand between the intellectual and the new order, and the need to make certain compromises and to manipulate circumstances do exert great influence on the intellectual's discourse and action. The intellectual will, certainly, have to make certain compromises and adjustments along the way, and to prudently move toward his goals. Yet these considerations do not take away from the fact that the intellectual would have, ultimately, to sustain himself in the face of the established power, and occasionally in the face of unreceptive supporters and sympathizers, through his moral grounding in universal transcendence, above and beyond all particular interests.

Notes

1. Parsons and, most recently, Habermas have attempted to achieve such a synthesis. See, for example, Parsons' The General Theory of Action (coauthored with Edward Shils), and Habermas's The Theory of Communicative Action.
2. See Chapter 2 for a more detailed discussion of the interaction. between the cultural and economic.
3. Marx, *Capital* vol. 1, pp. 725-34 and 762-72.
4. Ibid. pp. 781-94.
5. Ibid., p. 798.
6. Ibid., p. 900.
7. Lukacs, *History and Class Consciousness*, p. 47. Stress is mine.
8. Ibid., p. 19. Stress is mine.
9. Ibid., p. 135.
10. Robert C. Tucker, *The Marx-Engels Reader,* 2nd ed. (N.Y.: W.W. Norton & company, 1978), p. 155.
11. Ibid.
12. Karl Marx, *The German Ideology,* in Tucker, p., 159.
13. Ibid., p. 172.
14. Friedreich Nietzsche, *Beyond Good and Evil*, trans. Walter Kaufmann (N.Y.: Vintage Books, 1966), p. 104.
15. Ibid., pp.11-13.
16. Ibid., p. 104.
17. Brubaker, p. 59.
18. Richard L. Velkely, *Freedom and the End of Reason* (Chicago: The University of Chicago Press, 1989), p. 5.

19. Tucker, p. 158.

20. Jurgen Habermas, *The Theory of Communicative Action,* *Vol. 1,* trans. Thomas McCarthy (Boston: Beacon Press, 1984), p.189.

21. Tucker, p. 659. See also the introduction to Chapter 1.

22. Weber, *From Max Weber,* p. 280; see also Lash, p. 140; and Habermas, *Communicative Action,* Vol. 1, p. 193, 216.

23. Weber, *From Max Weber*, p. 286-7.

24. For further discussion on this point see Iredell Jenkins, *Social Order and the Limits of Law* (Princeton University press, 1980), pp. 333-5.

25. See Weber, *Economy and Society*, pp. 500-6.

26. Karl Mannheim, I*deology and Utopia*, p. 71.

27. Ibid., pp. 69-87; also Kiros, pp. 101-2.

28. Shils, *The Intellectual and Power*, pp. 25-6.

29. Weber, *Economy and Society*, p. 506.

30. Weber, *Economy and Society*. pp. 439-40.

31. Ibid., vol. 1, p. 450.

32. Ibid., p. 245.

33. Michel Foucault, Power/Knowledge, trans. Colin Gordon et. al. (N.Y.: Pantheon Books, 1980), p. 133.

34. ibid., p. 128.

35. Ibid.

36. Ibid.

37. See Shils, *The Intellectual,* pp. 40-3.

38. Ibid.

39. Gramsci, *The Prison Notebooks*, p. 5.

Conclusion to Part I

We began our examination of the process of modernization by trying to determine the essence of historical change. We saw that there are two basic models of development: the Marxian and the Weberian, the former places the locus of change in the economy, the latter in the culture. Marx attributed social change to the constant technological changes. New technologies give rise to new social organization, and ultimately to new political ideas and institutions. Marx assumed that workers' awareness of their historical role in bringing about new order would come automatically as soon as social conditions, themselves controlled by the state of technology, become ripe. Twentieth-century Marxists, beginning with Lenin, came to realize that not only is class consciousness not determined by structural change, but that class consciousness itself controls structural change. The direction of societal progress depends, ultimately, on the orientation of social actors, i.e. on the predominant cultural values and beliefs.

Leading twentieth-century Marxists came, eventually, to confirm the thesis advanced by the Marxian model's rivalry, the Weberian model. Weber taught that social development is in essence a process of cultural rationalization, whereby one worldview is replaced by another, leading to the emergence of new forms of consciousness, and ultimately new societal institutions and relationships. Perceiving modernization as essentially a process of rationalization need not be considered as an invitation to utter idealism. It is rather a rejection of material determinism and a reassertion of the primacy of ideas and values in determining societal institutions and practices. Marx was correct in insisting that historical directions are not determined by the whimsical will of individual agents, but by the structures of power embodied in social organization. He failed, however, to realize that power structures are determined by social cooperation, and, hence, by the beliefs and values which make such cooperation possible. Evidently, functionalist theorists repeat Marx's mistake when they contend that Third World modernization could be understood exclusively from a system-theoretical viewpoint. Indeed, functionalism reduces action to behavior when it insists that one can understand societal change by asking questions aimed at discovering how societal functions are attended to, or by finding out "who does what and when," while completely ignoring the purposes, motives, and commitments of social actors.

Modernization is at bottom a rationalization process. That is, it is an emancipatory project, aiming at eliminating the superstitious and irrational elements of culture, and therefore freeing the creative energies of the members of society. The emancipatory project is stimulated by an experienced disorder. The disorder manifest itself in two interrelated ways. On the level of consciousness, the disorder takes the form of cultural distortion, whereby the individual becomes increasingly unable to relate social ideas and values to his life situation. Cultural ideals and values appear to stand in contradiction with the aspirations of an increasing segment of society. On the level of reality, societal structures and institutions are turned into fetters, denying the individual the opportunity to grow and realize his potential. Political institutions cease to be the social embodiment of individual value commitments for an increasing number of people.

Finally, the replacement of disorder with order is contingent, first, on the people's ability to discover the cultural and social sources of distortion and deformation, as a necessary step for identifying the principles of order, and secondly, on the creation of social consensus on the desirability of the new principles of order. It is here that the role of the universal intellectual becomes crucial. Being equipped with the intellectual skills to analyze, synthesize and reinterpret reality, and the psychological authenticity to resist the pressure to adapt to prevailing societal conditions, the universal intellectual endeavors to bring order to his own internal world by redefining the relationship between the part and the whole, the universal and the individual, and then strive to extend the internally achieved peace and order to the surrounding society. By articulating the principles of order via discourse, the intellectual constantly tries to broaden the circle of social consensus in hope of establishing the articulated worldview as the predominant discourse.

We may conclude, therefore, that although the intellectual's ability to effect change is limited by the social and psychological conditions prevalent in society at a specific historical moment, its ultimately the intellectual activities that determine the direction of social change. It follows that one can in vain understand the thrust of development in a society by completely ignoring the internal intellectual and ideological debate. This is not to say, however, that by concentrating solely on the intellectual activities one can understand society's sociopolitical processes. The claim is rather that the analysis of the ideas and purposes articulated by the intelligentsia should be considered as an integral part of the overall study of society. Put differently, the claim is that a comprehensive approach to studying non-Western societies requires that the system-theoretical analysis be combined with an action-theoretical analysis.

PART II

The Modernization of the Arab World

Prelude to Part II

We concluded in Part I that modernization cannot be achieve merely by the introduction of Western ideas and institutions to developing countries, but requires a systematic rationalization of the structures of both consciousness and society. I argued that true modernization (modernization qua rationalization) cannot be attempted at the level of institutionalized action by replacing traditional forms with modern ones, but has to start at the level of theory by emancipating the creative and cooperative energies of the members of society, and eliminating the superstitious and irrational elements of culture.

In Part II we turn our attention to the modernization of the Arab society. My purpose in studying the process of modernization in the Arab world is twofold. First, to gain insight to the developmental processes in a non-Western society, as they have been guided by and reflected in the writings of leading Arab intellectuals. Secondly, to test some of the propositions and hypotheses of the conceptual framework advanced in Part I.

I have treated the Arab world, despite the significant political and social divisions that exist among Arab states, as one cultural bloc. It is true that what is referred to as the Arab world is far from being homogeneous. It consists of twenty sovereign states who, apart from their symbolic and occasional cooperation through the Arab League, have completely independent and frequently competitive, domestic and foreign policies. But behind the façade of power politics, there exists, as it will become soon apparent to the reader in the following chapters, a profound sense of commonality and a great deal of intellectual and cultural interactions. The cultural commonality of Arab countries is reflected in the lively debate among Arab intellectuals and the similarity of the political and social problems and concerns they all share.

In studying the evolution of Arab consciousness in modern times, I tried to discuss the ideas of those thinkers who have made remarkable contributions in shaping and reshaping contemporary Arab mind. I also tried to carefully select intellectuals representing the major ideological movements currently influential in Arab societies. I should point out, however, that the discussion is confined only to issues and concerns which have direct bearing on the subject-matter of this study, and is by no means reflective of all issues and concerns which have been subject to intellectual debate and contention.

Finally, by dividing my presentation to four phases, I am aware that the division is far from being perfect. For not only the tendencies identified with each historical phase do overlap, but some of our intellectuals do not fit neatly into one tendency or the other. Yet despite its imperfection, the schematic division should be helpful, I propose, for revealing the dialectics of the internal tensions and ideological rivalries which lie at the roots of the efforts to modernize Arab society.

Chapter 6

Voices of Reform

Throughout the better part of the nineteenth century and the early years of the twentieth, the regions of the Ottoman Empire were the ground of intense reformist activities, aimed at revitalizing Middle-Eastern societies. The period stretching over a century, from the turn of of the nineteenth century, when the Ottoman Sultan Salim III introduced his reformist program, until the collapse of the Ottoman Empire and its dissolution after WWI, represents the formative epoch in the modern awakening of Arab mind after many centuries of deep slumber. Among the intellectuals who played a crucial role in alerting the masses to the many challenges lay ahead, and urged the rulers and the ruled alike to take all necessary measures to reform social and political conditions four stand out: Rafa'a al-Tahtawi, Jamal al-Din al-Afaghani, Muhammad Abduh, and Abdul-Rahman al-Kawakibi.

Although our four intellectuals differed in their approaches to the internal and external difficulties facing the Middle Eastern society in some important ways, they all shared a number of common grounds. First, they were avowed anti-traditionalist, wasting no time or effort to condemn the blind imitation (*taqlid*) of the forefathers, a practice to which many Arab and Muslim scholars had by then fallen. Secondly, they were well exposed to Western thought, and came in direct contact with Western culture. This experience with alternative and, for the most part, superior ways of doing things convinced them of the need for a drastic social and political changes. Thirdly, despite the diversity of their attitudes toward the West, and the solutions they offered to social problems, they all displayed a strong commitment to Islamic values, and unwavering devotion to the goal of renaissance (*nahda*) and modernization (*tajdid*). These reformists had to deal with a wide array of difficult questions, the most troublesome of which was their struggle to define the relationship between Middle-Eastern and Western cultures. Mideast-West relationship continues to be a troubling area for Arab intellectuals even today, for, as it will be shown later, the West represents for many Middle Eastern intellectuals at once a civilizational model and a military and ideological foe.

Early Contacts with the West

The question of modernization, and the debate and conflict over modernizing approaches and measures, of the Middle East may be traced back to the early years of the nineteenth century, when the need to reform the military institution, and with it the education and administration systems, was felt by political and military leaders at the highest levels within the Ottoman ruling circles. Up until the eighteenth century, the Ottoman Empire was considered a Great Power, with a formidable military capacity and vast territories, stretching over the bulk of Eastern Europe and the Middle East. Yet by the end of the eighteenth century, it became apparent that the Empire was on a course of rapid decline. The state of decline was felt by Sultan Salim III (reigned 1789-1808), who was especially concerned about the deteriorating conditions of the Ottoman army, and the decline in the Empire's capacity to meet military threats from the rising European powers, most notably the Russian Empire. Salim III moved quickly to restructure the aging Ottoman military institution and modernize military industries. His plans to reform the military were, however, seriously challenged by the leaders of the army's elite forces, the *Janissaries* corps. After a fierce struggle, the Sultan's reform plans were defeated, and Salim had, ultimately, to pay with his life for his modernization efforts. The *Janissari* leaders successfully overpowered the Sultan, forcing him to abdicate the Ottoman thrown, and subsequently executing him.

The attempts at restructuring and modernizing the Ottoman military establishment were later resumed by Sultan Mahmud II, but only after he was able to eliminate the *Janissaries* and liquidate their leaders. Although the Janissaries' resistance to change was probably prompted by their fear that the restructuring of the army would most likely take away many of the privileges they enjoyed under the old order, their complaints were directed against the efforts to emulate, and borrow from, the "enemies of the faith."[1] Indeed, traditionalists would continue to resist, as will be shown later, reformist ideas and measures under the pretense that these ideas do not reflect the true Arab or Islamic ethos, since they were developed within an alien culture, and reflect the experience of another people.

For Sultan Mahmud II, as was for Salim III before him, the modernization of the Ottoman army meant that the outdated military training and equipments had to be replaced by new ones, developed after the European models. More specifically, modernization meant for the Ottoman Sultans that the Empire had to enlist the services of West European military experts and technicians. Indeed, the employment of West European military trainers and technicians was already underway during the reign of Salim III who, by commissioning officers from Britain, France, Italy, and Sweden to reorganize and rejuvenate the Ottoman military, had provoked the wrath of the *Janissaries*.[2] Mahmud II attempted, during the early years of his reign, to negotiate with the *Janissaries* and to strike a compromise with them. They, however, showed no signs of flexibility, completely rejecting the idea of modernizing the military, while insisting on maintaining the "old principles."[3] The rigidity of the *Janissari* leaders convinced the Sultan that the modernization of the Ottoman military could not proceed until the *Janissari* corps were dismantled. Mahmud II emerged from his confrontation with the Janissaries victorious. Using units of the recently created regiments known as the "modern order" (*nizam jadid*), and a great deal of maneuvering and deception, he was able to eradicate the *Janissaries*, in 1826, once and for all. The destruction of the *Janissaries* opened the way to Mahmud II to create a completely new military order, constructed after the European model.

The efforts to modernize the military were not confined to those of the Sultan at Constantinople. Muhammad Ali, the ambitious governor or Egypt, shortly followed in the footsteps of the Ottoman Sultans, embarking on a project of military modernization. Starting his career as an Ottoman military officer, he fought his way up to the leadership of Egypt, and was acknowledged by Constantinople as the governor of the Ottoman province of Egypt. He quickly became a formidable rival to the Ottoman Dynasty, and came close to controlling the entire Ottoman territories. Muhammad Ali began his efforts to build a modern military force by hiring ex-officers of European armies, mainly French and Italian. He established several military academies to teach modern military doctrines and techniques, and built a new industrial base to supply the military with modern weaponry systems.[4] However, he went farther than the Ottoman Sultans when he decided to sent missions of Egyptian nationals to receive training in Europe. He started sending students in small groups to receive training in Italy as early as 1813. The first large mission, consisting of forty four students, was sent to France in 1826. This unprecedented move to sent Muslim students to study in the West encouraged the Ottoman Sultan Saleem II to follow suit, sending Ottoman nationals to study in Western Europe, mainly in Prussia.[5] Undoubtedly, sending Muslim students to the West marked the beginning of profound cultural changes in Middle Eastern society.

Although the early reforms led by the Ottoman Sultan and his governor were directed almost exclusively toward the military establishment, the two Middle Eastern rulers soon realized that to keep the Ottoman military forces competitive with their European rivals, they had to introduce modern sciences to the education system, and hence decided to establish technical schools to teach pure sciences, such as mathematics and physics, since these sciences were excluded from the curricula of regular schools. Evidently both Muhammad Ali and his patron were driven toward reform by the desire to maintain or expand their power base. For not only were their reformist efforts directed, almost exclusively, at the military and the bureaucracy, but they showed no interest whatever in social and political reform.[6]

Yet despite the Ottoman rulers' desire to confine modernization to technical spheres, and the many precautionary measures which they took to safeguard against European cultural influences, the separation between the technical and cultural spheres of Western civilization proved untenable. Quickly, European ideas, customs, and habits began to penetrate the Ottoman society, creating social divisions and cultural tensions. Cultural tension and polarization became increasingly evident when those who received training in Europe came back to assume leading positions in the Ottoman bureaucracy. Having been exposed to a superior civilization, the Europe-educated students were deeply impressed by the advanced political and social institutions of Europe, and by the vigor and skills of Europeans.

Europe as a Civilizational Model

Among those students who had the opportunity to experience the European civilization first hand was Rafa'a al-Tahtawi (1801-1873), who came back to register his experience in a book published in Cario in 1265 (1849 A.D.). Al-Tahtawi received his higher education in al-Azhar University in Cairo, the most prestigious university throughout the Muslim world at the time, before he was sent by Muhammad Ali to Paris with the first education mission in 1826. In addition to being the religious instructor of the mission, he was to study French and familiarize himself with French literature. Al-Tahtawi was quite impressed by the advanced French society he came in contact with. Realizing that the quality of life in France was drastically different and remarkably higher than that of Egypt, he felt the need to reassure the reader of his memoir of the accuracy of his account of the French society. In the preface to his memoir of the Paris years, published under the title *Takhlis al-ibriz fi talkhis bariz*, he pleaded with the reader not to think that he was exaggerating in his account of the life in Paris, stressing that he was faithfully conveying his experience of the French civilization. "By God," he wrote, "I had had compunctions throughout the period I spend in this country about the lack, in the provinces (mamalik) of Islam of the [good] things enjoyed here."[7]

Al-Tahtawi's observations of the French life are of great historical significance because they provide us with a somewhat detailed contrast between the life in the Middle Eastern and Western societies in the mid-nineteenth century. Although al-Tahtawi only sporadically contrasted the Middle Eastern and Western cultures, his amusement and fascination by the advancement of European civilization tell us a great deal about the decadence to which the Muslim society had fallen. The disparity between the European and Middle Eastern societies is strikingly reflected in the following revealing passage: "The power of the *al-ifrange* [Europeans] had multiplied by their technical and organizational skills, as well as their fairness. Had it not been for the protection extended by the Almighty God, [the land of] Islam would have been nothing compared with their [the Europeans] strength, multitude, wealth, skills, and other [qualities]."[8]

Al-Tahtawi was impressed by various aspects of the French society. He was, for example, stricken by the literacy of the French people and the advancement of their educational institutions, pointing out that reading and writing was a common practice of even those who are engaged in "lowly" jobs such as artisans.

> You should know that the Parisians are distinguished among the Christians by their intelligence, brightness, and profundity,

unlike the Egyptian Christians, who are naturally inclined towards laziness and idleness. Not only are they disinclined toward blind imitation, but they are intent on learning the truth (nature) of all things through evidence. Even their commons know how to read and write. [Furthermore] all sciences, arts, and professions are described in books, including the lowly ones. Artisans need, therefore, to learn reading and writing in order to master their crafts; and experts in different fields try to contribute to their professions by either inventing something new, or refining what has been invented by others."[9]

Considering that the things which impressed al-Tahtawi the most about the French society were those which were lacking in the Egyptian society, this text undoubtedly underscores the decadent and stagnant conditions of the Middle Eastern society at the turn of the nineteenth century. Al-Tahtawi was greatly impressed by the diligent and hardworking French people, remarking that even the wealthy among them did not shun work.[10] He was, likewise, impressed by the social status of the French women. Not only did he encounter assertive and self-confident females, exhibiting the type of personality which he could only associate with male behavior, but came across well educated women with remarkable literary skills. Among the Parisian women, he noted, were some who had translated great literary works from foreign languages, and others had themselves authored important works. Al-Tahtawi was further fascinated by Paris's cultural life and its recreational facilities. Describing the theaters of Paris, he commented that in addition to the recreational atmosphere they create, the plays provide and important educational tool, conveying to the public instructive messages, wrapped within an attractive package.[11]

Perhaps the aspect of the French life which struck al-Tahtawi the most was the political. He alluded repeatedly to the principles of equality and liberty as being the central features of French political life, and attributed social and economic successes of the French society to a constitutional law, respecting the dignity of individuals and providing for the equality of all citizens. Commenting on the text of the French constitution, which he translated to Arabic and included in his memoir, he pointed approvingly to the various guarantees of individual rights provided for by French laws, especially to legal and political equality and freedom of belief and expression.[12]

Al-Tahtawi attributed the advancement of the French society primarily to the "fairness and equality" of French political order.

"Their minds believed," he wrote referring to the French people, "that justice and fairness are the basis of civilized kingdoms and the source of people's happiness. And the ruler and the ruled alike submitted to the principle [of justice]. Consequently, their country prospered, their sciences flourished, their wealth accumulated, and their hearts achieved satisfaction, so much so that you never hear anyone complain of injustice. Justice is indeed the foundation of civilization."[13]

Rafa'a al-Tahtawi was one of the very few Arab intellectuals who cared to register their experience in, and impression of, the West at this early stage of the modern encounter between Western and Arab cultures. Al-Tahtawi was greatly impressed by Western accomplishments and markedly fascinated by French society, so much so that he failed to notice any flaws in French life, and painted, in his memoir, a picture of almost faultless society. Perhaps the only area he referred to with some disapproval was the area of male-female relationship, and what he perceived as an excessive sexual openness and promiscuity.

Al-Tahtawi was very candid and open about his conviction in the need to borrow from the French experience and emulate the French civilization. He strongly defended Muhammad Ali's modernization project, arguing that learning Western sciences and enlisting the services of European expertise was the right course for improving the backward conditions of the Egyptian society.

> Since he [Muhammad Ali] was inaugurated, he, may the Almighty protect him, has been engaged in the treatment of her [Egypt's] ills, which, without his [care], would have become incurable, and reforming her decadent conditions, which would have become chronic. He has [further] sought from among the Europeans those who have mastered the inventive techniques and the beneficial professions, giving them fortunes out of his bounty. As a result, the common people, both in Egypt and abroad, have begun blaming him, out of ignorance, for employing, welcoming, and spending money on Europeans. What they do not understand is that he has been doing this not for the sake of their [the Europeans] Christianity, but for their humanity and scientific knowledge.[14]

One can feel in this passage the early signs of the internal tension created by the introduction of Western methods and ideas to Arab society, a tension which would gradually grow to reach, in less than one century, the level of social crisis when European social and political ideas began to take hold within the educated classes of Middle Eastern societies. Further, the struggle between the proponents and opponents of Western modernity would become more intense after the European colonization of Arab countries was completed by the end of WWI. Henceforth, Europe could not be seen anymore, after its imperialist intentions became apparent, as purely a civilizational model, but also as a symbol of aggression and a source of threat.

Europe as a Menacing Other

While al-Tahtawi saw in Europe a civilizational model to be admired and emulated, Jamal al-Din al-Afaghani, and his pupil Muhammad Abduh, perceived it as a source of threat and a foe to be feared and guarded against. Al-Afaghani was born in 1839 at As'ad-Abad, near Kabul in Afghanistan. He studied Islamic sciences in different parts of Afghanistan, Persia, and Iraq.[15] In March 1871, al-Afaghani arrived in Cairo, Egypt where he met his eminent pupil Muhammad Abduh. Henceforth the two reformist leaders would work in unison to create political awareness in the Arab society.

Al-Afaghani pursued, throughout his life, two principal goals: The struggle against imperialism and the unification of the Muslim community (*Ummah*). He took every opportunity to warn the Muslims of the threat of European colonialism in general, and British in particular. For the latter, he argued, surpassed other European powers in their ambition and shrewdness. Rather than using naked force to extend their dominion over other nations, the British, he contended, usually resort to trickery and deception to achieve their goals. They, further, target those nations which are rich in natural resources, but weak in military power, or lowly in spiritual strength.[16] Very often they disguise their real imperialistic objectives under the pretense of helping the rulers to quiet popular revolt, or, alternatively, they offer their support and assistance to the people themselves in their struggle against oppressive rulers. In either case, they move quickly to subjugate the people and to reduce the rulers into puppets working under the direct command of the colonial administration.[17]

To underscore the aggressive and exploitative nature of colonialism, al-Afaghani cites the American and Irish experiences with the British colonialism.

> If a state should depart from [the norms of colonial rule] and deal with its colonies with some equity, avoiding injustice, oppression, and persecution, this should be the manner of the English with their American colonies. For they both, the English and the American, share common language, religion, denomination, and morality. Such [similarity] should invoke the compassion [of the English] and inspire them to avoid using violence [against the Americans]. But alas! All colonial rule are the same. And we all know how much the Americans had to suffer under the oppression of the English rule, being subjected to all forms of persecution and rubbed of their money by all kinds of taxation.[18]

As to the Irish, al-Afaghani pointed to the plight of the Irish under the English rule, and to the fierce arm struggle between the two very close nations. Having pointed to the flight of many Irish to America, and to the engagement of those who stayed behind in a bloody struggle with the British authority, thereby putting their lives at a great risk, he asked: "Is the flight of the Irish and their constant confrontation with death as a result of their revolt against the English a sign of their repulsion to justice and hate to happiness? [Could this be the reason of their revolt] when we know that humans are naturally inclined towards them [i.e., justice and happiness]."[19]

Al-Afaghani's relentless attack on European colonial powers notwithstanding, he recognized and acknowledged the positive aspects of European culture. He admired the vigor of Europeans and called upon the Muslims to acquire those values which gave the West its superiority. Responding to an accusation that he had had personal animosity and hatred toward the English people, he noted that the resentment and harsh criticism he expressed were directed only towards the oppressive colonial policy of the English government, and not toward the English society as a whole. No one can ignore, he proclaimed, that the English are among the most advanced nations, and that they are among the first to adhere to the principle of justice and to respond to the plight of the oppressed. He added, however, that this is their manner only among themselves.[20]

Likewise, he expressed his admiration to the firmness, ambition, and daring of the European people. The European bravery and vigor, he argued, propel them to aim at high goals and to confront all sorts of challenges no matter how difficult they may be. "Their great love of glory," he wrote referring to the Westerners, "led them to see in its pursuit not only food for their souls, but also nourishment for their bodies."[21] He, therefore, called upon Easterners to follow the good example of the West, and to vigorously seek high and glorious objectives. [22] Further, al-Afghani did not blame the plight of Eastern nations exclusively on colonialism, but equally blamed the Middle Easterners for their weakness and inability to defend themselves against foreign aggression. He strongly believed that the helplessness of the Muslim people was but the natural consequence of their scientific and moral decline. After all, colonialism is at bottom "the domination of nations distinguished by their strengths and sciences of weak and ignorant nations." "It is a law of nature," he observed, "that the 'strong and knowledgeable' should govern the 'weak and ignorant'."[23]

Al-Afghani, along with Abduh, endeavored to combat fatalism, which plagued the bulk of Muslim societies by the turn of the nineteenth century. It was widely accepted then that Muslim decadence was natural, as it reflected an advanced stage in the continuous moral decline since the time of the Prophet. It was also believed that this trend was inevitable and beyond human control.[24] Al-Afghani rejected this interpretation of history, which was advocated by traditionalists, insisting that Muslim decadence had been precipitated by moral and intellectual decline, and that the superiority of the West, and its triumph over the Muslims, was a temporary stage in the continual struggle between the East and the West. He attributed Western military superiority to its scientific advancement, arguing that the French and English had been able to conquer Muslim lands not by the virtue of being French or English, but because of their superior and more advanced scientific capabilities.[25] Furthermore, al-Afghani saw a positive aspect of the rivalry between the East and the West, contending that the Western invasion of the Muslim land had a stimulating effects on the Muslims, and would eventually awaken them from the state of slumber that had dominated their lives for centuries.[26]

Al-Afghani recognized, however, that scientific development could not be achieved merely by training Muslims to use Western technology. For technology and scientific innovations are but artifacts, reflecting the ethos of a people and their philosophical outlook. What was needed for the Muslims to progress was a new spirit and direction.

> If a community did not have a philosophy, and all the individuals of that community were learned in the sciences with particular subjects, those sciences could not last in that community for a century. . . . The Ottoman government and the Khedivate of Egypt have been opening schools for the teaching of the new sciences for a period of sixty years, and they are yet to receive any benefit from those sciences.[27]

Al-Afaghani ascribed the Muslim failure to catch up with the West in science and technology to their deficient outlook and faulty perspective, arguing that Islam had created in the early Muslims the desire to acquire knowledge. Thus, they quickly assumed a leading role in scientific research, first by appropriating the sciences of the Greeks, Persians, and Indians, and later by moving these sciences to new frontiers.[28] He accused contemporary Muslim scholars ('ulama) of wasting time and energy on trivial matters, instead of addressing the important questions and issues facing the Muslim community (Ummah). He therefore called upon the 'ulama to probe into the causes of Muslim decline and devastation, instead of occupying themselves with minutia and subtleties.[29] Rather than providing strong leadership for the community, he proclaimed, 'ulama had become obstacles hindering its development. By dividing science, which has a universal nature, into Islamic and European, the 'ulama have deprived the Ummah of technology, allowing the West thereby to surpass the Muslims in military capacity. "Ignorance had no alternative," he wrote, 'but to prostrate itself humbly before science and to acknowledge its submission."[30]

The other chief goal al-Afaghani endeavored throughout his life to accomplish was the unification of the Muslim people under one Islamic government. Establishing a unified Islamic state, he thought, could be the first step toward reforming the decadent conditions of the Muslims. He believed that such a state could revitalize the Muslim Ummah and mobilize the masses to meet the European challenge. To achieve this goal, al-Afaghani tried first to persuade the rulers of India, Persia, and Egypt, as well as the Sultan Abdul-Hamid, the head of the Ottoman Empire, with whom he had close personal relations, to islamize the practice and policy of their governments. He soon realized that Muslim rulers were neither receptive to his ideas, nor interested in Islamic reform. Gradually, he began to address his reformist ideas to Muslim intellectuals in particular, and the public in general.

In 1879 he went to Paris, after he was expelled from Egypt by Khedive Tawfiq for his increasing political activities, where he established, along with Muhammad Abduh, an Arabic newspaper called *Al-'Urwa al-Wuthqa* (The indissoluble Bond). Now al-Afaghani openly held Muslim rulers responsible for the disunity of the Muslims. Muslim rulers have, he argued, put their self-interests before those of the *Ummah*, and hence allowed the division of the Muslim world into small entities. It is incumbent upon Muslims, he asserted, by their faith to come together under one banner, and join forces to meet the challenge of imperialism. Al-Afaghani contended that the division of the Muslim world into small units defies the teachings of Islam, and thus should not be condoned by Muslims.[31]

> Actually, the schisms and divisions which have occured in Muslim states originate only from the failure of rulers who deviate from the solid principles upon which the Islamic faith is built and strayed from the path followed by their early ancestors.[32]

The division of the Muslim world into small states, he maintained, was artificial, induced by the struggle for power among various rulers. As such, this division did not reflect the real sentiments of the Muslim masses who had been, on the contrary, united from the very beginning only by the bonds of Islam, disregarding any other type of bonds such as race or ethnicity.[33]

Al-Afaghani insisted that Islam, and only Islam, was to be the basis of the unity of the Ummah. He conceded that people are naturally inclined to seek the support of those who share with them their language and ethnic background, their national character. But when a people submit to the authority of God and his revealed law, he contended, they will have no need to appeal to their ethnicity, having accepted one universal law.[34] He rejected the notion that a unity based on religious grounds is likely to stir fanaticism, accusing the British of disseminating such ideas so as to be able to dominate Muslim regions, having divided them into small manageable units. It was by dividing the Muslims into small rivaling sects, the British, he proclaimed, were able to establish their hold over India.[35]

The Menace From Within

Muhammad Abduh, who spent the first part of his public life working closely with al-Afaghani and was committed to the goals of combating colonialism and achieving Muslim unity, became convinced in his latter years, that the principal menace threatening the *Ummah* lies within its boarders. He came to the conclusion that the problems of the Muslim people are at bottom cultural and social problems, and believed that the road to progress starts with intellectual reform and cultural rejuvenation.

What were the causes of Muslim stagnation (*jumud*)? Abduh posed the question and responded by pointing to two sources: bad politics and intellectual decline. The politics of oppression and selfishness was to be blamed for the decline of the Muslims, and the distortion of the principles of Islam. The true principles of Islam were bent and misinterpreted, and stripped of their moral essence. Muslims were, therefore, left in a state of despair after the vital content of Islam, which once inspired the Muslims, have been taken away. Islam, Abduh asserted, has been reduced today to few rituals such as prayer, fasting, and pilgrimage, as well as a few meaningless statements.[36]

But if the rulers are guilty of subversive activities for the purpose of maintaining their grip on power, the Muslim scholars (*'ulama*) are equally responsible for the Muslim decline for they have failed to confront the serious problems facing the Ummah, and to enlighten the people as to how they can go about solving them.[37] Even worse, the *'ulama* have adopted a fatalistic outlook, believing that nothing can be done to overcome the plague encompassing the Muslim community. Abduh explains:

> Those idle and stagnant say, repeating the saying of the enemy of the Qur'an: The end of time has arrived, and the day of judgment is about to start, and that corruption which has befallen the people and the *recession* which has inflicted religion are only signs of the age. It is, therefore, useless to work to [rectify these deviations], for all efforts [in this regard] are fruitless, and all movements [in this direction] are pointless.[38]

The fatalistic attitude of Muslim scholars was reflected in their resistance to innovation and creativity, as well as in their blind adherence to the opinions of their forefathers. To prevent contemporary Muslims from resorting to original reasoning and to inhibit fresh reading of the divine revelation, traditionalist *'ulama* raised the early generation of Muslims to the level of sanctity and infallibility, and resorted to all repressive measures to combat original minds.[39] Abduh went farther to openly accuse traditionalist *'ulama* of being the enemies of Islam; they kept the Muslims weak by depicting natural sciences as perverted, admonishing Muslims to refrain from learning them. "The truth is where there is proof," Abduh wrote, "and those who forbid science and knowledge to protect religion are really the enemies of religion."[40]

Abduh rejected the notion put forth by orientalists that the decline of the Muslims was attributed to Islam, arguing, on the contrary, that their stagnation is due to the decline in the commitment of the Muslims to the true principles of Islam.[41] Abduh devoted a great deal of his efforts to clarify the principles of Islam, defend it against its detractors, and repudiate what he perceived as a misreading of the Islamic revelation and a distortion of the true principles of Islam. He asserted that the teachings of Islam are still capable, if adhered to, of prompting the *Ummah* forward. For, to begin with, Islam has freed man from the mythical notion that his fate could be controlled by the will of other human beings, or manipulated by stones, trees, stars, and others.[42] Further, Islam cautioned against blind immitation (*taqlid*) of the forefathers, and asserted that preceding in birth is not a sign of superiority in learning or knowledge. On the contrary, those who are born at latter historical epochs have better opportunities to utilize the knowledge accumulated over time.[43]

Abduh perceived the crisis of the *Ummah* as a rationality crisis, and felt that he had to reemphasize that thinking is not merely the reiteration of the views and opinions of early Muslim scholars, but should include original reasoning as well. In his book *Al-Islam wa al-Nasraniya* (Islam and Christianity), he numerated five basic Islamic principles, three of which emphasize the centrality of human reason. Discussing what he called the first basic principles of Islam, he argued that Islam requires that true belief has to be based on evidence, and should satisfy the requirements of rational judgment. By appealing to human rationality, Islam has, therefore, elevated reason to the seat of authority.[44] Abduh went even further to argue for the primacy of reason over revelation when the two come into contradiction. Does this mean that Abduh believed that reason was the ultimate basis of truth, or that revelation occupied a subordinate position in relation to reason? Not at all. Abduh insisted that reason and revelation are coeval, complementing each other. Without revelation, reason is doomed to go astray, and without reason, revelation is incomprehensible. As such, they may not contradict each other, and at any time a contradiction between the two occurs, we should regard such contradiction to be more apparent than real. When a contradiction between the principles of reason and a revealed text becomes apparent, we should accept the judgment of reason and "bracket" the implications of the text. That is, we can either admit our inability to comprehend the text or reinterpret the text in ways that would eliminate the apparent contradiction, provided that our new reading of the text does not violate the formally accepted linguistic rules.[45]

Abduh's hasty and obscure treatment of the interrelationship between reason and revelation made him vulnerable to attacks from both traditionalists and secularists. His casual and loose use of the terms reason and revelation made his discussion of the relationship between the two open to a great deal of speculation and misinterpretation. In his highly acclaimed book *Risalat al-Tawhid,* he made an attempt to clarify the concept of reason. He contended that all theologians and philosophers, agree that human reason can discern good and evil deeds by evaluating their effects even in the absence of external criteria supplied to it by revelation. He claimed that animal and child behavior, as well as human history can provide us with many evidence in support of this proposition.[46] Human beings can, by applying utilitarian criteria, agree in general terms on what constitute good or bad deeds. However, as soon as they move from dealing with actions in general, to evaluating specific acts, they are likely to disagree among themselves pursuant to their individual tastes and interests. He concluded, therefore, that human reason cannot single-handedly guide the activities of humans unless it is enlightened by revelation.[47] It is not clear, for instance, whether Abduh uses the term reason in reference to the principles of formal logic, or to a comprehensive system of propositions which can be used as criteria for sound judgments and reasonable actions. Nevertheless, Abduh confronted a vital issue that remained unattended to in the Muslim world for centuries, reminding his contemporaries that revelation itself would be rendered incomprehensible if it is deprived of human reasoning

The Roots of Arabism

Before we conclude this general outline of the formative years of what is generally known in Arab literature as the Arab or Muslim renaissance, we need to briefly review some of the ideas presented by another influential figure in modern Arab history, namely those of Abdul-Rahman al-Kawakibi (1848-1902). Al-Kawakibi was born at Aleppo in Northern Syria. He worked as a journalist early in his life, and established two newspapers in 1878 and 1879. Both papers were closed by the Ottoman authorities who decided that the material published in them was subversive. Al-Kawakibi published two major works, *Um al-Qura* (the mother of towns) and *Taba'i al-Istibdad* (the characteristics of tyranny). In the first book, al-Kawakibi set out to discover the causes of the "idleness" (*futur*) which had befallen the Muslims in the last few centuries.

> What is the cause of the [state] of idleness which has, for centuries now, permeated the Muslims, whoever they are, wherever the live, and whatever their religious or political views may be, both on the individual and collective levels? We can clearly recognize this [state of idleness] when we compare between Muslims and non-Muslims in two neighboring regions or villages, or even between a Muslim and non-Muslim families in the same village. We will, then, find that the Muslims are always lagging behind, in their activities and organization, in all aspects of life, personal and public alike. We will find them, likewise, less meticulous (skillful), in every profession, in comparison with their [non-Muslim] counterparts, though they are distinguished--everywhere, from their neighbors by their moral character--i.e., their honesty, courage, and liberality.[48]

Al-Kawakibi realized that the crisis confronting the Muslim society is, at bottom, a cultural one. The problem lies in the first place in the belief and value system of the Muslim population as they are manifested in the attitude and behavior of the Muslims. The cultural basis of Arab decline becomes transparent when one realizes that non-Muslim Middle Easterners, who after all share the same social and political environment, have escaped the state of idleness. Having determined the general character of the problem, al-Kawakibi turns to discuss in some detail the specific aspects of this cultural crisis. Among the important aspects discussed by al-Kawakibi are:

First, the deeply rooted fatalism in the minds of latter-days Muslims. Muslims have come to believe that they have no control whatsoever over the historical development of society. Al-Kawakibi attributed this belief to the scientific decline of the Muslims which made people unable to analyze and understand the causes of social changes, thereby attributing it to supernatural causes in order to disguise their ignorance.[49]

Secondly, the widespread subversion of Muslim scholars by political authorities. The "official" scholars, as he referred to them, have become hired guns, ready to employ their expertise in the service of the personal ambitions of rulers in return for monetary compensation and political privileges.[50]

Thirdly, the antagonism toward natural sciences which is widespread among the 'ulama, who insist that only religious sciences are worthy of being studied. The anti-science 'ulama have condemned the study of mathematics and physics, accusing anyone attempting to study them of heresy, thereby creating the conditions which ultimately led to the disappearance of these sciences from Muslim society, while science continued to flourish in the West.[51]

Fourthly, The widespread illiteracy among Muslim Women, who have been kept at home uneducated. The current conditions of women, al-Kawakibi remarked, are in complete contradiction to the tradition of early Muslim society, when women were literate, and great many of them became scholars and scientists.[52] Lacking training and education, contemporary Muslim women, al-kawakibi asserted, are unfit to rear and raise bright children.[53]

To deal with the current cultural crisis of the Muslim society, al-Kawakibi, in agreement with al-Afaghani, believed that political reform was needed. A new political order, under which all Muslim regions were to be united, had to be forged. He suggested that a federation, structured after the German or American model, should be established.[54] The new political order, he argued, should have the following features:[55]

1. The establishment of an Arabic caliphate, with the caliph chosen from the tribe of Quraysh. Makkah was to be the new capital.

2. The caliph would have a direct political authority on the region of Hijaz. His rule would, further, be limited by the authority of a shura (consultative) council, established exclusively for the Hijaz region.

3. A general shura council, representing all Muslim provinces (sultanate) and principalities (emirate), to be created. The council to be headed by a president chosen by the caliph.

The Model suggested by al-Kawakibi deserves two comments. First, al-Kawakibi was careful to limit the executive authority of the caliph, who was to be the head of the proposed union, to the province of Hijaz, the Eastern region of Arabia, a limitation which accords with his views regarding the centralization of authority. Al-Kawakibi was critical of the political programs, adopted by the Ottoman government in the second part of the nineteenth century, which aspired to achieve more centralization of power. (The program was also criticized by al-Afaghani who tried unsuccessfully to persuade the Sultan Abdul-Hamid to abandon it.) Al-Kawakibi believed that a centralized system was inappropriate to a Muslim union. For one thing, it would impose a narrowly designed legal and administrative code on a highly diverse people, with different habits, customs, and nationalities. But for another, it would make the system very rigid, unable to respond to the specific needs of the various elements within the Empire.[56]

The second point deserving comment is the new emphasis on the Arabs as the people who are more qualified to rule the proposed Muslim federation. Indeed al-Kawakibi depicted the natives of the Arabian Peninsula as a people better equipped to play a leading role in the new political order, because of the purity of their origin, and their "uncontaminated" doctrines as well. As he put it:

[The people of Arabia are more equipped to lead the Muslims because], as you know, the people of the peninsula, who constitute about seven to eight millions, all of whom are Muslims, puritan in their beliefs, and most of whom belong to the Hambali and Zaidi sects. Among these people religion has emerged, and is verbalized in their language. They are, therefore, the people and bearers of religion, and its defenders and protectors. Rarely have they mixed with outsiders, or have appeared among them anyone who called to an unorthodox religions doctrines so as to distinguish himself.[57]

By emphasizing the centrality of the Arabs among the Muslim people, and their distinct character, al-Kawakibi sow the seeds of Arab nationalism. In fact the revolt of Sharif Hussain, the governor of Makkah, himself a decendent of Quraysh, against the Ottoman in 1917 in unsuccessful bid to create an Arab state in the Middle East, could be read as an attempt to fulfill al-Kawakibi's vision.

Concluding Remarks

By the end of the formative years of Arab renaissance, a number of trends emerged, trends which would later shape the political and intellectual life of Arab society. The four intellectuals discussed in this chapter represent a profound revolt against the backward status quo, all of whom have been influenced, in one way or the other, by the rising European powers. Europe presented, at once, a source of inspiration and a model to be emulated and followed on the one hand, and a source of threat and a foe to be feared and confronted on the other. The ambivalent feeling toward the West, a feeling which later became intensely troubling after the colonization of the Middle East, is transparent in the writings of the four reformists. While admiring Europe for its scientific and political accomplishments, they resented and distrusted, with varying degree of intensity, the Europeans either for posing a potential threat (al-Tahatawi), or for their imperialistic and aggressive policies toward Muslim regions (al-Afaghani).

We can also recognize, at this early stage, the emergence of two competing models, or frames of reference, which were presented as promising alternatives to the status quo: the Western model, embodied in the Western civilization, and the Islamic model, exemplified in the early Muslim community. Al-Tahtawi, along with numerous Lebanese intellectuals, called for the Westernization of the Arab society, and the adoption of Western cultural forms. Whereas the other three intellectuals invoked the Islamic historical model, calling upon Muslims to re-embrace the ideals of the early Muslim community, and to reform the current social and cultural structure. As it will be shown in the next chapters, the two models soon collided as society became increasingly polarized into two major social blocs.

Clearly, the two models did not appear to the four leading reformists to be mutually exclusive. Al-Tahtawi and Abduh, have argued that many of the European practices reflected a direct application of Islamic principles abandoned by the Muslims themselves. Abduh, for instance, once said: "We went to Europe and saw Islam, but did not see Muslims, and came back to the Muslim land to see Muslims but not Islam." On the other hand, many Western ideas and institutions, such as the representative government or federalist system, were included in the historical model advocated by al-Kawakibi and Abduh.

Notes

1. Muhammad Abdul-Latif al-Bahrawi, Harakat al-Islah al-Uthmani fi Asr al-Sultan Mahmud al-Thani (1808-1839) (Cairo, Egypt: Dar al-Turath, 1978), p. 118.

2. Ibid., p. 108.

3. Ibid., p. 180.

4. Abdul Rahman al-Rafi'i, Asr Muhammah Ali, 4th ed. (Cairo: Dar Al-Ma'arif, 1982), pp. 326-42.

5. Ibid., pp. 407-8; also al-Bihrawi, p. 200.

6. Ibid., p. 321.

7. Rafa'a Rafi' al-Tahtawi, Takhlis al-Ibriz fi Talkhis Baris (1265 A.H.) in Usul al-Fikr al-Arabi al-Hadith 'Ind al Tahtawi, Mahmud Fahmi al-Hijazi (Cairo: al- Hay'at al-Masriya al-'Ama lilkitab, 1974), p. 141.

8. Ibid., p. 148.

9. Ibid., p. 208.

10. Ibid., p. 210; also pp. 288-292.

11. Ibid., p. 256.

12. Ibid., pp. 237-40.

13. Ibid., p. 40.

14. Ibid., p.148.

15. Jamal al-Din al-Afaghani, Al-A'mal al-Kamila, Vol. 2, ed. Muhammad Imara (Cairo: al-Mu'asasa al-'Arabiya, 1981), pp. 20-29.

16. Ibid., p. 71.

17. Ibid., p. 72.

18. Ibid., p. 73.

19. Ibid., p. 147.

20. Ibid., p. 83.

21. Ibid., p. 91.

22. Ibid.
23. Ibid., p. 72.
24. Muhammad Abduh, *Al-Islam Din wa Hadarah*, Tahir al-Tinaji, ed. (Cairo, Egypt: Al-Hilal, n.d., p. 148.
25. Jamal al-Din al-Afaghani, "Lecture on Teaching and Learning," in *An Islamic Response to Imperialism*, Nikkie R. Keddie, ed. (Berkely, CA: University of California Press, 1968), p. 17.
26. Al-Afaghani, *Al-A'mal al-Kamilah*, Vol.2, pp. 335 and 339.
27. Al-Afaghani, "Lecture on Teaching and Learning,"p. 17.
28. Ibid., p. 18.
29. Al-Afaghani, "The Benefit of Philosophy," in Keddie, pp. 120-1.
30. Al-Afaghani, "Lecture on Teaching and Learning," in Keddie, p. 17.
31. Al-Afaghani, *Al-A'mal al-Kamilah*, Vo. 2, pp. 28-33.
32. Al-Afaghani, "Islamic Soliderity," in Keddie, p. 23.
33. Al-Afaghani, *Al-A'mal*, V.2, p35.
34 Ibid., pp. 34-5.
35. Ibid., pp. 42-4.
36. Muhammad Abduh, *Al-Islam wa al-Nasraniyah Ma'a al-'Ilm wa al-Madaniya*, 7th ed. (Cairo: Dar al-Manar, 1367), p. 150.
37. Ibid., pp. 140-41.
38. Ibid., p. 177-8.
39. Ibid., p. 134-37, and 154.
40. John Esposito, *Islam in Transition:Muslim Perspectives* (N.Y.: Oxford University press, 1982), p.19.
41. Abduh, *al-Islam and al-nasraniyah*, p. 145.
42. Muhammad Abduh, *Risalat al-Tawhid* (Cairo: Dar al-Ma'arif, 1966), p. 144.
43. Ibid., 147.
44. Abduh, *al-Islam wa al-Nasraniyah*, p. 72-3.
45. Abduh, *al-Islam wa al-Nasraniya*, p. 74.
46. Abduh, *Risalat al-Tawhid*, p. 73.
47. Ibid., p. 78.
48. Abdul-Rahman al-Kawakibi, *Um al-Qura in al-A'mal al-Kamila*, ed. Muhammad 'Imarah (Cairo: al-Hay'ah al-Masriyah al-'Amah, 1970), p. 146.
49. Ibid., p. 150.
50. Ibid., pp. 160-5.
51. Ibid., pp.170-1.
52. Ibid., pp. 264..
53. Ibid., pp. 261-2.

54. Ibid., p. 315.
55. Ibid., p. 313.
56. Ibid., p. 254.
57. Ibid., p. 139.

Chapter 7

Growing in the Image
of the West

The Project of Westernization

By the turn of the twentieth century the number of Middle
Easterners who were attracted to Western ideas and practices was
on the rise, and Western institutions found many proponents in
the Arab world. Throughout the better part of this century, the
bulk of Muslim intellectuals have been actively working to apply
European measures to deal with social problems, advocating
Western ideas and methods, or, in some cases, openly calling for
the complete Westernization of the Arab world.

Among the foremost advocates of Westernization, and one of
the early writers to attack the Islamic historical model, was Taha
Hussain, an Egyptian writer and probably the most influential
novelist and literary critic in the twentieth-century Arab world.
Hussain was born at Mafaghah, a small Egyptian town, in 1889.
He received his secondary education in his town, before moving
to Cairo to study at the al-Azhar University in 1902. Hussain did
not stay long at al-Azhar, for he was shortly expelled for his
"radical views." He later joined the newly established University
of Egypt, graduating in 1914 with a doctorate in Arabic literature.
In the same year he left to France on a scholarship from the
University of Egypt, where he spent the next five years preparing
for a doctorate in sociology.

Hussain started his literary life by publishing, in 1926, a
provocative book, which he entitled *Fi al-Shi'r al-Jahili* (on pre-
Islamic poetry). The book created an uproar in Egypt, forcing the
publisher to withdraw it from the market, and subsequently
destroy its copies. Hussain republished a modified version in
1927 under the title *Fi al-Adab al-Jahili* (on the pre-Islamic
literature).[1] Hussain's thesis, as it appears in the modified
version, does not deserve all the uproar created around it.
Hussain's main contention is that the *jahili* (pre-Islamic) poetry
does not reveal to us the true nature of the pre-Islamic life. The

pre-Islamic poetry, Hussain alleged, was forged by Muslim poets, and falsely attributed to pre-Islamic poets.[2] Hussain, further, argued that the life in the pre-Islamic epoches of Arab history is better reflected in the Quran and, therefore, should be sought in the Quran, rather than in pre-Islamic poetry; for while the latter is subject to a great deal of doubts, the former's authenticity is beyond any shadow of doubt.[3] Whereas the Quran reveals to us a picture in which the pre-Islamic Arabs are depicted as a feverishly religious people, who fiercely resisted Islam, the pre-Islamic poets have provided us with a completely different picture, in which religion took a back seat to other this-worldly concerns.[4]

Hussain's critics, however, did not see in his work a purely scholarly effort to verify the authenticity of the pre-Islamic poetry, or to discover the true features of pre-Islamic life. Rather, they were quick to condemn Hussain's work as a subversive attempt to undermine the authority of the Quran, and to insult and profane the most sacred text in Islam.

Our interest in Taha Hussain's work, from the perspective of this study, is twofold. First, the book illustrates the influence of Western ideas on Middle Eastern intellectuals. Secondly, the book reflects the increasing tension, often reaching the level of explosive collision, between the supporters of tradition and the advocates of modernity.

From the early pages of his book, Hussain makes his intention abundantly clear. Although the subject-matter of the book is the pre-Islamic poetry, Hussain's main objective is to attack orthodox methods of research, repudiate traditional thinking, and introduce new principles of scientific research. He begins his discussion by distinguishing between two methods or approaches: the traditional and the modern. The method of the traditionalists (*ansar al-qadim*) is based on consensus and unanimous agreement. Contemporary Arab literary critics, he argues, do not entertain any doubts about the authority of the pre-Islamic poetry because early scholars throughout the Arab world have all agreed on its authenticity. By so doing, traditionalists have closed the door on any attempt at creative or original interpretation (*ijtihad*), following thereby in the footsteps of traditional jurists and theologians.[5]

The method of the modernists (*ansar al-tajdid*), on the other hand, is based on a completely different approach, Hussain proclaims. Unlike traditionalists, modernists do not base their judgments on authority. "They [the modernists] have been endowed," Hussain writes, "by neither the faith nor the trusting nature of [the traditionalists]. For God has given them minds which find enjoyment in doubts and satisfaction in restlessness and vicissitude."[6] The method employed by the modernists, Hussain asserts, has great consequence, for it leads to nothing less than "the revolutionization of [Arabic] literature." In addition, the new approach would ultimately "result in changing history, or what people call history. For it would lead those [who adopt it] to doubt the things they were never allowed to doubt before."[7]

But what is the nature of this revolutionary method which Hussain wants to employ to revolutionize Arabic literature, and even change Arab history? Hussain tells us that this new method is nothing other than critical subjectivism, which was introduced by Descartes early in the sixteenth century. "I would like to apply to literature," Hussain announces,

> the philosophical method invented by Descartes for examining the true nature of things at the beginning of modern times. Everyone knows that the basic principle in this approach is that the researcher has to neglect all previously acquired knowledge, and confront his subject matter with a completely clear mind of everything told about it.[8]

It is not Husserl's phenomenology, nor Kant's critical philosophy, either of which represents a markedly more advanced and drastically more refined version of Descartes's critical subjectivism,[9] but rather the latter's critical approach was the method of choice for Hussain. Perhaps Hussain reasoned that before Middle Eastern thought can become ready for a Husserl or a Kant, it has first to experience a Descartes. At any rate, Hussain's application of the Cartesian method to the study of literature has led him to some interesting conclusions, which outraged his traditionalist detractors.

It is beyond our interest in this study to follow the detailed arguments and counter-arguments evolving around the question of the authenticity of, or the lack of it in, pre-Islamic literature. Hussain's thesis has been discussed exhaustively by countless Arab writers.[10] What is of interest to us is rather the cultural struggle between the Western-inspired ideas and the traditional outlook, which was brought to the fore as a result of this, and similar, confrontation between modernists and traditionalists. Hussain's traditionalist critics fought back fiercely, accusing him of heresy and insanity, and called for his dismissal from the teaching position he held at the University of Egypt. Among his outspoken critics was Mustafa Sadiq al-Rafi'i. Al-Rafi'i, a highly influential writer at the time, was outraged by Hussain's ideas, directing his anger and unsparing attacks against both Hussain and the president of the University of Egypt; the latter provoked al-Rafi'i's anger for his steadfast defense of the notion of intellectual freedom, and for his support of Hussain's right to speak out his mind freely. Al-Rafi'i was especially upset that Hussain was able to find a sanctuary in the University of Egypt, which employed him, published his controversial book, and refused to fire him despite all the pressure from influential religious authorities. Rather than responding to Hussain's thesis through intellectual arguments, al-Rafi'i exploded in full rage and indignation, condemning the author not the thesis, calling him all possible names, and questioning his integrity and character. This emotional confrontation, and the lack of meaningful communication, continue even today to characterize the intellectual rivalry between the supporters of the Muslim historical model and the advocates of the Western civilizational model, or, to put it in terms currently popular in Arab literature, between the supporters of authenticity (*asalah*) and the advocates of modernity (*hadatha*). To al-Rafi'i, Hussain was a spokesman of a foreign culture, and had to be condemned as a "traitor." Summarizing his views of Western civilization, he wrote:

> Western civilization has liberated the human mind, allowing it to be original and innovative. But with it, it freed the human appetite to enjoy its lusts, and to satisfy its unbridled desires. . . This civilization has [therefore] brought to its people social ills unknown before.[11]

The best solution to the ills of the Western civilization, al-Rafi'i argued, is to adopt preventive measures against it, or to put it more bluntly, to use repressive measures against its advocates. "They [Westerners] will not find a cure to the ills of civilization except by refraining from it. When they realize this, they will forbid people, by the force of law, from getting in touch with its arts, or even imposing a partial [state of] ignorance on them by force."[12] In other words, to solve the problems associated with modern civilization, al-Rafi'i suggested, the West should voluntarily commit a suicide, and give up its innovativeness and assertiveness. For if the West can regress back to the level of cultural decadence experienced by the Middle Eastern society, the traditional culture would be able then to compete with Western culture. This would save the traditionalists the hardship of undertaking the painful task of social and cultural development. If Western civilization would only give up its scientific and political achievements, the lazy minds and souls of the traditionalists can sit back and watch the West sinking back into the Middle ages, when the Western and Arab civilizations were still standing on competitive grounds.

In little over a decade, Hussain published another provocative book, *Mustaqbal al-Thaqafa fi Misr* (the future of culture in Egypt). The book received a great deal of attention and became the subject of a great controversy. The book deals with the question of development in general, and cultural change in particular; it analyzes the current conditions of the Egyptian society, and suggests measures for effecting social progress. Hussain begins his arguments by posing a question and then spending the rest of the book answering it. "Does Egypt belong to the East or to the West?" Hussain asks. "I do not, naturally, mean," he explains, "the geographical East or the geographical West. I rather mean the cultural East and the cultural West."[13]

But what is the significance of determining whether Egypt belongs to the East or the West? And how would this determination influence the future of the Egyptian culture? To find answers to these questions we have to follow Hussain's arguments little further. He begins by positing two propositions. First, he contends that the future conditions of Egyptian society have to emanate from current conditions, and cannot depart drastically from present norms. Secondly, he posits that the future of the Egyptian society is closely connected with its distant past. "I do not want us to contemplate the future of culture in Egypt," he writes, "except by reflecting on its distant past, and near present. Because we do not want, and cannot afford, to sever linkage between our past and present."[14]

Hussain, then, turns back to Egypt's distant past, three millennia ago, to the time of the pharaoh, to demonstrate that the Egyptian culture was back then part of the European culture, the Greek culture that is. He argues that pharaonic Egypt was in harmonious relationship with the "Western" nation of Greece, while it was engaged in a bloody conflict with the "Eastern" nation of Persia.[15] He points to the cultural exchange that took place between the Egyptians and the Greeks during the reign of Alexander the Great. "The Egyptian mind, during the reign of

Alexander," he contends, "influenced, and was influenced by, the Greek mind, sharing many, if not all, of the latter's characteristics."[16] This is what happened in the distant past, but what about the near past? Hussain recognizes that pharaonic civilization was superseded by over one millennia of continuous Islamic civilization, but rejects the notion that the Islamic culture has restructured the Egyptian mind. He rather contends that as Christianity was forced to readjust to fit into the European culture, failing thereby to reshape the European mind, which continued to be faithful to its Greek roots, so did Islam change so as to conform with local cultures, thereby failing to change the Egyptian mind, or, for that matter, what Hussain calls the "Mediterranean mind." "If it is true that Christianity did not change the European mind, and was not able to deprive it of its Greek heritage, or strip it of those characteristics it acquired by being part of the Mediterranean region, it should be [equally] true that Islam did not change the Egyptian mind, or the minds of other Mediterranean people."[17] Hussain concedes that most Egyptians see themselves as part of the East, not only the geographical, but the cultural as well.[18] He dismisses this belief as a misconception, arguing that religious similarity among Middle Eastern societies, though can be the "basis for economic exchange, is not sufficient to be a basis of cultural unity."[19]

Hussain returns from the distant past to the present to find that the old close ties between the Egyptian and European society have been renewed in the last few decades. He notes that the Egyptians have copied the European life in all aspects.

> Europe built railroads and telegraph and telephone lines, so did we. Europe uses tables [for dinning], and produces [different kinds] of dinning wear, tools, and food, so do we. We have gone further to emulate Europeans in their clothing, and even their lifestyle, without being selective or cautious; nor have we distinguished between what is good and what is not, or what is appropriate and what is inappropriate [when emulating the Europeans]. . . . Even our moral life, on all levels, is purely European. Our political system is purely European, we have copied it from Europe without being cautious or hesitant.[20]

If the Egyptian society has already become in practice a European society, as Hussain asserts, why is it necessary, then, for him to prove the obvious? Hussain realizes that the Europeanization of the Egyptian society is incomplete. For one thing, only the "upper" social classes have been Europeanized (*al-tabaqat al-raqiya*), while the vast majority of Egyptians have not. But for another, Hussain recognizes that the development of the upper classes, and the Europeanization of the Egyptian society, and by implication other Middle Eastern societies, has been superficial. What has been Europeanized is people's taste, not their intellect. They have acquired the European appetite, but not the European assertiveness, creativity, productivity, or scientific curiosity. Even the parliamentary system and the democratic rule, a source of great pride to Hussain, which he thought were so entrenched in society that no Egyptian would be willing to give them up,[21] were not deeply rooted in society. Hussain himself was allowed to live enough to see the democratic system vanishing in the air in 1952.[22]

Be that as it may, Hussain contends that Western culture remained on the surface, unable to penetrate deep into the heart of the Egyptian society, because Egyptians have been reluctant and selective in adopting European culture. In order to ripe the fruits of modern civilization, Egyptians would have to follow the example of the Japanese, who, though were exposed to Western civilization for a shorter period of time, stand today on equal footing with the West, because they have not been hesitant in adopting Western ideas and practices.[23] In short, to stand on competitive ground with the Europeans, the people of Egypt, Hussain contends, have to become Europeans themselves; they have, that is, to embrace the European culture in all of its aspects, both the "good" and the "bad."

> The road to [civilization] cannot be travelled on empty words, superficial semblance, or compromised positions. The road is rather straightforward, with no curves or detours. It is a single and distinct road, with no alternatives. The road is this: we have to follow in the footsteps of the Europeans, and adopt their ways, in order to become their equals; we have to become their partners in [modern civilization], in its good and evil, in its sweetness and bitterness, in its attractive and repulsive aspects, and in its elements which can be celebrated and those which should be faulted.[24]

Evidently, what Hussain resented the most was the duplicity of those who, while enjoying the fruits of the Western civilization, reject Western culture which, after all, lies at its foundation. To Hussain, resisting Western culture, after all that have been borrowed from the West, was counterproductive, especially when it is realized that among the elements of Western life which have been excluded are those which can help the Egyptian to move from the consuming to the producing end of civilization.

Hussain realized that among the main objections that would be, and was, raised in the face of his invitation for the complete Westernization of the Egyptian society was the question of religious differences between the Europeans and the Egyptians, and the contradiction between some European beliefs and practices and Islamic teachings. His response to those who pointed to the down side of the European culture was to remind them that the Muslim society is not, and had never been, without its own flaws and shortcomings. "We should remind those who, though are sincere and good, [oppose European culture]," he wrote, "that the European life is not purely sinful, . . . for purely sinful life does not lead to progress . . . and that our present, and past life, is not purely good . . . for pure goodness does not lead to decadence."[25]

It should be emphasized here that Hussain's invitation to the Westernization of the Egyptian society was not, at the same time, a call for the repudiation of the Egyptian national identity. For he himself called upon the government to preserve Egypt's national character by stipulating that national language, religion, and history were to be mandatory subjects in the curricula of all primary and secondary schools, private and public alike.[26] The Westernization, or the Europeanization as he would put it, was to him a pragmatic matter, and a necessary step in the road to civilization. Hussain saw Europe as both source of science, technology, and progressive culture, and a bearer of a mighty military power, threatening the very existence of Egypt's national character. To meet the European military threat, European culture had to be adopted. As he explained:

We need indeed to become equal to the European nations in their military strength, so as to be able to defend ourselves, and to say to our English friends after few years: go home, we have become capable of protecting the [Suez] canal. But [we have to remember that] he who desires an end, desires [also] the means leading to it; and he who desires strength, desires its causes; and he who desires a strong European army, desires, as well, a European culture and European education system which prepare the youths to build a strong, and mighty army.[27]

Yet Hussain's attempt to counterbalance his call to adopt Western culture with a call for preserving the national character of Egypt was not well thought, nor was it systematically treated. It was not clear, for instance, how it was possible for the Egyptians to cut ties with their Islamic cultural milieu and historical heritage, and embrace European historical experience. Nor was it clear how, and in what ways, could Islamic ideas and practices be reconciled with those of the Europeans. Obviously, Hussain's notion of Westernization and cultural change involved a great deal of confusion about the constituting components of culture in general, and the role of religion in shaping the various aspects of culture in particular. Hussain, evidently, underestimated the difficulty of reconciling Islam with modern secular culture. For unlike Christianity, Islam includes, in addition to moral norms, legal norms as well; and Islamic teachings address themselves not only to individual morality, but to communal rights and obligations. The importance of the Islamic legal code for the Arab, and Muslim society in general, may be appreciated by realizing that, historically, the most influential intellectual figures were not theologians, as was the case in Christian Europe, but jurists and doctors of law. Furthermore, the notion of separation of state and church, widely accepted in the West, was completely absent in the Islamic tradition. Apparently, Hussain was mislead, as were many orientalists and Arabists by the almost complete Westernization of the Egyptian upper class.[28] Nevertheless, by raising the question of cultural change, Hussain brought to light an important issue, contributing to the intellectual debate on the question of cultural modernization.

Arab Nationalism

Not all Arab intellectuals agreed with Taha Hussain that the modernization of Arab culture can only be achieved through radical Westernization. In fact Hussain was in the minority, among Arab intellectuals, on this issue. The overwhelming majority advocated more selective and restrained borrowing from the West. The bulk of Arab intellectuals fall within a loosely clustered movement of Arab nationalists. This movement comprises a highly diverse group of intellectuals who, despite all of their differences, share two common denominators. First, they insist that although the modernization of the Arab world hinges on the Arab ability to adopt Western forms, they caution that such borrowing has to be done in such a way that the Arab national identity can be preserved. Very often, Arab national identity is reduced to a pride in the Arab heritage and the historical accomplishments of the ancestors, and a desire to achieve political unity. The form and the extent of this unity is, however, subject to debate and contention. Secondly, Arab nationalists, by and large, reject the authority of the Islamic historical model in determining the political or social structures of future Arab society. In the remainder of this chapter, I will briefly review the core concepts of Arab nationalism, as they were advanced by Sati' al-Husari, the father of Arab nationalism, and Michel Aflaq, the founder of the most influential political party in the Arab world, the Ba'ith Party.

Sati' al-Husari was born at Sana, Yemen in 1880 to a Syrian family. He received his education at Constantinople, and was appointed as chief administrator, by the Ottoman government, in the Balkans province. He became a close adviser to Faysal Ben Hussain when the later was crowned as the King of Grand Syria (Lebanon, Jordan, and Syria) in 1920. He flew to Egypt when the French army entered Damascus and declared Syria a French Colony. He later rejoined King Faysal when the later become the King of Iraq. In 1947, he moved to Egypt and was later appointed as the director of the Institute of Advanced Arab Studies. Al-Husari spent his life advocating the ideas of Arabism, and fiercely defended it against its detractors.

Although the reference to the Arabs as a distinct nation with special historical mission could be found, as we saw earlier, in the writings of al-Kawakibi, it was in the writings of al-Husari that Arab nationalism became a full-fledged concept. For while the former continued to hold that the Arabs were, politically and culturally, an intrinsic part of the Muslim *Ummah* (community), the latter insisted that the Arabs constituted a distinct cultural group to the exclusion of other Muslim peoples, and that political unity was only possible when it was based on nationalist grounds.

Al-Husari's theory of Arab nationalism was a replica of the one advocated by the German nationalists J. G. Herder and J. G. Fichte. In a lecture delivered in 1928 before the Baghdad Teacher Club, at Baghdad, Iraq, he discussed at some length the basis of nationalism. Al-Husari began his argument by posing a question: "What are the elements that comprise nationalism and constitute a nation?," he asked, and immediately replied: "the unity of origin and stock."[29] Al-Husari argued that by "unity of origin" he did not mean to imply similarities based on blood relations or pure ethnicity, for such purity could not exist in modern times. Rather, "unity of origin" refers to mental and "psychological" similarity, as opposed to physical and material one.[30] What is important, therefore, is not the actual "unity of origin," al-Husari contended, but rather the mere belief in this unity. The belief in the unity of a people is, however, not purely ideological, for its bases are embedded in society itself, and these bases, he argued, are two: the commonality of language and of history.[31] Language is the spirit of a nation, he insisted, because by establishing communication within a linguistic group, it brings them together and prevent their dissolution in other groups. History, likewise, is the memory of a nation and its consciousness. The commonality of historical experience gives the people who share this experience a distinct national character. Al-Husari cautioned that by the term "history" he did not mean the written history of the nation, but rather its living tradition–the history which is embodied in people's consciousness, thought, and customs.[32]

Al-Husari discussed two other elements which are considered by some theorists as constitutive components of national unity, namely religion and the general will. He distinguished here between two types of religion: national and global. National religions are those which limit membership to one ethnic group, such as Judaism. In such a religion, religious beliefs definitely constitute a major element of nationalism.[33] Global religions (e.g., Christianity and Islam), on the other hand, aspire to unite different nations under one belief system, and, therefore, cannot be considered as an intrinsic part of the components of nationalism. He concluded, therefore, that "Muslim unity" cannot replace "Arab unity," for history shows that Muslim unity failed, under the Abbasid Caliphate, to unite all Muslim peoples under one political banner.[34] Yet it could be shown that a consistent reading of Arab history does not allow us to make any historical inference in support of Arab national unity. Al-Husari ignores, for instance, that the Abbasids were able to unit four Muslim nations (Arabs, Persians, Kurdes, and Turks) while failing to unite all Arabs. As to the general will, he hastily dismissed it as insignificant component of nationalism, arguing that the will of a people can only be measured through referenda and voting, and since people's opinions, measured through voting, changes quickly pursuant to the nature of the prevailing ideas and the predominant propaganda, relying on referenda to determine the unity of a people would transform the nature of a nation from "natural grouping" to some sort of organized parties.[35] Al-Husari's argument boils down to this: the general will should not be one of the components of nationalism, for its inclusion would undermine the linguistic conception of the nation-state, should the people choose a multinational form of political community. Al-Husari further argued that the concept of the general will was forged by the French theorists, such as E. Renan, in order to disguise their imperialistic desire to control the German regions of the Alsace and Lorraine.[36]

It is worth noting that al-Hursari's nationalist inclinations have not manifested themselves until the Ottoman Empire was dismantled after WWI. It may be argued that al-Husari resorted to the concept of Arabism because it became apparent to him, after the collapse of the Ottoman Empire, that Arab nationalism was the only hope for bringing unity back to the fragmented Arab regions. He did not have simply an intellectual interest in studying the question of nationalism. Rather, Arab unity was his passion and life project, and was clearly willing to bend certain facts, and overlook certain truths, when these did not fit into his theory. He misrepresented, for instance, the history of the Middle East so as to make it supportive of his thesis, as we noted earlier, and even quoted intellectuals and political figures out of context, thereby reversing their views, to show that they agreed with his ideas. For example, he misrepresented the position of al-Afaghani, describing him as a leading nationalist theorist, and as a strong advocate of national unity, thereby, denying that al-Afaghani was an advocate of Muslim unity.[37]

Al-Husari believed that with the collapse of the Ottoman Empire, and the division of the Arab world into small territorial (*qutri*) states, the Arabs were in need of a new national identity to replace the religious identity which united them for four centuries with the Turks under the Ottoman state. They were in need, that is, of a nationalist ideology which could unite them together, and allow them to join the club of nation-states. He was especially inspired by the unification projects carried out successfully by German and Italian nationalists in the nineteenth century, and made his admiration explicit in various articles and speeches. In an introductory lecture delivered in Cairo before the faculty and student body of the then newly established Institute of Advanced Arab Studies, al-Husari told his audience that modern European states have all been established on what he termed the "nationalist principle," while the Arabs were divided into small fragments.

"Why? Why have we been, thus far, lagging behind?," he asked and immediately went on to cite three reasons for the lack of national awareness and unity among the Arabs. First, Arab nationalism continued, throughout the Ottoman rule, to lark beneath the surface because of the Arabs' commitment to the "state of Islamic Caliphate."[38] Secondly, because the Arabs early exposure to Western civilization was through their contacts with British and French cultures, Arabs were influenced exclusively by the political ideas and practices of these two European cultures. However, the French and the British were both well established powers, with global imperialistic ambitions. They both disdained and discouraged nationalist ideas and sentiments because they wanted to keep other European nations divided so they could be easily dominated. However, the "nationalist principle" ultimately triumphed, despite the resistance of the French and British, transforming both Italy and Germany into two great powers.[39] Finally, the absence of national consciousness among the Arabs is the immediate result of the conspiring efforts of major colonial powers who have restructured the Arab world so as to insure the continuation of Arab disunity, and continued to encourage sectarian tendencies in an effort to perpetuate territorial division.[40]

Yet beyond his interest in the general question of Arab unity, and his analysis of the grievous consequences of the state of disunity prevailing in the Arab world, al-Husari did not pay adequate attention to the tremendous difficulties and numerous problems surrounding the question of Arab unity. Nor did he appreciate the significant impact of social and economic conditions on the possibility of political unity. For al-Husari, Arab unity was the first step toward building more advanced and more viable society; he believed that political unity was possible despite the significant economic, political, and social differences which existed between Arab regions.

Since al-Husari met Faysal Ben Hussain, the leader of the revolution which aspired to unite the Arab under one national state, he became increasingly obsessed with the question of political unity, and the desire to unite the Arabs, using the strategy adopted by German and Italian nationalists. If the Germans and Italians could build a nation, he insisted, the Arab could do the same as well. He clearly failed to see the drastic difference in both the internal and external conditions between Arabs and the two European nations. Internally, the Arabs were not at the same level of intellectual, scientific, or industrial advancement experienced by the German or the Italian nations at the eve of their unification. Externally, the international political structure, and the system of balance of powers, which was at work in nineteenth-century Europe, were drastically different from those which prevailed in twentieth-century Middle East.

Al-Husari's efforts, nevertheless, were not in vain, for the cause he struggled throughout his life to advance found many supporters among Arab intellectuals, first in Syria and later in Egypt and Iraq. In Syria, and later in Iraq, the Ba'th party, established in the thirties by Michel Aflaq and Salah al-Bitar, carried the banner of Arab nationalism, and was able, by infiltrating the military, to capture political power in early 1960s. In Egypt, the Free Officers, under the leadership of Jamal Abdul Nasser, came to power in 1952, and soon adopted a version of Arab nationalist ideology similar to that of the Ba'thists.

Despite al-Husari's political involvement as a close adviser to King Faysal, he was more of an educator and publicist than a political activist. Michel Aflaq, the co-founder of the Ba'th party was, on the other hand, a gifted politician and strategist, and the chief ideologue of the Ba'thist party. Born in Damascus in 1910, Aflaq received his primary and secondary education in its schools, before he went to study philosophy in France. He returned to Syria in 1932 where he worked as a high school teacher. Along with Salah al-Bitar, Aflaq established the Ba'th party in 1943 and served as its secretary general from 1943 to 1965. He served as a minister of education in the first Ba'thist government and was later forced into exile in 1966 after a successful military coup, which brought to power rivaling elements of the same party. He went to Iraq where he was welcomed and appointed as the secretary general of the national command of the Iraqi branch of the Ba'th party, and continued to hold this honorary position till his death in 1989. Aflaq helped developing the three objectives of the Ba'th party, which, along with the equivocal notion of the "eternal mission" of the Arab nation, constitute the Ba'thist creed.

Aflaq was more of an ideologue than a profound thinker. In expounding his ideas he rarely delved into their deep theoretical roots, and, hence, many of the ideas he propounded lacked theoretical clarity and systematic coherence. Frequently, his argument produced more heat than light, providing more inspiration than enlightenment. For example, in a statement addressed to the youth, in 1940, Aflaq denied that the concept of Arab nationalism has its roots in the nationalist theory developed by German philosophers, arguing that "Arab nationalism is not a theory, but the source of all theories; nor is it the product of thinking, but its nourisher, nor is it an artistic expression, but art's spirit and source. It does not stand in opposition to freedom, for it is freedom itself."[41] He contended, likewise, that Arab nationalism required no rational justification, since it was, in the first place, a "sentiment" and "love," proclaiming that "he who fall in love does not search for the reasons of his love." He went further to say that "even if a person were to look for [reasons], he will not find any clear reasons [for his love]. And when a person becomes incapable of loving unless he can find obvious reasons, this clearly means that the love he [once] had in his heart has either diminished or vanished."[42] Using the same romanticist tone, he equivocates in two separate statement made in 1956 and 1950, the meaning of the Ba'thist slogan: "One Arab nation with an eternal mission." This eternal mission is in the first place, he argued, a faith and conscience. "The Arab mission," he proclaimed, "is faith, before being anything else. It does not diminish of its importance that [faith] is its deep core, for faith [always] precede clear knowledge. And indeed there are things which are innate to humans, desiring no proofs or studies."[43] But we are yet to understand what the notion of "eternal mission" refers to. Aflaq, then, goes on to argue that the Arab mission, though eternal, is not fixed. In the past the eternal mission was embodied in the moral values of Islam, values whose influence was deeply felt by non-Arabs as well. However, the mission of Arabs is no longer universal, but has to be understood today as a mission of a people unto themselves. That is, the Arabs' mission today is to form one united political community, with advanced social and economic structures.[44]

Although Aflaq was not a systematic thinker, he was an astute political leader and strategist. Early on in his career, he established three objectives to his party: freedom, socialism, and Arab unity, and insisted that these objectives had to be realized in their given sequence. Freedom from colonial rule and foreign domination had to be had first, for neither social progress nor Arab unity are possible as long as the Arab territories fell under European control. Socialism had to be achieved next, because, he believed, Arab unity can be accomplished and maintained only after the social and economic structures of Arab society have been modernized.[45]

For Aflaq, Socialism meant a peculiar type of socialism, an "Arab socialism." He rejected the Marxist version of socialism arguing that Marxism was the childbrain of Western thought. It emerged in response to its "bigoted nationalism and swollen industry."[46] He cited three reasons for his rejection of the Marxist type of socialism. First, Marxism, being a product of Western society, does not respond to the internal problems of Arab society. Marxism calls upon the Arabs to deal with problems and fight enemies unknown to Arab society, therefore distracting them from dealing with the real problems and confronting their real enemies. Western socialism has, hence, to be Arabized and adjusted to the peculiar conditions of the Arab society.[47] Secondly, communism is not merely an economic system, but a comprehensive system, based on the principle of materialism. It threatens to replace the Arab spiritual beliefs and moral values with materialism and atheism. As such, Marxism aspires to destroy those elements which the Arab need to preserve and nourish if they to ever become a developed nation. "Look at how the Arabs were in the past." Aflaq remarked:

> They sought the sky, and were able, therefore, to command the earth. But when they confined themselves to the objective of acquiring earthly possessions, they lost both the earth and heaven. The Arab will not reclaim, today, their command over their lives until they believe in eternity, and they will not be able to reclaim their lands until they believe again in paradise.[48]

Finally, communism is rejected by Aflaq because it undermines nationalism and calls for globalism. Such an invitation to give up national claims is, he asserted, unthinkable at a time when there is a need for Arab unity and solidarity in the face of colonial threats and aggression.[49] Aflaq concluded that socialism could not be "the first philosophy," but only an economic doctrine within the Ba'thist creed. Western socialism has to be modified to fit into Arab conditions; and when it does, it will be reduced, according to Aflaq, to a moral principle, stressing the need for equitable distribution of wealth, and ascertaining that equality should prevail in Arab society.[50]

As Aflaq rejected communist groups for their materialistic and anti-nationalistic beliefs, he equally rejected religio-political organizations for their traditional and backward views. He insisted, however, that his rejection of politically organized religion was not a rejection of religion *per se*. He asserted that the Arab past, especially during its glorious Islamic phase, cannot, and should not be repudiated. It has inspired, and will continue to inspire, the Arab spirit, and should be utilized to propel the Arabs forward. "The movement of Arab Ba'th[51] inherits from Islam," Aflaq contended, "its renovative spirit and revolution against traditionalistic values. It [also] acquires from Islam the virtues of faith and excellence, and detachment from personal interests and earthly temptations."[52] Yet Islam which inspired the admiration of Aflaq was a historical experience, a bygone glorious period in the history of the Arabs which they can recall with pride and be inspired by, but not as a set of living principles which may command the present or guide social progress toward the future. Islam played a leading role in the past, and should be praised and commended for that. But today, it is Arab nationalism, and only Arab nationalism, which may qualify as an ideology capable of leading the Arabs on the road to economic prosperity. As he put it:

> If we look at the Arab past, we find that religion was the driving force at the advent of Islam. . . . Economic reformation, then, was a consequence of deep religious faith. Today, however, nationalism is the driving force in this period of Arab life. And as they [the Arabs] responded, in the past, to religious call, and were, hence, able to accomplish economic reform, they can today achieve social justice, and equality among citizens, and [can] ensure freedom among all Arabs, by putting their faith in nationalism alone.[53]

Concluding Remarks

The first epoch in modern Arab history witnessed the awakening of the Arab mind under the impact of Western challenge, and its revolt against traditional ideas and institutions. The second epoch experienced the emergence and strengthening of the liberal and national movements. In many ways this period could be seen as a continuation of the first. For Arab nationalists, following in the footsteps of the Reformist School, entered into confrontation with both the forces of foreign domination and traditionalism. Even liberal writers, such as Taha Hussain, despite their open invitation to Westernizing Arab life, were operating in accordance with the same strategy. As we saw earlier, Taha Hussain justified his call to Europeanizing Egypt by invoking the need to adopt Western ideas and practices in order to make Egypt coequal to European powers, and, therefore, capable of defending itself against European imperialism, and to force the British to pull their troops out of the Suez canal.

Yet the second epoch was different from the first one in some important respects, namely, the replacement of the Islamic model, adopted by the early reformists, with the European model, embraced by liberal and nationalist writers, with varying degrees of modification and adjustment. This alteration in the frame of reference should not surprise us when we realize that the reformist school, was able to successfully undermine traditional ideas, while failing in substituting new ones in their stead.

The second epoch also witnessed and increased polarization of Arab society into two blocs, the supporters of the Islamic model and the proponents of the Western model. The balance between the nationalist and Islamist groups was throughout this period, tipping toward the former, who by the late fifties were in control of the political and intellectual life in most Arab states. Further, the polarization of social and political forces was assuming a dangerous level, for it was accompanied by unhealthy disengagement between the Islamist and nationalist forces. Communication and intellectual interaction were almost nonexistent between the two, and there was a constant attempt, by both groups to depict each other as "traitors" and "agents" of foreign interests. It was during this period that the first bloody confrontation between the Islamic and nationalist movements took place in Egypt, in which the Muslim Brethren and the Nasserits clashed.

Notes

1. Since I do not have access to the early version of the book, my comments are confined to the modified second edition.

2. Taha Hussain, *Fi al-Adab al-Jahili* (Cairo, Egypt: Dar al-Ma'arif, 1927), p. 65.

3. Ibid., p. 70.

4. Ibid., p. 73.

5. Ibid., p. 63.

6. Ibid., p. 64.

7. Ibid.

8. Ibid, p. 68.

9. See Chapter 4 for a detailed discussion of Descartes's critical subjectivism.

10. A myriad of articles and books were written in the 1920s-30s by prominent writers including Khudari Hussain, Sayed Qutb, Zaki Mubarak, Rafa'a al-Tahtawi, and others.

11. Mustafa Sadiq al-Rafi'i, *Tahta Rayat al-Quan* (Cairo, Egypt: al-Maktabah al-Tijariyyah al-Kubrah, 1963), p. 359.

12. Ibid., p. 261.

13. Taha Hussain, *Mustaqbal al-Thaqafa fi Misr* (1938) in The Collected Work of Taha Husain, Vol 9 (Beirut, Lebanon: Dar al-Kitab al-Lubnani, 1973), p. 17.

14. Ibid., p. 16.

15. Ibid., p. 20.

16. Ibid., p. 29.

17. Ibid., p. 32.

18. Ibid., p. 24.

19. Ibid., p. 25.

20. Ibid., p. 41.

21. See Ibid., pp. 44-5.

22. The parliamentary rule was abolished by Jamal Abdul Nasser on the twenty third of July, 1952. It only took an executive order signed by Nasser to dismantle the Egyptian "democratic" experiment.

23. Ibid., p. 49.

24. Ibid., p. 54.

25. Ibid., p. 62.

26. Ibid., pp. 81-98.

27. Ibid., p. 56.

28. See for example Daniel Turner's *The Passing of Traditional Society*. For a discussion of Lerner's work see Chapter 1, p.

29. Sati' al-Husari, *Abhath Mukhtara fi al-Qawmiyyah al-Arabiyyah*, vol. 1 (Beirut, Lebanon: Dar al-Quds, 1974), p. 39.

30. Ibid., p. 42.

31. Ibid.

32. Ibid., p. 44.

33. Ibid., pp. 45-6.

34. Ibid., p. 134.

35. Ibid., p. 52.

36. Ibid., pp. 10-20.

37. Ibid., p. 139; also his discussion of al-Afaghani's thought in his book What is Nationalism.

38. Ibid. p. 19.

39. Ibid., p. 20.

40. Ibid., p. 22, 28.

41. Michel Aflaq, *Fi Sabil al-Ba'th* (Damascus, Syria: Dar al-Tali'ah, 1959), p. 27.

42. Ibid., p. 29.

43. Ibid., p. 76.

44. See Ibid., pp. 67-82, and 109-110.

45. Ibid., pp. 172-4.

46. Ibid., p. 74.

47. Ibid., pp. 72074.

48. Ibid., p. 90.

49. Ibid.

50. Ibid., pp. 97-8, 86-9.

51. The term "Ba'th" is an Arabic word meaning "resuscitation."

52. Ibid., p. 143.

53. Ibid., p. 88.

Chapter 8

Islamic Reassertion

While the nationalist movement, in its both the liberal and socialist branches, was on the rise, conquering new grounds and increasingly dominating political and intellectual life, the Islamic movement was disoriented and defensive. Islamist intellectuals were busy defending Islam against the accusation that it was responsible for the decline of the Muslim society, and apologizing for those aspects of Islam which appeared repugnant to modern taste. This trend started, however, to change by the late 1960s, when the ideas of Sayed Qutb began to spread throughout the Arab world. The sixties and seventies witnessed also the translation into Arabic, from French, of the work of Malek Bennabi, an Algerian-born, French-educated writer, whose ideas gave a new momentum to Islamist intellectuals. In this chapter we will examine the ideas of Qutb and Bennabi, especially those which have had a great impact on the Islamic movement, and Arab society in general. It should be noted that while Qutb exerted a tremendous influence on the public, Bennabi's influence has been almost completely confined to intellectual circles.

Sayed Qutb: The Islamic Vanguard

Sayed Qutb was born at Qaha, a small town in the Egyptian province of Asyut, in 1906. After completing his primary education in his town, he moved to Cairo where he received his secondary and college education. Graduating with a degree in Arab literature, Qutb soon established himself as an acute literary critic. In 1949 he was sent by the Ministry of Education to the United States, where he spent two and half years studying American school curricula. He came back disillusioned with Western civilization, and publicly condemned the American culture as excessively materialistic, devoid of all spiritual value.

He joined the Muslim Brethren in 1951 and was appointed as the editor-in-chief of the Brethren's major newspaper in 1954. He was arrested in the same year, and was accused, with other Brethren members, of engaging in subversive activities against the state. He was released from prison in 1964 to be arrested few months later on the charge that he was a party to an unsuccessful attempt to assassinate the president and overthrow the government. This time he was sentenced to death by the State Security Supreme Court in 1966, and was executed in the same year.

Perhaps the most influential and widely read work of Qutb is his book *Ma'alim fi al-Tariq* (Milestones), which he published in the year he was released from prison in 1964. The book was written during his imprisonment (1954-64), and constituted a drastic departure in tone, attitude, and substance from all that was written by Islamist writers prior to its publication. The book begins with an ominous warning:

> Mankind today is on the brink of a precipice, not because of the danger of complete annihilation which is hanging over its head– this being just a symptom and not the real disease–but because humanity is devoid of those vital values which are necessary for its healthy development and true progress.[1]

He goes on to accuse Western civilization of driving mankind to this blink state of affairs, failing thereby to fulfil its moral responsibility to the rest of humanity, and to call upon the Muslims to step forward and reclaim the leadership of mankind from Western powers.

> It is essential for mankind to have new leadership! The leadership of mankind by Western man is now on the decline, not because Western civilization has become poor materially or because its economic and military powers have become weak. The period of the Western system has come to an end primarily because it is deprived of those life-giving values which enabled it to be the leader of mankind. . . . At this crucial bewildering juncture, the turn of Islam and the Muslim community (*Ummah*) has come to fulfill the task for mankind which God has enjoined upon it.[2]

But how is that possible? What should the Muslims do to fulfill their moral responsibility and save the human race of an imminent disaster? What qualifications does the Muslim community have to take the lead from the West? Qutb dismisses the idea that the Muslim leadership has to manifest itself through advancement in material production or technology, for, he contends, "Western ingenuity has made remarkable progress in this area, that it will take [the Muslims] at least several centuries to surpass it!" Rather, Muslims can provide leadership to mankind by supplying humanity with a "worldview" and a "way" which would allow mankind to enjoy the material advancement they have attained, while fulfilling their spiritual and moral needs.[3]

Having placed the problem confronting Muslim society in a global framework, linking it with what is portrayed to be a global problem, Qutb then goes on to explicate this global problem, and to spell out a very general solution. Qutb organizes his system of ideas around three key concepts: "*Jahili* society," "Islamic society," and "the Islamic vanguard." He contends that all societies could be subsumed under one of two, mutually exclusive, societies: Islamic and *jahili*. Qutb developed the concept of *jahiliyyah*, or *jahili* society, to analyze modern society and expose its shortcomings and deficiencies. The term *jahiliyyah* was first introduced in the Quran in reference to the faithlessness of the pre-Islamic Arab society and its ignorance of divine guidance. Sayed Qutb, however, adopted the term and gave it a new definition. According to Qutb, the *jahili* society is one that has been established on rules, principles, and customs which have been founded by men without regard to, or in ignorance of, divine guidance.[4] In such a society, Qutb argues, man's unrestrained greed and self-aggrandizement become the overwhelming forces that dominate social, economic, and political relationships among its members, leading to injustice and exploitation of some persons, classes, races, or nations by others.

> [Jahilliyyah] roots are in human desires, which do not let people come out of their ignorance and self-importance, or in the interests of some persons or some classes or some nations or some races, whose interests prevail over the demand of justice, truth and goodness.[5]

Qutb concludes that all current societies are *jahili*: communist societies are *jahili* because they deny the existence of God and his revealed commandments; Jewish and Christian societies are *jahili* because they have distorted their original teachings. Even contemporary Muslim societies are *jahili* because their social practices and legal principles are not founded on, but are in contradiction with, the teaching of Islam.[6] Qutb also criticizes modern society on the ground that it has been based on racial, ethnic, or national foundations. The criteria which are used to differentiate modern nation-states from one another emphasize the animal, rather than the human, aspects of man–i.e., his physical attributes. While the means of subsistence, territories, and boundaries might be an appropriate basis to bring animal stocks together, Qutb argues, human associations must be based on moral values and beliefs, and the free choices of people. In a word, human societies should be founded on shared ideology and outlook, rather than nationalistic and ethnocentric bonds.[7]

Islamic society, on the other hand, is based on harmony between God and man, and the unity of religious and sociopolitical principles, and on man's duty to his fellow man and his duty to God. Qutb defines Islamic society as one in which Islamic law (*shari'ah*) rules, and where Quranic and prophetic injunctions are observed and practiced; and he clearly stresses that Islamic norms have ceased to be the governing principles in contemporary Muslims society.

> [The] Muslim community does not denote the name of a land in which Islam resides, nor is it a people whose forefathers lived under the Islamic system at some earlier time. It is the name of a group of people whose manners, ideas and concepts, rules and regulations, values and criteria, are all derived from an Islamic source.[8]

But how does this process of resurrection of Islamic society begin? How can *jahiliyyah* be replaced by Islam? Qutb's answer was that bringing an Islamic society to life requires the emergence of an Islamic vanguard.

The transformation of the *jahili* society to an Islamic one is not a natural process that takes place apart from human efforts, Qutb stresses. Nor is it a supernatural process carried out directly by divine power in isolation of human agency. Rather, changing the prevailing conditions from *jahili* to Islamic is a long and tedious process that requires the struggle of the Muslim masses. To convince the Muslim masses, who have come to believe that they have no control over the evolution of history, that their current beliefs do not emanate form an Islamic perception, Qutb points

out to the struggle of the first generation of Muslims under the
leadership of the prophet of Islam, stressing that the triumph of
the early Islamic movement against *jahiliyyah* was the result of
human endeavor.[9] The struggle to establish an Islamic society,
Qutb contends, should be initiated and led by a vanguard. The
vanguard must confront the *jahili* society on two levels:
theoretically, by refuting the ideas and arguments of the
jahiliyyah and exposing its corruption; and practically, through a
well organized movement, equipped with all the strength it can
acquire to combat a powerful *jahiliyyah*.

When *jahiliyyah* takes the form, not of a 'theory' but of an
active movement in this fashion, then any attempt to abolish
this *jahililiyyah* and to bring people back to God which presents
Islam merely as a theory will be undesirable, rather useless.
Jahiliyyah controls the practical world, and for its support there
is a living and active organization. In this situation, mere
theoretical efforts to fight it cannot even be equal, much less
superior, to it.[10]

By theoretical struggle, Qutb did not understand intellectual
efforts aimed at developing political, economic, or even social
theories in which Islamic principles and values are applied to the
problems of twentieth-century Muslim society. Theoretical
struggle meant that the Islamic "worldview" (*'aqidah*) should be
introduced, by the vanguard, to the masses, so that people may
be educated about the true principles and values of Islam, and
taught the real meaning of the Islamic revelation. Qutb was very
critical of any attempt to translate Islamic principles into theories,
prior to their acceptance by the Muslim masses. People have to
believe that Islam is a revealed message from God, and embrace
it in its totality before the details of the Islamic system are
elaborated: this is how Islam was first introduced at the time of
its revelation, and, hence, this is how should be presented today
to the people. Qutb contended that those who are calling upon the
Muslim to present the details of the system which can guide
twentieth-century society are making mockery of the Islamists,
for they are asking to see the details of a system, while the
principles from which this system is derived have not been yet
embraced by society.[11] Those who ask Muslims to present a
modern Islamic legal code do not, first, understand that Islam,
unlike theory, cannot address itself to hypothetical conditions, or
legislate to social conditions derived from non-Islamic practices,

but deals only with real circumstances and legitimate conditions. These people, secondly, have ill-intent, for they would like to see the energies of the Islamists wasted on theoretical issues.[12]

Qutb's understanding of the term "theory" is problematic and perplexed. This perplexity could be detected in his failure to distinguish, for instance, between legal theory and legal code, i.e., between the abstract legal doctirnes and the practical rules derived by applying legal doctrines to concerte situations. He, further, failed to realize that he was himself engaged in theorizing activities by interpreting Islam and Islamic ideas. He should have realized that what he referred to as *the* "Islamic worldview," which he elaborated in his writings, was only *a* reading of the Quranic text by a human mind, placed in specific spatial and temporal setting, and subject to all the historical conditions and social limitations associated with this setting.

What is even more troubling about Qutb's "worldview" is that he reduced the problems facing the Muslim society to a simplistic struggle between good and evil, faith and infidelity, or morality and immorality. No more do these problems appear as cultural and civilizational problems, resulting from a drastic decline in the intellectual, industrial, and organizational capacities of the Muslim people, alongside the moral decline in Muslim character. With Qutb, the problems of the Muslim society became exclusively moral problems, and could be solved simply when a significant number of people declare their commitment to the "Islamic worldview."

Qutb went further to redefine the terms "development" and "underdevelopment," and introduce new criteria for advancement and progress. A developed society, Qutb insisted, is not a society which is on the cutting edge of material production, but one which displays moral "superiority." A society which is high on science and technology but low on morality is backward; while a society which is high on morality and low on science and material production is advanced. By so defining the question of development, Qutb was able to take away the guilt associated with underdevelopment, and provide a quick fix to a seemingly complex and intricate situation. The feeling of relief and self-confidence was obtained, however, at the expense of sacrificing clarity and sound judgment. As a result, many Muslim organizations began to see their role in terms of converting the *jahili* society to "Islam," and engaging in fierce, and frequently bloody, struggle with political authorities. Advancement and progress are no more to be accomplished by emphasizing science, industry, innovation, education, and social reform, but through revolution, confrontation, distinction, and dedication to the Islamic movement.[13]

Despite his revolutionary ideas and sharp criticism of the prevailing sociopolitical system, Qutb shunned and rejected the use of violence to change it. He insisted that a truly Islamic state can only be established among people who are properly educated in the teachings of Islam, and who are self-motivated to implement these teachings in their daily life. Any attempt to use violent tactics to overthrow the ruling elite and install an Islamic elite in its stead, he contended, would be a grave strategic mistake; first, because Islam cannot be imposed on the people by the state, for Islam is a belief system in the first place, and sociopolitical system afterward. Secondly, such an approach would inevitably violate the tenets of the Islamic ideology.

During his interrogation in 1964–in connection with an alleged plot to assassinate Nasser, and overthrow the incumbent government–Qutb told his prosecutor that "establishing an Islamic system requires a prolonged effort of education and propagation, and could not be done through coup d'etat." Qutb went on to say that "the overthrowing of the established regime does not bring about Islamic rule. Clearly, the obstacles that stand before the establishment of an Islamic system are big enough to require long time [of work], and elaborate preparations which might take several generations."[14]

Qutb strongly believed in a gradualistic approach in which the Islamic movement would struggle to expand its power base, and gain support of the masses through communication and mobilization. He further advised the Islamists not to become impatient and rush their efforts to bring about a revolution before the sociopolitical conditions warrant such a move, warning that any premature attempt to overthrow the ruling power could lead to bloodshed, and would eventually culminate in a disaster.[15] Yet by using certain conceptions and categories, such as *mufasalah* (disengagement), *jahiliyyah* (ignorance), *isti'la'* (supremacy), and *dar al-Harb* (territory of war), Qutb unwittingly paved the way for radical groups, providing them with a terminology, which they could use to justify an all-out war against current society. He argued, for instance, that the Islamic movement must distinguish itself from the surrounding *jahili* society. Such a distinction, he maintained, was necessary so that the Islamists could become independent from the prevailing *jahiliyyah*, channeling their energies to build the growing Islamic movement, rather than support the *jahili* regime.[16] Although Qutb tried elsewhere to shed more light on how a distinction and independence could be maintained between the two, his statements remained equivocal, lacking a clear and practical expression.

> This [replacing *jahiliyyah* with Islam] cannot come about by going along few steps with *jahiliyyah*, nor by now severing relations with it and removing ourselves to a separate corner, never. The correct procedure is to mix with discretion, give and take with dignity, speak the truth with love, and show the superiority of the Faith with humility.[17]

Likewise, by stripping the Islamic identity from modern Muslim societies, and by subsuming them under peculiar categories, such as "jahili society," and "dar al-Harb," Qutb helped Muslim radicals to use classical solutions, initially designed to tackle different circumstances, to deal with a society that can be classified as un-Islamic, and a state that could be called a territory of war. In fact, some of the passages of Qutb's last book, *Ma'alim fi al-Tariq*, could be easily interpreted as an open invitation to the use of violence against current Muslim society, especially if they are read apart from the few passages in which Qutb emphasized a gradual approach and a long-term strategy.

> Any country which fights the Muslim because of his belief and prevents him form practicing his religion, and in which the *Shari'ah* [Islamic law] is suspended, is dar al-Harb [territory of war], even though his family and his relatives or his people live in it. . . .[18]

Malek Bennabi: Building a Civilization

Unlike Qutb who confined the problems of Muslim society almost completely to the conceptual spheres of cultural life, Malek Bennabi saw these problems manifesting themselves through far more complex patterns, involving three interrelated spheres: the realm of ideas (cultural system), the realm of persons (personality system), and the realm of things (economic/technological system).

Malek Bennabi was born at Constantine, Algeria, in 1905. He received his primary and secondary education in Algeria, and then went to Paris where he received a Bochelour of Science degree in electrical engineering in 1935. Rather than working in the field of his training, Bennabi devoted the rest of his life to writing and lecturing on the question of underdevelopment in the Third World. He wrote and published his work in French up until 1956 when he left Paris for Cairo. In 1963 he was appointed as the director of higher education in Algeria in the first government established after Algeria declared its independence from France in 1962. In 1976 he resigned his post and spent the last few years of his life lecturing and writing. Bennabi died in Algeria in 1973.

One theme permeates almost all of Bennabi's writings, namely that the problems of Muslim societies are, at bottom, civilizational problems. He divided modern societies into two principal categories: industrial and underdeveloped. These two categories of society occupy two distinct geographical areas. Industrial societies are clustered around, what Bennabi termed, the Moscow-Washington axis, whereas underdeveloped societies are clustered around the Tangier-Djakarta axis (the area stretching from Tangier in the Northern region of Morocco to Djakarta, the capital of Indonesia). Bennabi contended that the differences between these two categories of societies are by no means limited to differences in the primary means of production employed in either of these two areas, but is reflected in all aspects of life.

The difference would become immediately apparent for a person who encounters life in these two types of societies in its totality for the first time, say a visitor from the outer-space. If an outer-space visitor would come to visit the planet earth, and if that visitor were to be given a tour first to those societies located along the Moscow-Washington axis, and then another tour to the Tangier-Djakarta societies, he would immediately recognize the marked differences in the quality of life, personality composition, and life style between the two areas. Generally speaking, the visitor would notice that life on the Moscow-Washington axis is highly organized, houses and streets are well designed and equipped, towns and cities are linked with an extensive communication and transportation systems, people are active and industrious. But as soon as the visitor moves to the other axis he would be surprised to see a completely different picture. He would immediately notice that life on the Tangier-Djakarta axis is for the most part disorganized: huge areas of fertile land is left unutilized, rampant idleness and inaction, and primitive industry and production; the countless smoke chimneys, which distinguish the numerous factories and industrial centers along the Moscow-Washington axis, are almost non-existent here.[19] Yet our visitor would be truly astonished if he were to travel back in time ten centuries and make the same trip along the two axis. For he would see that the conditions which were prevalent then were exactly the opposite. That is, in the eighth or ninth centuries, the Southern axis enjoyed material advancement, efficiency, and organization, and maintained a scientific and economic edge over the Northern axis.[20] According to Bennabi, the significance of this observation is that the two axes represent not merely two distinct geographical areas, but rather two separate *historical blocs*, or simply put two civilizations. The two civilizations or historical blocs have been in constant competition in which the material expansion of the one corresponds to the contraction of the other. The situation today is as such that our outer-space visitor is exposed only to one scene of a long episode. As things stand at this historical moment, the outer-space visitor observes, on the one hand, a Northern bloc in which people are active, and where the raw material and time are efficiently utilized, and, on the other hand, a Southern bloc in which people are inactive, and where time and resources are wasted. This comparison, Bennabi argued, clearly shows that the crisis of the Afro-Asian person is at bottom a civilizational crisis, and has to be dealt with accordingly.

Bennabi argued that there are two sides to the backwardness of Muslim societies. One is external, relating to the efforts of the industrial countries to keep the South under its domination and to exploit its resources; the other is internal, having to do with the historical decline of Muslim culture. He, however, insisted that the internal aspects of the problem are far more significant in holding Muslim society back and preventing its progress. For, he maintained, although European colonialism has in the past eccelorated Muslim decline, and continues to work diligently to delay Muslim renaissance, colonialism, in the final analysis is only a symptom of the disease which plagues Muslim society, and not the disease itself. The real disease is rather the *susceptibility* of Muslim societies to colonialism. That is to say, colonialism would have not been possible, had the Muslim culture been able to produce the type of society which could stand economically and technologically on equal footing with Western powers, and muster the military might which could

repulse European aggression. The European domination of the
Muslim world has been the consequence of the latter cultural
decline, and, therefore, it can be terminated only when the
internal conditions which allows this form of relationship to exist
are eliminated.[21]

Bennabi insisted that the central problem of the Muslim society
is not really whether this society has the wealth or the material
capacity to satisfy the needs of its people. Rather, the main
problem is that the individual lacks the intellectual skills and the
practical training and experience to deal with the economic, social
and political challenges confronting him, as well as the ability to
translate the theoretical solutions to practical measures.[22] It is this
lack of efficacy on the part of the individual members of society
is what larks behind the apparent stagnation of Arab-Muslim
peoples. The question of development can, therefore, be reduced
to the question of finding and creating the sociocultural
conditions which can precipitate the emergence of "efficacious"
Arab personality, leading to the transformation of society from a
backward to an advanced one.

Yet rather than working on the task of creating those internal
conditions which can precipitate cultural rejuvenation, and hence
lead to real social progress, Arab intellectuals, Bennabi charged,
have been preoccupied with verbal warfare against colonialism,
blaming foreigners for Arab backwardness, and condemning
colonial powers for their unsavory and ill-intent towards the
region.[23] Further, since they were awakened to the call of al-
Afaghani, Arabs have been wondering aimlessly, failing to
develop a well defined plan that could guide their efforts, or
embark on a civilizational project, with fairly determined
objectives. Consequently, in a little over a century, Arabs and
Muslims have hardly made any progress, while the Japanese
have become, as early as the 1900s, the rivals of Western
powers, even though Muslim efforts to modernize date to several
decades earlier than those of the Japanese.[24] Why then were the
Japanese able to modernize their society in less than half a
century, while the Arabs failed to do so in over a century?

Bennabi's answer was that while the Muslims were busy
buying modern commodities from the West, and *accumulating*
modern products, the Japanese were busy building a modern
society, and acquiring the internal elements which would allow
them to produce modern commodities themselves. Real
development could be achieved not by acquiring modern
products, but by raising Muslim society to the level of modern

civilization. This means that Muslims would have to cease *accumulating* modern products and start *building* a civilization. For while the process of accumulation might endow a backward society with the feeling and appearance of modernity, and allow it to enjoy the fruits of modern industrial society in a short period of time, accumulation is a losing enterprise in the long run. For no underdeveloped society is capable of going on buying things indefinitely. Soon national resources would be exhausted in the illusive project of buying a ready-made civilization for itself. But the process of accumulation is a losing enterprise for more fundamental reason, for this proposition is predicated on the fallacy that acquiring the fruits of a civilization enables a people to acquire the civilization itself, that the effects have the power of bringing about their causes.[25]

To bring about real progress, Muslims need therefore to shift their focus form the process of accumulating the product of modern civilization, to the process of producing modern goods themselves. More specifically, the Arab society needs to acquire the elements of civilization and create the conditions which facilitate the development of these elements. According to Bennabi, civilization consists of three elements: *man,* who produces civilized forms of life through his ideas and technical skills; *soil*, or the natural resources, which constitute the raw material which man, through his ideas and skills, transforms into useful things; and, finally, *time*, since ideas and skills cannot instantaneously transform raw material into advanced tools and equipments; for time has to be entered into the equation so that ideas could be developed, technical skills could be refined, and more elemental tools and equipments could be produced.[26] Bennabi put the three elements of civilization into the following formula:

$$Civilization = Man + Soil + Time$$

He, further, cautioned that the relationship between these three elements of civilization is not simply additive, but interactive. And like all interactive relationships one may find in nature, the interaction of these three elements is contingent on the presence of a stimulus whose main function is to facilitate and accelerate interaction. If we look in the "laboratory of history," Bennabi argued, we will find clearly that all civilizations have their roots in religious sentiments. For history will tell us that the Buddhist civilization has its roots in Buddhism, Islamic civilization in Islam, and Western civilization in Christianity.[27]

The general formula which we arrived at shows that the question of civilization cannot be solved by importing the available products of another civilization. . . . Its solution, rather, requires solving three partial questions: the question of man, by determining the conditions which reconcile him to progress and history; the question of soil (material resources), by specifying the conditions which allow their social utilization; and the question of time, and how to inculcate its true meaning (and significance) in individual, as well as social consciousness.[28]

But rather than embarking on civilizational project, aiming at reconciling the Arabs and Muslims to the progress of history, and building the intellectual and psychological conditions which would facilitate the social utilization of natural resources, Muslims opted to the easy route of buying the products of industrial nations. "It is indeed much easier to buy a Cadillac ," he noted, "than to develop the ideas which are necessary for its production."[29] This insistence on enjoying, here and now, the fruits of another civilization, rather than taking the pain and spending the time to develop the necessary skills to produce one has resulted in the emergence of a materialistic tendency, a tendency that manifests itself in the excessive desire, and unsatiable appetite, for modern "things" that one finds especially among the ruling elites in the Middle East. It is instructive, Bennabi remarked, that the Muslim world has rejected the Marxist-type of materialism, despite its deep concern for the plight of the oppressed, because of its animosity to human spirituality, but at the same time the Muslims fell an easy prey to Western materialism. This behavior is indicative, he contended, of the fact that the contemporary Muslim can be amused, like a child, by bright and fancy objects, more than the ideas that lie behind them and contribute to their very existence.[30] And like children, contemporary Muslims have been accumulating all kinds of modern "things," not necessarily because these "things" satisfy urgent needs, but simply to imitate the West. That is to say, contemporary Muslims are driven to acquire "things" not by a rationally determined needs, or intellectually examined reasons, but by a child-like envy and desire to imitate (*taqlid*) more advanced peoples.

Contemporary Muslims have an ambivalent attitude towards modernity: while working hard to preserve Muslim cultural life, and insulate it from Western influences, they actively seek to enjoy and utilize the products of modern civilization, which emanates from Western cultural roots. Consequently, the cultural and social spheres of contemporary Muslim society have been almost completely disjoined and split asunder. Muslim societies can in vain hope for a real progress, Bennabi concluded, so long as modernization is confined to the social structures, while cultural structures are kept in a sabbatical state.[31]

The absence of genuine modernization in social spheres is, therefore, the direct result of the stagnation in the cultural spheres. Cultural stagnation manifests itself psychologically in the indifferent attitudes with which contemporary Muslims confront the mounting problems facing them, and intellectually in the lack of innovativeness and creativity. The problems of the Muslim world, Bennabi insisted, are not simply problems of poverty, productivity, or efficiency which could be easily located in the economy, but run "deep" in the cultural spheres. He conceded that it would be extremely difficult in a progressive society, in which both the social and cultural aspects of society are constantly changing, for any one to decide where the locus of change is located. However, the locus of change becomes transparent in certain extraordinary events. Such an event, he noted, was the rebuilding of the German industry after the complete destruction of Germany's infrastructure in 1945. The destruction of Germany's infrastructure did not signal the end of the German civilization, for the Germans were able to rebuild from scratch their economy in less than two decades.[32] He concluded that the locus of change has to be located in people's values and thoughts, not in the economic wealth of a nation.

Bennabi pointed out that there are today two approaches to thinking about societal change. The first one stems from the Hegelian system, and views social change as dependent on cultural change. The other is found in the Marxian system, and considers cultural change to be the dependent variable. He further argued that although the Marxian analysis is valid when applied to Western society, it falls apart when it attempts to extend its analysis to Muslim society. For while the cultural elements in the former are well structured, these elements are still in a chaotic state in the latter. That is to say, while the aim of social theory in the Western world is to restructure the already established sociocultural system so as to improve the quality of life of all citizens, the goal in the Muslim world is to build the system itself.[33]

Bennabi concluded that despite all the changes that have occured in the Muslim society over the last century, they do not amount to a true Arab or Muslim renaissance. For a true renaissance, such as the one experienced by fifteenth-century Europe, has to be directed primarily at restructuring the intellectual and moral life of the individual, and not to be mistaken for the cosmetic operations whose aim is to disguise the ugly face of underdevelopment, and to impute a false sense of development. The Muslim renaissance begins, he held, when the Muslim personality is liberated from those obstacles and yokes which prevent the ordinary individual from becoming an effective and efficient person. Muslim renaissance is, therefore, contingent on a process of cultural renovation. That is, Muslim heritage has to be purged of those ideas and values which pull the Muslim back, preventing him from developing those psychological elements which are conducive to efficient life. According to Bennabi, the process of cultural renovation is a dual process, involving two interrelated sets of activities. The first set of activities is destructive, aiming at isolating repressive ideas and values, so as to make their groundlessness and perversion transparent for all to see, as the first step toward their ultimate repudiation and elimination from the cultural fabric of society. This phase of cultural renovation[34] was manifested, Bennabi pointed out, in the history of Western civilization in the work of such eminent thinkers as Thomas Aquinas, who devoted his life to the project of purging the Western culture from its Augustian and Averroesian elements.[35] The second phase in the process of cultural renovation involves primarily constructive and innovative activities, whereby thoughts and actions are systematized so as to ensure the maximum utilization of human and natural resources. The phase was presented in the Western culture, Bennabi contended, in the innovative Cartesian thought.[36]

Even though his ideas were grounded in the Islamic frame of reference, Bennabi was regarded by most Islamists as an outsider. And in many respects he was. He located himself in al-Afaghani's and Abud's Reformist School, and disagreed with the strategy adopted by mainstream groups in the Islamic movement, according to which open confrontation with nationalist institutions was the best approach for combating corruption, misuse of national resources, and social inequality. For he insisted that these problems were cultural and social in the first place, and political afterward. In a lecture delivered in 1960, Bennabi cautioned his audience that democracy cannot be reduced to democratic institutions. Democracy, he told his audience, is not merely a political system, but a moral and social system as well. Before manifesting itself on the political arena, democracy should become transparent in the attitudes and social practices of a people.

> Democracy is not, as it might appear to the superficial viewer . . . purely a political process, a process of transition of authority to the public, or a constitutional article declaring the sovereignty of a people. . . . Democracy is not, at bottom, the regulation of the use of political power between two parties, between a sovereign and a people for instance. It is rather embodied in the emotional and sentimental composition [of the individual], as well as in the subjective and objective norms.[37]

Democracy presupposes the emergence of the "free" person, the new person who believes in those values which constitute the backbone of democracy. The free person who stands comfortably at the positive middle of the negative extremes: tyranny and servitude. In other words, democracy can only flourish in a culture which condone neither authoritarian nor subservient personality.[38] Bennabi insisted that combating tyranny and dictatorship can not be achieved by changing a government or adopting a democratic constitution, or even invoking an Islamic text. To defeat tyranny and establish a democratic rule, the principle of democracy has to become a social value, while those cultural elements which contribute to the nourishment of both authoritarian and subservient personality would have to be repudiate once and for all.[39]

We noted earlier that Bennabi thought about Muslim underdevelopment along two lines. On the one hand, the internal conditions which make Muslim society unable to efficiently utilize its resources, and which, hence, make it susceptible to outside manipulation, and, on the other hand, the external conditions which contribute significantly to the perpetuation of the state of backwardness, and which is reflected in the imperialistic ambitions of industrial powers. To reduce the effects of the outside forces, Bennabi believed that developing nations would have to cooperate among themselves, by creating a political bloc, and a community of interests, to counteract the influence of the industrial bloc, and to work in harmony to defeat exploitative intents of Western colonialism. Bennabi received with enthusiasm the news about the convening of the Bandung

Conference in 1955. He placed a great hope in the Conference, and believed that it would facilitate cooperation and harmony among Afro-Asian nations, thereby creating the political and economic conditions that would enable these nations to counteract and, hence, reduce the negative influences of the North (i.e., Moscow-Washington axis) on the development of the South (i.e., Tangier-Djakarta axis).

In 1957 he published *L'Afro-Asistisane: concusions la Conference de Bandoeng*. The book repeats many of the themes discussed earlier, using them to underscore the historical importance of the Bandung Conference, and to list the various benefits that the participant countries would be able to enjoy. To Bennabi, Bandung Conference was as important to the twentieth-century Afro-Asian countries as was Berlin Conference to nineteenth-century European countries. But while the latter was consumed with the problems of power, and the need for ensuring peace in Europe, the former had to be concerned with the problems of survival and the need to ensure that Afro-Asian countries would not be violated and penetrated with impunity by industrial powers.[40] He pointed to the aggressive and exploitative policies adopted by Western powers toward the Afro-Asian countries, and called for the political and economic cooperation among the countries represented in Bandung Conference, to counteract the military alliances of industrial countries, and to undercut the strategy of "encirclement," employed by advanced nations to subdue any developing nation which may attempt to assert its own rights and interests. Bennabi cited, for example, the cooperation among NATO members to defeat the measures taken by the Iranian national government which were aimed at transforming control of the national petroleum industry from foreign oil companies to an Iranian national company in the early 1950s. When the United Nations formed in 1952 a committee to investigate the alleged monopoly which existed on the international market, the U.N. secretariat was forced, under pressure from the U.S. government to classify the report submitted by the committee.[41] This refusal on the part of Western nations to extend the moral and legal principles, applied internally within their boarders, to Third World countries (e.g., extending the application of anti-trust laws to the international market) was a strong indicator to Bennabi that Afro-Asian countries need to collectively develop mechanisms which they could use to defeat the imperialistic intents of industrial nations. In the introduction to the second Arabic translation of

L'Afro-Asiatisnal (1971), Bennabi conceded that the idea behind Bandung Conference was defeated, adding that "Bandung Conference of 1955, and later Cairo Conference of 1957, have both combined all the conditions which would have made a Third World revolution possible, except one condition–the intellectual spark which was crucial for setting [the revolution] in motion."[42] "The idea [of Afro-Asian solidarity] died, or rather was killed, in its infancy; and those who killed it were ignorant."[43] For Bennabi, the failure of Bandung Conference was, once again, an example of how the cultural aspect of underdevelopment could prevent the structural development of Third World countries.

Concluding Remarks

Malek Bennabi and Sayed Qutb presented two distinct models of modern Islamic thinking. Both agreed that Islamic principles and values were relevant to modern life, and that their adoption by contemporary Muslims was essential for the future development of the Muslim world. Both shared the same concern about the backwardness of the Muslim society. But beyond that they presented a markedly different approaches to dealing with the problems facing contemporary Muslim society. The essential difference in the views of these two eminent Muslims thinkers came to the fore in an exchanged between the two, sparked by Bennabi's criticism of Qutb, when the latter decided in the fifties to change the title of one of his books from "Toward a Civilized Islamic Society" to "Toward an Islamic Society," whereby the word "civilized" was dropped from the title. Bennabi attributed Qutb's change of mind to a defensive and apologetic attitude, preventing Muslim thinkers to look honestly at the true state of their society and, hence, keeping them back from dealing with the fundamental causes of Muslim backwardness. Qutb rejected Bennabi's assessment arguing that the term "civilized" was redundant and superfluous in the early title since true Islamic society is by its very nature a civilized society. For a civilized society, Qutb insisted, is not a scientifically and technologically advanced society, but one in which moral and humane values prevail.[44] Bennabi, on the other hand, distinguished between the theoretical acceptance of certain beliefs and values, and the actual application of these values to practical situations. An individual, or a group of individuals, may readily accept the validity or truth of certain ideas, but continues nevertheless to live in complete contradiction to the letter and spirit of these ideas. "It is said," Bennabi wrote, "that the Muslim society lives in accordance with the principles of the Quran. It would be more accurate to say, however, that it [Muslim society] speaks in accordance with the principles of the Quran, but lacks the 'practical logic' to [translate the uttered words into] Islamic behavior."[45] This makes the problems of the Muslim society "civilizational problems."

The impact of Qutb's thought on the Arab consciousness was far more pervasive and profound. The ideas of Qutb became very popular among Islamists throughout the Arab and Muslim world. The impact of Bennabi, on the other hand, was more limited among Muslim activists, but made, and continues to make, significant impact in intellectual circles. Bennabi underscored the need for a reevaluation and critical inquiry into the cultural heritage of the Muslims, considering cultural renovation as the first step toward a true "Muslim renaissance." As we will see in the next chapter, his invitation to undertake a critical evaluation of cultural heritage became the paramount concern of Arab intellectuals throughout the seventies and the eighties.

Notes

1. Sayed Qutb, Ma'alim fi al-Tariq, 9th ed. (Beirut, Lebanon: Dar al-Shuruq, 1982), p. 5.
2. Ibid., p. 6.
3. Ibid., pp. 9-10.
4. Alexander S. Cudsi and Ali E. Hillal Dessouki (ed.), *Islam and Power* (Blatimore: The Johns Hopkins University, 1981), p. 7; Tariq and Jacqueline Ismael, Government and Politics in Islam (London: Frances Printer, 1985), p. 110.
5. Quoted in Asaf Hussain, *Islamic Movement in Egypt, Pakistan, and Iran: An Annotated Bibliography* (London: Mansell Publishing Limited, 1983), p. 10.
6. Ibid.
7. Sayed Qutb, *Milestones,* Cedar Rapids (Iowa: Unity Publishing, Co., n.d.), pp. 95-6; see also by the same author *Hadha al-Din* (Cairo: Dar al-Qalam, n.d.), p. 85; and *Al-Mustaqbal li-Hatha al-Din* (Cairo n.d.), p. 9.
8. Qutb, *Milestones*, p. 9.

9. Qutb, *Hadha al-Din*, pp. 3 & 51.
10. Qutb, *Milestones*, p. 46.
11. Ibid., pp. 38-41.
12. Ibid., p. 50.
13. Ibid., pp. 118-21.
14. Jabir Riziq, *Madhabih al-Ikhwan fi Sujun Nasser* (Cairo: Dar al-Nasir Lil-Tiba'ah al-Islamiyyah, 1987), p. 146.
15. Qutb, *Hadha al-Din*, p. 35.
16. Qutb, *Milestone*, p. 47.
17. Ibid., p. 140.
18. Ibid., p. 125.
19. Malek Bennabi, *Ta'amulat* (Damascus, Syria: Dar al-Fkr, 1985), pp. 101-103; also his *Fikrat Komonwilth Islami* (Cairo, Egypt: Maktabat Amar, 1971)
20. Ibid., pp. 106-7.
21. Ibid., p. 129.
22. Ibid., p. 125.
23. Ibid., p. 129.
24. Ibid., p. 162.
25. Ibid., p. 164-7.
26. Ibid., pp. 168-9; 197-9.
27. Ibid., p. 198-9.
28. Ibid,. p. 199
29. Malek Bennabi, *Fikrat Kamonwolth*, p. 15.
30. Ibid., p. 14.
31. Ibid., p. 24-5.
32. Malek Bennabi, *Mushkilat al-Thaqafa*, 4th ed. (Damascus, Syria: Dar al-Fkr, 1984), p. 45.
33. Ibid., p. 38.
34.This phase corresponds to the early stage in what Weber termed cultural rationalization.
35.Ibid., p. 71.
36. Ibid.
37. Malek Bennabi, *Ta'amulat*, pp. 70-1.
38. Ibid., pp. 66-7.
39. Ibid., pp. 72-6.
40. Malek Bennabi, *Fikrat al-Afriqiyyah al-Asyawiyyah*, p. 110-12.
41. Ibid., p. 62-3.
42. Ibid., p. 12.
43. Ibid., p. 13.
44. See Sayed Qutb, *al-Ma'alim*, pp. 116-22.
45. Malek Bennabi, *Mushkilat al-Thaqafa*, p. 87.

Chapter 9

In Search of Authenticity

The spread of Qutb's and Bennabi's ideas in the late sixties and throughout the seventies coincided with the increased assertiveness of the Islamic movement in the Arab World. Although it is very difficult to establish causality between the increased popularity of the writings of the two thinkers and Islamic resurgence, the introduction of Qutb's and Bennabi's ideas, though not the only one, was definitely an important factor at play during this period. One can find several other factors contributing to the rise of Islamic consciousness among Arab, including the successful Islamic revolution against the shah regime in Iran. The recent assertiveness of Islamic identity and Islamic ideas among Arabs has had a noticeable impact on nationalist intellectuals, who have, by now, realized that they cannot win the struggle for their modernist project without tackling head on the theoretical basis of religious ideas, that is, without reinterpreting the Islamic heritage and using it in support of their claims to legitimacy.

Nationalists find themselves increasingly under pressures to answer to the charge that their ideas and methods are unauthentic. Nationalists have been accused by their Islamist rivals of being the agents of Western domination, and the facilitators of the "cultural invasion" by Western values and tastes, whose effects would be, if succeeded, undermining the last defenses of the Ummah against foreign domination.

Beginning with the sixties, the substantive elements of nationalist thought started to develop along two distinct models: Marxism and liberalism. In this chapter we will examine the ideas of two influential Arab thinkers, representing the two major trends in the nationalist movement. Tayeb Tizini and Muhammad 'Abid al-Jabiri have respectively applied the Marxist and liberal ideological framework to study Arab culture. Despite all their differences, the two writers stand on the same ground in their rejection of the Islamist framework, and endeavor, each from his own distinct perspective, to undermine the claims of the resurgent Islamic movement. Similarly, both writers set out to rebut the charges that their Marxist or liberal ideas lack authenticity, and, hence, legitimacy, for both writers realize that grounding their ideas and thoughts in authenticity has increasingly become important for their validation. The strategy they use to confront their critics is simple: they disarm their critics from the very weapons the latter employ to discredit their ideas, by tracing the roots of Marxism and liberalism to the Arab and Islamic tradition.

Arab Marxism

Tizini, an avowed Marxist, has embarked on a highly ambitious project, aiming at a comprehensive evaluation and reinterpretation of the history of Arab thought. He has already announced a project of twelve volumes, of which he has so far published three. Tizini entitled his huge undertaking "A Project of Modern Review of Arab Thought From its Beginning Till the Contemporary Phase." The first tome, consisting of a little over thousand large size pages, is clearly the most important of all, for it provides the theoretical and systematic framework used by the author to analyze the history of Arab thought. As Tizini himself puts it: "we may consider this introduction [i.e., the first volume of the project] at once the theoretical and systematic resultant of all the volumes."[1]

The first volume, entitled *Min al-Turath ila al-Thawra* (from heritage to revolution), is divided to three parts. Part one is a prelude, occupying the first forty five pages, clarifying some of the terms used by the author and preparing the reader for the next two parts. Part two provides a detailed classification of the different trends in modern Arab thought, and a critical analysis of the main themes, ideas, and methods advanced by modern Arab thinkers. Whereas the third part is devoted to the development and elaboration of the author's theoretical framework, termed "*al-jadaliyyah al-tarikhiyyah al-turathiyyah*" (historical heritagial dialectics), which, he insists, provides a "scientific" approach for understanding Arab intellectual history. He concedes right at the beginning that his proposed theory is "nothing more than a 'heritagial' particularization of the dialectic and historical materialism."[2] In other words, Tizini's "historical heritagial dialectics" is the outcome of applying Marx's historical materialism to the study of the Arab history.

But why does Tizini find it necessary now to deal with the question of "cultural heritage" in general, and "Arab cultural heritage in particular" ? That is, if Marx's historical materialism is still valid in interpreting Arab history, as part of world history, why does not Tizini, following in the footsteps of other Arab Marxists, dismiss off hand Arab cultural heritage as part of the ideological superstructure of foregone historical epoches? He cites three factors as the source of the renewed interests in the question of cultural heritage. First, the recent change in the economic and social infrastructure, as well as in the political and ideological superstructure, which takes place in a number of Arab countries, and the need for the theoretical clarification of this change. Secondly, the need to counteract the efforts of the declining social forces, who in an attempt to prevent their downfall have been working to resuscitate religious and national Arab past. Finally, the need to respond to the ongoing attack, led by global imperialism against the growing progressive forces in the Arab regions. Tizini seems to suggest that the third factor, global imperialism, has both provoked and guided the other two factors.[3] Be that as it may, what Tizini fails to cite as a factor in the renewed interest in the question of "heritage" is the increased pressure placed on Marxist and liberal writers to locate their ideas within the historical framework of Arab thought, a concern of Tizini which becomes quite apparent as he progresses further in his study.

Tizini classifies the various tendencies in Arab thought along ideological and epistemological lines. Ideologically, the various theoretical trends could be divided, he contends, into two major groups, pursuant to their class commitment. First, the Arab Left, who are committed to the promotion of the interests of the proletarian classes (*tabaqat kadiha*), and to whom Tizini himself, he tells us, belongs. Secondly, the rest of Arab intellectuals, who are committed to advancing the interests of the "oppressive" and "anti-progressive" classes. The latter are, in turn, divided to five subgroups: 1) *salfawiyyah* (atavism), 2) *'asrawiyyah* (modernism), 3) *talfiqawiyyah* (syncritism), 4) *tahyidawiyya* (neutralism), and 5) *merkazawiyyah awrubiyyah* (Eurocentrism). Epistemologically, Tizini distinguishes between two categories. First, those who fail to see the historical nature of ideas, and who are accordingly subsumed under the label "ahistorical and aheritagial thought;" and secondly, Tizini's "historical and heritagial dialectics," which, he proclaimed, is the only theory capable of providing an accurate interpretation of Arab intellectual history.[4]

Atavism, both in its religious and nationalist forms, emerged in the wake of the external threats, confronted the Arabs at the turn of this century. The former found its citadel in the Islamic period of Arab history, the latter in the *jahili*, or pre-Islamic period. Both sought protection in the past to guard against the threat of cultural annihilation posed by Western cultures, for they knew of no better way to combat it.[5] The two forms of *salfawiyyah* (atavism) may have been able to create a sense of national solidarity, he argues, but at the expense of perpetuating the control of the semi-bourgeois, semi-feudal backward classes, who have been successful in using the "glorious past" to maintain their domination over society. Thus, atavism has protected the Arabs from the domination of the "outsiders" (*al-aghyar*) only to ensure the domination of the national elites (*al-akhyar*).[6]

Turning to the study of Arab history in its medieval period, a period corresponding to the time of glory when Islamic civilization was at its zenith, Tizini makes two general remarks. First, he concedes that Arab society in this period does not fall into any of the five historical epochs, established by historical materialism. He hastily subsumes it under the Marxian category of "Asiatic production." Tizini does not find it worthwhile to investigate whether, and to what extent, the medieval Arab society matches the Marxian description, even though Marx developed his "Asiatic production" notion while he was studying the forms of production in India and China, and not in the Arab society.[7] Secondly, Tizini rightly rejects the notion that Islamic historical thought was homogeneous. He distinguishes between the progressive and regressive elements in the history of Arab thought, i. e., between those who wanted to push Arab and Islamic thinking into new frontiers, and those who fought to preserve the status quo, and to emphasize past accomplishments.[8] This distinction seems important in the wake of the fact that many Islamists and nationalists writers treat Arab history, stretching over a millennium, as if it was a homogeneous whole. He does a good job in exposing the reactionary attitude of leading Muslim scholars near the end of the medieval period (*al-'asr al-wasit*), an attitude which was manifested in those scholars who warned against the 'evil' consequences of innovation (*ibtida'*), even when innovation did not violate the dictates of

Islamic texts, as well as in the severe limits placed on the use of reasoning.[9] Medieval Muslim scholars, following in the footsteps of Abu al-Hassan al-Ash'ari, whose theological system became predominant by the turn of the eleventh century, restricted their intellectual activities to the study and interpretation of Islamic texts. Although Ash'ari scholars continued to pay lip service to the importance of independent reasoning, they reduced the role of reasoning to those activities aimed at defending doctrines against critics and detractors. Thinking and reasoning could no more be used to understand nature and society.[10]

In contrast to the reactionary elements of medieval Arab thought, Arab philosophers (*al-falasifa*) represented the progressive elements. Not only were the philosophers interested in understanding nature and society, but they were also open to foreign ideas and thoughts. Tizini turns here to address the question of "authenticity," raised by contemporary nationalist and Islamist writers. He rejects the narrowly defined criteria of Arab or Islamic authenticity, in which ideas and methods are perceived to be authentic only if they can be firmly grounded in the Arab or Islamic traditions. Tizini finds in the Arab philosopher and Muslim jurist Ibn Rushd (Averroes) a powerful weapon to be used against the *Salfawiyyah*. Ibn Rushd was a renowned Muslim jurist, whose religious knowledge and commitment to Islam were above reproach. He was the chief justice of twelveth-century Cordoba. Ibn Rushd was also a leading physician and philosopher who fiercely defended Greek philosophy against the all-out attack carried against it by Ash'ari scholars, including the very influential jurist and theologian Abu Hamid al-Ghazali. Ibn Rushd rejected the notion advanced by the Ash'ari scholars that it was not fit for Muslims to rely on, or borrow from, ideas developed under other religions. Greek philosophy was especially attacked because of its pagan roots. He argued that Greek ideas and methods were intellectual tools, and like all tools their use should not be limited to any specific religion.[11]

Tizini goes, further, to trace the roots of materialism, secularism, and even socialism to Ibn Rushd. As he puts it:

What is of great importance here is the position which Averroesism (al-Rushdiah) assumes vis-a-vis the question of cultural heritage, a position stemming from Averroes's overall theoretical framework. This position is manifested, first, in Averroes's materialism, which takes the form of pantheism. This [position] is, secondly, manifested in his secularism, which appears clearly in his distinction between philosophy (al-hikma) and law (al-shari'a). Thirdly, and finally, [the position] is manifested in his social and political progressiveness, which transpires in his support for the principle of collective ownership of social wealth.[12]

Not only does Tizini equivocate the ideas of Ibn Rushd, but he is evidently willing to misrepresent the latter's thought in order to realize the objectives he set out to achieve. First, Tizini misrepresents Ibn Rushd when he equates the latter's alleged pantheism with materialism. For if one can invoke Ibn Rushd's pantheism as an example of materialist thinking, one should be able, by the same token, to list Hegel's pantheism as an instance of materialism. Secondly, Ibn Rushd's secularism is a far cry from Tizini's secularism. For Ibn Rushd called for the development of two different sets of principles and methods to be applied to the study of natural phenomena on the one hand, and moral and legal activities on the other. He had never entertained the thought that legal principles or social regulations could be made in isolation of the directives of revealed texts, let alone to advocate the complete abandonment of revealed values and principles. Whereas Tizini's secularism reflects an orthodox Marxist position which, unlike liberal secularism, is not satisfied with the depoliticization of religion, but sees in it a negative force standing in the way of progress and, hence, has to be eliminated or suppressed. Finally, Ibn Rushd's support of collective ownership of social wealth is not peculiar or new in the history of Islamic legal thought, for almost all Muslim jurists since the inception of Islam have held the view that social wealth, such as water, minerals, and uncultivated land are public property which may not be claimed exclusively by anyone. But this conception is far removed from the socialist ideas of collective ownership of the means of production.

Having discussed Arab and Islamic atavism, Tizini turns to the second category in his typology of contemporary Arab intellectual trends, i. e. modernism. Modernism stands on the opposite side from atavism, for it calls, in the main, for the complete repudiation of the past and the dissolution of Arab culture in Western culture. He further divides modernism into three subbranches in which Western Marxism and Western liberalism are placed along side religious renovation. These three groups, he argues, were overwhelmed by Western accomplishments. Western (or liberal) Marxism is faulted for its "syncritism," and tendency to compromise Marxist principles to liberal ideals. Western liberalism, or modern nihilism as Tizini would like to call it, is condemned for opening Arab frontiers to Western imperialism. And religious renovation is rejected for combining its modernizing overtone with a religious undertone, thereby compromising the interests of the Arab proletariat.[13]

This typology becomes even more perplexed when Tizini goes on to discuss the category syncritism. Here, Zaki Najib Mahmud, a leading Arab logical positivist, is placed in the same category with Sayed Qutb and Malek Bennabi. The reason for putting the three together, despite the ideological and methodological differences that separate one from the other, is that they all, Tizini proclaims, have attempted to strike a balance between Arab or Islamic atavism and modernism. It seems quite absurd to classify Mahmud and Qutb under one category just because both appear to be willing to intellectually engage their opponents when Tizini well know that Mahmud's ideas are grounded in logical positivism, while Qutb's thoughts are anchored in Islamic idealism. Tizini chooses to classify contemporary Arab thought not on the basis of the substantive views of the intellectuals in consideration, but rather on the basis of the formal positions these intellectual assume vis-a-vis the temporal framework in which their ideas are anchored. Tizini's typology could have been far more useful had he informed his classification by the substantive positions of Arab thinkers. However, he completely ignored the ideological commitments of Arab intellectuals, while insisting that he is undertaking a systematic analysis of ideological trends. This confused and confusing approach to analyzing Arab intellectual life, consequently, contributes nothing to the clarification of the intellectual scene. On the contrary, it equivocates the political and ideological positions of various Arab intellectuals, for when Sayed Qutb and Muhammad Abduh, who struggled for establishing Islamic revelation as the source of moral and legal regulations, are placed in the same category with Taha Hussain and Zaki Nagib Mahmud, who strongly believed in the need to Westernize Arab cultural and social life, and insisted that religious principles should not intervene in Arab political life, the result is a great confusion in political and theoretical positions.

We turn now to examine the far more important part of Tizini's first volume, i. e. his theory of "historical heritagial dialectics." For this theory constitutes the analytical framework which he uses to reconstrue the history of Arab thought. I would like to state right at the beginning that it is not my intention to undertake a comprehensive critique of Tizini's theory, for obviously such a task falls outside the scope of this study. My purpose is rather a limited one, namely to underscore the urgent need felt by Tizini, and other nationalist writers, to legitimize socialist and liberal thought, by tracing their roots to historical Arab thought.

The theory of "historical heritagial dialectics" employs two primary concepts: "the prevalent national phase" and "the historical heritagial selection." From these two concepts arises a web of secondary concepts: "the historical substance," "the heritagial substance," "heritagial inspiration," "historical adoption," and "Historical isolation." The "prevalent national phase" represents the present moment of the historical development of society. This moment reflects, in turn, the temporal region in which the past and the future overlap, or, to put it more accurately, the region where the forces of the past confront the forces of the future. In the case of Arab society, the struggle takes place between the backward classes (a combination of pretty bourgeois and feudalist classes) and progressive classes (blue collar workers and peasants). Tizini holds that although class struggle is at bottom an economic and social, it can be won only on the ideological plane. That is, Marxist intellectuals would have to reinterpret Arab history so as to purge it from its regressive elements, and to demonstrate that Arab intellectual history has been moving, through its enlightened elements, toward Marxist thought. This process requires that the progressive elements of the Arab past be carefully documented as the first step toward mobilizing these elements to create a brilliant and promising future.

Documenting the past requires that the concepts of history and heritage be distinguished. According to Tizini, history refers to past events as they are documented in historiography, while heritage points to elements of the national history which continue to exert influence on the present. As he puts it:

> While the historical past continuously approaches the present, without becoming part of the present, "heritage" represents the continuity of the past in the present. That is, the two [i. e., history and heritage] combined constitute, in their progressing ends, "heritage." Consequently, the dialectical relationship between the lines of continuity and discontinuity becomes transparent through the relationship between "history" and "heritage."[14]

Apparently the term "heritage" is used by Tizini to denote those cultural elements (values, beliefs, customs, traditions, etc.) which are historically transmitted from one generation to another. The relationship between "history" and "heritage" is, moreover, dialectical since the cultural heritage of a people represents the subjective understanding of the objective historical material. Cultural heritage can be changed when new historical knowledge is brought to bear on it. Likewise, historical substance can be enlightened when cultural heritage is enriched by rational and scientific elements.

But how can the "historical heritagial dialectics" make use of "historical substance" and "heritagial substance" in ways that would contribute to the progressive development of the "prevalent national phase"? To answer this question Tizini introduces the other primary concept in his theory, the concept of "historical heritagial selection." The process of "historical selection" aims at identifying the historical elements of Arab thought which may contribute to the rise of "the emerging national phase." The process of selection itself consists of three components: two positive, "heritagial inspiration" and "historical adoption," purporting to incorporate the progressive elements in Arab history to the "emerging national phase," and the third is negative, "historical isolation," aiming at isolating and eliminating reactionary elements. These three tools, then, would allow Tizini to flip through the Arab and Muslim history, analyzing the various ideas and theories developed in the past, isolating and rejecting those which do not contribute to future progress of the Arab society, adopting those ideas and theories which are epistemologically correct, and enlisting those elements which, though lacking in theoretical coherence, have ideological value in that they could be used for strengthening and legitimizing the adopted ideas.[15]

Yet for those readers who have become increasingly perplexed by the ever-growing web of intricately interwoven concepts, known collectively as "the historical heritagial dialectics," Tizini provides another reminder that his theory is only a particularized formulation of Marx's historical materialism, adapted to fit into the specificity of the Arab culture. "The relation of historical and heritagial dialectics," Tizini writes, "to historical and dialectical materialism is that of a branch to trunk. It is, in this sense, a subjective and internal relationship."[16] Having established the proximity of his theory to the Marxist theory of history, Tizini spends the next sixty pages in an effort to demonstrate that historical materialism is not a theory imposed on the Arab history from without, but that it, rather, reflects the genuine needs and demands of the Arab society. To do so, he introduces what he calls the "law of inner and outer dialectics,"[17] which he uses to redefine the relationship between the "Self" and the "Other." The "Self" whose national identity and authenticity is to be maintained and protected against the threats of the "Other" should not be taken, Tizini remarks, as the whole of Arab or Muslim history. Rather, the "Self" should be confined to the "prevalent national phase," while the "Other" has to be redefined so as to include both the contemporary *West* and the Arab or Muslim *past*. Both the contemporary West and the national past do exert positive as well as negative influences on the national present. Since the rules of inclusion and exclusion must be determined on the basis of what is more conducive to national development and progress, the Western-Other should be incorporated and included in the definition of the "Self", while the reactionary elements of the national past should be ejected and excluded from the definition of the "Self."

> When we consider that 'the prevalent national phase' is influenced by the 'Other' in two ways: one is contemporary and direct, the other via 'the national past' in its historical and heritagial context, we shall realize that this 'other' is included in the formation of the 'prevalent national phase,' thereby becoming part of 'the inner.' This is what need to be emphasized by the 'historical heritagial dialectics.' It has to be recognized, however, that the 'Outer-Other,' by being transformed into 'inner-ego,' becomes, in effect, part of the characteristics of the 'prevalent national phase' and ceases to be recognized as an 'Other,' except for the purpose of analytical study.[18]

With this formulation, Tizini shifts the center of authenticity from the past to the present. That is to say, the criteria of authenticity are included in the definition of the present. For an idea or a practice to be authentic it need not, any more, correspond to principles or values rooted in the Arab or Islamic past. On the contrary, past principles and values are authentic only insofar as they continue to be relevant to the needs of contemporary life. Tizini brilliantly turns the table on his critics by redefining the criteria of authenticity. To be authentic now means to be committed to the advancement of historical materialism.

It has become clear by now that the "historical heritagial selection" is a process, or a combination of processes, purporting to reinterpret and redesign the national culture and prepare it to make the transition from the "prevalent national phase," which, as Tizini tells us, is the equivalent to what Lenin termed the "social formation," to the "emerging national phase." More specifically, the purpose of the process of "historical selection" is to create the subjective (cultural) and objective (structural) conditions which can bring about a cultural and social revolution. In spelling out the subjective and objective conditions needed to effect progress, Tizini follows closely the Marxist-Leninist lines of thinking. Socially, a socialist revolution has to take place, in which the "proletariat masses" (*al-jamahir al-kadiha*) overthrow, of course under the leadership of the "revolutionary organization" (*al-tanzim al-thawri*), the bourgeois ruling classes and restructure society in accordance with Marxist-Leninist dogmas. The socialist revolution has to initiate the process of "socialist transformation" (*al-tahwil al-ishtiraki*) which aims at achieving three goals: social-industrial revolution, national-unificational revolution, and cultural-ideological revolution. Culturally, the proletariat masses, again led by the revolutionary organization, would have to rearrange the cultural and ideological superstructure of society so as to make it compatible with the socialist goals of society. The aim here is the "creation of the comprehensive and innovative socialist personality," and the replacement of the "cultural elite" by an "acculturated people".

After over a thousand pages, and countless theorems and concepts, we find ourselves returning back to our point of departure, to the theory of historical materialism. To our surprise, Tizini has found nothing to be amended or modified in the Marxist-Leninist conception of history. After a strenuous and sophisticated intellectual exercise, and the repeated allusion to the specificity of the Arab society and culture, he ends up prescribing to the Arab people the same medicine which once administered to the Soviet people by the Bolshevik revolutionaries.

What is significant about Tizini's project is this renewed interest in studying the cultural forms and intellectual history of the Arab people. By committing himself to the study of the cultural history of the Arabs, Tizini dedicates his life, and his outstanding intellectual talents, to the task of clarifying and reinterpreting the Arab past, albeit a clarification relying exclusively on Marxist ground. It is unfortunate that he approaches his subject-matter with already formed concepts, and deeply entrenched ideas. Tizini seems to be totally committed to Marxism to the extent that he does not believe that Marxist doctrines should be enlightened and reevaluated by the results of his examination, but rather that Arab history has to be rearranged to fit the Marxist premises. His Marxist prejudices notwithstanding, by critically analyzing cultural aspects of Arab history, and raising questions about the validity and "authenticity" of cultural values and beliefs, Tizini's writings are likely to stir a very needed debate about the validity and adequacy of cultural and social forms of traditional thought.

Finally, Tizini affirms, in his own peculiar way, the importance of ideas, beliefs, and values in shaping the future. The ideological superstructure is once again shown, by an avowed Marxist-Leninist, to have a strong hold on the economic infrastructure, and even to have the primacy in determining the future through the formation of individual and social consciousness.

Arab Liberalism

Unlike Tizini, whose primary interest in studying the Arab-Islamic heritage is to use it in support of his Marxist ideas, Muhammad 'Abid al-Jabiri approaches his subject-matter with a desire to discover the constants and variables of Arab heritage. His contribution to the clarification of Arab thought and culture is both informative and original. Al-Jabiri's intellectual project consists of two major thrusts. The first thrust involves a critical analysis aimed at uncovering what he perceives as the contradictory nature of modern Arab intellect. His brilliant critique of modern Arab thinking is outlined in his book *Al-Khitab al-Arabi al-Mu'asir* (contemporary Arab discourse), published in 1982, as well as in numerous other papers. The second thrust of al-Jabiri's project involves his efforts to trace the contradictions of modern Arab intellectualism to its historical roots. In *Naqd al-'Aql al-Arabi* (the critique of Arab mind), consisting of two large volumes published consecutively in 1984 and 1986, he attributes the confusion of modern Arab thinking to the fusion of three distinct epistemological frameworks into one syncritic system by latter-days Muslim scholars (twelfth century onwards), concluding that "Arab renaissance" is contingent on the restructuring of the Arab mind. In what follows, I attempt to sketch a general outline of al-Jabiri's project.

Al-Jabiri expressed his intention to embark on a project dealing with the problematics of Arab thought in the introduction of a book, published in 1980, entitled *Nahnu wa al-Turath: Qira'at mu'asirah fi turathina al-falsafi* (we and heritage: contemporary readings of our philosophical heritage), where he succinctly summarizes the major thrust of his project:

> Modern and contemporary Arab thought is, in general, an ahistorical thought, lacking the minimum level of objectivity. Its reading of [cultural] heritage is an atavist reading, sanctifying and revering the past, and seeking in it ready-made "solutions" to the problems of the present and the future. An if this [analysis] is true for the religious trend, it is equally true for other trends, since each has its own *salaf* (historical model) to look up to and depend on. Therefore, all Arabs borrow their projects of renaissance from some sort of a past: either the Arab-Islamic past or the European 'past-present,' or from the Russian, Chinese. . .experiments, and the list goes on and on. This sort of mental activities [reflects] a mechanical type which seek ready-made solutions for all emerging problems in some [historical] source.[19]

Like Tizini, al-Jabiri is concerned with the concepts of *authenticity* and *modernity*, and the tension that exists between the two in contemporary Arab thought. For him, the "authenticity-modernity" tension stems form much deeper contradiction, rooted in the very structure of the Arab mind. He holds, therefore, that any attempt at reconciling the authentic and the modern has to address itself to the root causes which brings the two into direct confrontation. This means in practice that a comprehensive critique of contemporary Arab thinking is the first step toward the social modernization of Arab society.

Since the question of authenticity is rooted in the Arab-Islamic heritage, the latter has to be examined by approaching it on two levels: the ideological and the epistemological. Ideologically, those elements which have merely historical value should be used to clarify the genesis and development of the various intellectual trends; such clarification should allow us to understand how the current structure of Arab mind has evolved, and how it can be restructured so as to effect a true Arab renaissance. Epistemologically, those elements of Arab intellectual history which continue to be scientifically valid, should be incorporated into the contemporary body of knowledge and be employed to enrich and advance modern life.[20]

Having called for the reexamination of Arab heritage on the ideological and epistemological planes, he goes on to assert that the epistemic substance of the Islamic philosophy, and all pre-contemporary philosophies for that matter, has become completely irrelevant and useless. Consequently, only the ideological elements of the Arab intellectual heritage are useful today, he concludes, for they can help in clarifying historical trends leading to the current predicament of the Arab mind.[21] Yet throughout his work, al-Jabiri's use of the terms ideology and epistemology is equivocal, if not confused. It is not clear, for example, whether by the epistemic (al-ma'rifa), or epistemic substance (al-mada al-ma'rifiyah), of the Avacinnian (Ibn Sina's) philosophy he refers to its scientific (natural science) or philosophical (human and social knowledge) aspects. But since al-Jabiri is only interested in the social and metaphysical aspects of Avacinna's intellectual work, one may wonder how Avacinnia's philosophical analysis, or those of Aristotle or Kant for that matter, has no epistemic value whatsoever. Al-Jabiri's assertion that the epistemic substance of all pre-contemporary philosophy is irrelevant to modern life becomes more problematic and perplexing when we realize that he himself employs the concept of antinomy, introduced by Kant, to explain the internal contradictions of contemporary Arab thought.[22]

In 1982, al-Jabiri published his book *Al-Khitab al-Arabi al-Mu'asir* (The contemporary Arab discourse), in which he attempted a comprehensive critical analysis of contemporary Arab thought. Here he argues that Arab thought has been, for the last century, revolving around two questions: the question of "authenticity" associated with the idea of cultural heritage, and the question of "modernity," linked with the idea of European technological advancement.[23] But what causes contemporary Arab thought to continuously revolve around these two concepts, unable to make any significant progress? He provides throughout his discussion a number of reasons for the intellectual stagnation of Arab thought, which may be reduced to one fundamental reason, namely the absolute authority the historical model has on the Arab mind. Arab intellectuals are committed to either of two civilizational models: "The European civilization whose effect has been the awakening of [the Arabs] to confront a cultural and military challenge, and to force them to face the problematic of 'renaissance;' and the Arab-Islamic civilization which constituted, and still does, a crucial driving force in the process of self-assertion in the face of these challenges."[24] As a result of this strong attachment to historical models, Arab thinking has become utopian, completely detached from reality, and constantly dealing with theoretical (hypothetical) possibilities. Modern Arab thought has been shaped by the three-sided relationship existing among (a) the experienced backwardness of contemporary Arab society, (b) the Arab-Islamic historical model, and (c) the European model. Yet rather than confronting reality as it is, and working toward constructing the future on the basis of what is practically possible, Arab intellectuals, al-Jabiri contends, have been living in a world created by their fantasies, and have been pursuing untenable dreams.

Among the constants of contemporary thought which cause al-Jabiri to make his harsh assessment is the linkage Arab intellectuals make between the prospect of an Arab renaissance, on the one hand, and the inevitable "collapse" of the West, on the other hand. The collapse of the West, it is asserted, will correspond with the "rising" of Arab society to the "leadership" of humanity.[25] This belief in the inevitable collapse of the West and its replacement with an Arab civilization is the direct result, he contends, of the internal logic of Arab intellect, a logic based on *analogous reasoning,* whereby the resolution of present problems is always achieved by making reference to some sort of an experienced past (*qiyas al-gha'b 'ala al-shahid*). Today Arabs see their modern renaissance in the lens of their past renaissance. The underlying assumption is that as the Arabs were able, at the inception of Islam, to built a civilization which inherited both the Roman and Persian civilizations, they should be able today to build a modern civilization that will inherit Western civilization. Yet this "fantasy" about the immanent collapse of the West and the inevitable rise of the Arabs is based completely on analogous reasoning that deals exclusively with theoretical possibilities, a reasoning which is utterly indifferent to existing reality and objective conditions. It is a fantasy precipitated by the belief that for the "Self" to rise and progress, the "Other" which stands in the way of progressive future has to go first. Al-Jabiri points out that this "analogous reasoning," preoccupied with the desire to find similarities between the present and the past, and, hence, is completely oblivious to the significant differences between the two, thereby basing its conclusion on two fallacies. The first fallacy results from the failure of contemporary Arab intellectuals to see that part of the "Other" that prevents Arab progress is the

Arab past itself, reflected in the cultural heritage handed down form previous generations, furnishing the very ideas and methods of thinking responsible for Arab backwardness. The second fallacy entertained by contemporary Arab thought lies in the Arab intellectual's inability to realize that Arab liberation from, and independence of, Western control need not be associated with Western decline. Rather, it requires that the Arab mind be able to enter into a "critical dialogue" with both Western culture and its own Arab heritage. Western culture should be read historically, and its propositions and conceptions should be understood relatively. Also the bases of Western development should be identified, and, then, introduced into Arab culture and thought.[26] Similarly, liberation from the control of the intellectual heritage does not mean that this heritage has to be neglected or rejected, but has to be understood, sorted out, restructured, and surpassed.[27]

Al-Jabiri concludes that "Arab national discourse" is at once a *problematic* and *metaphysical*. It is problematic (*ishkali*) because it posits problems which either have no practical solution, or the subjective and objective requisites for their solution are lacking. It is metaphysical, on the other hand, because it deals with purely theoretical possibilities, that have no grounding in reality. These possibilities have not been formulated by an objective analysis of the actual conditions of contemporary society, nor have they been articulated in response to real needs. Rather, the possibilities are necessary for the satisfaction of the psychological needs of their advocates. That is, they ensure the internal cohesiveness of the ideologies built around the various historical models subscribed to by Arab intellectuals. These characteristics are shared by the three predominant intellectual discourses in the Arab World: the *salafiyyah* (religious atavism), the liberal, and the national socialist.

The *salfawiyyah*, for once, has called, since its inception in the writings of Muhammad Abduh, for the liberation of the Arab-Islamic thinking from all contradictions and distortions which have been accumulating in the last millennium. Yet rather than understanding the genesis and causes of these contradictions in order to restructure the Arab mind, *Salfawiyyah* has elected to completely overlook the evolution of Arab thought, and to start anew by building on early Islamic thought. However, al-Jabiri notes that by so doing, *salfawiyysah* has been able to overcome not only Arab "contradictions," but Arab "rationality" as well. For the early Islamic thought predates the period when the rules of science and systematic thinking were established. The *Salfawiyyah's* call is, hence, an invitation to revert to the pre-rational – i.e., the irrational – era of Arab intellectual history. The result is that although the "*Salafi* mind" continues to pay lip service to reason and rationality, it has reduced reason to a negative force restricting the expansion of intellectual activities to uncharted territories, so to speak. Reason, in other words, is being manipulated by religious scholars and used to ensure the continuous predominance of the Arab-Islamic tradition.[28]

On the other hand, Arab liberals call for the total repudiation of Arab intellectual heritage, at the time they invite their co-nationals to embrace Western culture in its entirety. "How is it possible," al-Jabiri asks, "for the Arab to proclaim a history other than his? How is it possible to strip himself out of his past, let alone his milieu and environment?"[29] This makes the Arab liberal stand on the same footing with the Arab *salafi*, for both seek the future in some historical model. The former finds its model in the Arab-Islamic era which preceded the "corruption" of the Arab mind by "outside" influences, while the latter seeks its model in the pre-colonial Western thought, before the corruption of Western ideas by imperialist ambitions.[30]

Finally, the same tendency exists among social nationalists. For here too the ideological content of nationalist thought has been developed by contemplating theoretical possibilities, in an attempt to counterbalance the claims of the ideological rivals. Nationalist thought has emerged in response to three foes: colonialism, religious atavism, and communism. Nationalists managed to incorporate, as part of their strategy to defeat their adversaries, the very ideas which their rivals used to validate their claims to power. From the *salfawiyyah* they have adopted the ideas of the glorious past, of course after substituting the Arab for the Islamic past. And so Islamic unity advocated by the Reformist School has been replaced by an Arab unity. From communism, the nationalists have embraced the idea of socialism, after transforming it from a global Communism to a "national Arab socialism." Finally, in response to colonial domination, nationalist have advocated the principle of independence. The result has been that the principles of "unity," "liberation," and "socialism," which nationalists declare as their permanent objectives, have been reduced to pure slogans, having no effects whatever on actual practices. Al-Jabiri attributes the failure of Arab nationalists to realize their objectives primarily to the lack of any grounding of these ideas in reality. For example, when Arab nationalists posit the objectives of unity, liberation, and socialism as preconditions for any social and economic development, they deal with these issues exclusively on the theoretical plane; i. e., they postulate as a reality those conditions which make Arab unity and progress possible. Indeed, nationalist theorists pay no attention to the objective conditions existing on the ground which make such goals out of reach. Therefore, when Arab nationalists emphasize the historical and linguistic bases of Arab unity, they fail to see that cultural and political differences between Arab states which make the realization of this unity impossible under current circumstances

Why has not, then, the contradictory nature of contemporary Arab discourse become apparent to the bulk of Arab intellectuals? To answer this question, al-Jabiri appeals to the concept of naqa'd (antinomies), a concept introduced and discussed at some length by Kant in *Critique of Pure Reason*. Al-Jabiri argues that since contemporary Arab thought deals with modern problems only after the latter are abstracted and isolated from the social surrounding, the contradictory nature of the propositions advocated by Arab intellectuals is equivocated and obscured. Contradictions, that is, are reduced to antinomies which can be neither firmly established nor systematically refuted.[31]

To deal with the intellectual crisis of Arab thought, radical solutions have to be attempted. Al-Jabiri suggests that the Arab mind has to be analyzed and reduced to its basic constituting elements. Such an analysis should permit a critical differentiation in which the progressive elements can be singled out and restructured so as to make Arab culture more conducive to progress and more responsive to the needs of a modern society. What is needed is, in short, a critical project which would bring about an Arab epistemological revolution, similar to the one undertook by Kant, a project that would aspire to do to Arab cultural heritage what the Kantian revolution did to Western culture. What is need is *"naqd al-'aql al-arabi,"* a critique of the Arab intellect.

The critique of Arab mind has been al-Jabiri's primary mission, and the *Naqd al-'Aql al-Arabi* is thus far his principal work. The book was published in two volumes, subtitled *Takwin al-'Aql al-'Arabi* (the formation of Arab mind) (1984), and *Bunyat al-'Aql al-Arabi* (the structure of Arab mind) (1986).[32] The first volume is devoted to studying the evolution of Arab intellectual life. To study the Arab mind, one has to examine its products, i.e. the cultural elements through which the

Arab mind manifests itself. Al-Jabiri begins his analysis by posing a provocative question: "What has hitherto changed in Arab culture since the pre-Islamic period (*al-jahiliyyah*)?" In response to this question al-Jabiri proclaims that nothing has changed. Any Arab, he argues, can read the work of poets, novelists, or legal scholars from the pre-Islamic times onward and feel as if they are all his contemporaries. The work of Arab intellectuals who belong to various epochs of Arab history is accessible to contemporary Arabs.[33] But how could an intellectual history which spans over one and half millennia, and has influenced and is influenced by countless civilizations and cultures, be so homogeneous and static? He argues that the uniformity of Arab thought throughout much of its history becomes intelligible when we realize that the basic structure of Arab culture was established once and for all during the "Age of Recording." For the Age of Recording was not only the time when all Islamic sciences were classified and recorded in textbooks, but was also the time when Greek and Hellenistic sciences were translated into Arabic. Even the pre-Islamic poetry was written and forged in the same period. In other words, the "Age of Recording" established the rules and principles (e. g., legal, linguistic, logical, grammatical, etc.) which constituted for later generations the "authoritative framework" that guided intellectual activities all the way down to the contemporary era.[34]

Al-Jabiri contends that the "Age of Recording" has witnessed the emergence of three distinct epistemic systems, which soon entered into fierce rivalry over the control of intellectual life:

1. *al-nizam al-ma'rifi al-bayani* (the epistemology of explication). This theory of knowledge, he argues, was the first to appear in the Arabic-Islamic intellectual history. The disciplines which came under the authority of this system were the Islamic sciences, including grammar (*nahu*), language (*lugha*), jurisprudence (*fiqh*), rhetoric (*balaghah*), and theology (*kalam*). This epistemology is characterized by its heavy dependence on the analogous reasoning (*qiyas al-gha'b 'ala al-shahid*), and its rejection of the principle of causality.

2. *al-nizam al-ma'rifi al-'urfani* (the epistemology of gnosticisim). This system was introduced to Arab thought through the translation of Hellenistic and Persian literature. Gnosticism is reflected in the ideas and doctrines of the *shi'i* sect as well as in *sufi* philosophy. The followers of this approach believe that human knowledge is essentially intuitive. It can be

acquired through unmediated interaction between the subject and object.

3. *al-nizam al-ma'rifi al-burhani* (the epistemology of inference). This system was introduced to the Arab world when the Greek sciences were translated into Arabic. Being a late comer, it had to compete with the other already established epistemologies. This system was established by the Islamic philosophers who were greatly influenced by the ideas of Aristotle, and to lesser extent by those of Plato. Al-Jabiri believes that this system had reached its zenith in the philosophy of Ibn Rushd in the twelfth century.

Although these epistemic systems had had early on clear lines of demarcation and following, gradually these lines became blur, and eventually the three distinct systems intermingled and were reduced to one flux. The result was that irrationalism dominated Arab intellectual life, putting the whole Arab-Islamic civilization on a steep course of decline.[35] The rise of irrationalism was precipitated not only by the arbitrary integration of the three markedly distinct, and drastically heterogeneous epistemic orders, but also because of the unbalanced growth of gnosticism at the expense of the two other orders.

Is there any solution to the mounting problems confronting the Arab intellect? How can modern Arab thinking escape the seemingly chronic intellectual crisis it finds itself in? Al-Jabiri suggests that a crisis of such depth and magnitude requires a radical solutions; namely, Arab intellectual history has to be rewritten, and the Arab mind has to be restructured on a new foundation. The restructuring of the Arab mind and Arab consciousness does not mean that contemporary consciousness should be replaced by historical models borrowed from the past. Rather, it means that Arab culture has to be redesigned so as to, first, free contemporary consciousness from the authority of the past, and, secondly, ensure that Arab culture is conducive to innovative thinking, characteristic of modern thought.[36] Furthermore, Arab history should be rewritten in such a way that the modern Arab can read his history as an evolution, a series of historical moments in which the latest moment supersedes and embodies all previous moments. In other words, if Arab history can be read by contemporary Arabs, as European history is read by contemporary Europeans, as the "becoming" (*sayrurah*) of the present, then no modern Arab would dare to call for the resuscitation of past epoches, as no European entertains today such a possibility.[37]

Concluding Remarks

The recent appearance of the concept of authenticity in the work of Arab Marxists and liberals, and the return to the study of the cultural heritage of the Arab people, represents a drastic shift in the attitude of two ideological groups who have for long insisted that traditional and historical ideas were irrelevant to futural possibilities, and clearly underscores the dilemma facing the Arab society. Both Tizini and al-Jabiri realize the need for the restructuring of the Arab mind, both offer some sort of a frame of reference for guiding social progress and development, and both insist that the restructuring of culture and society must be made in such a way that social progress is directed toward satisfying the current needs of society.

The increased interest in the concept of authenticity makes a meaningful exchange and a two-way communication among the major ideological groups a real possibility for the first time since the interest in development arose in the first half of the nineteenth century. For although authenticity and heritage have been, all along, a central concerns of the Islamic movement, the interest in these ideas is new to other Arab ideological movements. The significant contribution made by Tizini and al-Jabiri lies in redefining the relationship between the "Self" and the "Other" on the one hand, and the concepts of "authenticity" and "modernity" on the other.

Doubtlessly, the eighties have witnessed the beginning of a dialogue between ideological movements who, till then, were experiencing almost a complete lack of intellectual exchange. This recent development is quite significant. For one thing, it certainly enhances the prospect for a profound and far-reaching self criticism, making thereby the beginning of a process of true rationalization possible. But for another, the inception of a meaningful dialogue among major ideological groups, who for decades have talked past each other, is a necessary step toward the realization of a general consensus, without which genuine social cooperation is hardly possible.

Notes

1. Tayeb Tizini, Min al-Turath ila al-Thawrah (Damascus, Syria: Dar Dimashq, 1979), p. 30.
2. Ibid., p. 32
3. Ibid., p. 7-8.
4. Ibid., pp. 36-8.
5. Ibid. p. 260.
6. ibid., p. 288.
7. Ibid., p. 58.
8. Ibid,. p. 207.
9. Ibid., pp. 154-62.
10. Ibid., pp. 154-63.
11. Ibid., p. 934.
12. Ibid., p. 94.
13. Ibid., pp. 309-420.
14. Ibid., p. 631.
15. Ibid., pp. 733-56.
16. Ibid. p. 664.
17. Ibid., p. 687.
18. Ibid., p. 689.
19. Muhammad 'Abid al-Jabiri, Nahnu wa al-Turath (Bierut, Lebanon: Dar al-Tali'ah, 1980), p. 17.
20. Ibid., pp. 58-9.
21. Ibid., pp. 59-60.
22. See al-Jabiri, Al-Khitab al-Arabi al-Mu'asir (Beirut, Lebanon: Dar al-Tali'ah, 1982), p. 134-5.
23. Ibid., p. 34.
24. Ibid., p. 18.
25. Ibid., p. 27.
26. Ibid., p. 189.
27. Ibid.
28. Ibid., pp. 35-6.
29. Ibid., p. 63.
30. Ibid., p. 36-7.
31. Ibid., p. 132-4.
32. Al-Jabiri has recently published a third volume under the tilted Al-'Aql al-Siyassi al-Arabi [the Arab political mind] (Beirut, Lebanon: Markaz Dirasat al-Wihda al-Arabiya, 1990).
33. al-Jabiri, Naqd al-'Aql al-Arabi, Vol. 1:Taqwin al-'Aql al-'Arabi, pp. 38-9.

34. Ibid., p.61-3.
35. Ibid., pp. 191-2.
36. al-Jabiri, *Ishkalyat al-Fikr al-Arabi al-Mu'asir* (Casab lanca, Morocco: Mu'asat Yanshurah Lil-Tiba'ah wa al-Nashr, 1989), p. 30-31.
37. Ibid., pp. 27-8.

Conclusion to Part II

The drive to acquire modern sciences and technologies in the Middle East was precipitated by the desire of the ruling elites to maintain military parity with outside powers. But soon Middle Easterners came to realize that the technological and industrial backwardness they had been experiencing were only symptoms of the decadent conditions of society. By the close of the nineteenth century, it became quite apparent to leading intellectuals that the failure to achieve scientific and industrial progress was the result of the absence of the cultural and social conditions needed for facilitating such progress. Although early modernists (e.g. the Reform School) tried to bring about change by restructuring Middle Eastern consciousness, later modernists became increasingly impatient with the slow pace of change, and opted for more radical solutions. Taha Hussain, for example, reasoned that the cultural forms inherited from the past were so deformed and corrupt that it was impossible to reform them. Cultural heritage had therefore, he insisted, to be abandoned once and for all, and replaced by a new worldview imported from Europe. Henceforth the strategy of importing modern ideas and institutions, along with modern commodities, from Western societies became the favorite approach for many Middle Eastern leaders. As Bennabi pointed out, Arab elite believed that if they can accumulate modern ideas and products, they would ultimately be able to buy for themselves a ready-made modern civilization rather than undergoing the painstaking alternative of making one.

The modernist strategy, however, prompted a fierce response from the traditionalists. The latter could hardly see any good coming from the West, for their eyes were fixed on the negative aspects of Western modernization. As a result, Arab modernists and traditionalists entered into a political and ideological struggle aiming at winning the hearts and minds of the Arab masses. By the late 1950s, the struggle took a different twist when modernists were able to dominate the political scene, and used state power to introduce modern institutions and ideas, and dictated to society modern programs and plans.

The strategy of Arab modernists, which has a striking resemblance to the modernization scheme advanced by modernization school, proved, by the late 1970s to be a fiasco. Rather than effecting modern reform, it helped strengthening traditionalist and radical tendencies. But why did the strategy fail? Clearly several theoretical and practical factors could be pointed out. I contend, nonetheless, that the most crucial factor behind the grand failure of Arab modernists is their inability to understand the process of modernization itself. That is, Arab modernists, guided by either Marxist-Leninists ideas or modernization schemes, failed to recognize the interconnectedness of consciousness and society, culture and structure, or thinking and producing. They believed that they could change social behavior by implanting institutions and ideas developed and matured in the confines of another culture. They soon discovered, however, that democratization and industrialization could not by brought about by holding elections or by building industrial facilities. For in order for these institutions and facilities to function properly, they have to be integral parts of a meaningful world. But meaning can never be generated from without; it has to be subjectively generated from within the field of significance of the conscious self. Evidently, Third World "modernists", failing to appreciate the importance of persuasion and dialogue in solving cultural problems, have, by and large, elected to almost exclusively rely on the power of the state to impose modernization plans on people.

The strategy adopted by Arab modernists has not only been oblivious to the interconnectedness of thinking and being, but it is also unmindful of the temporal interconnectedness of past and future. The cry of authenticity and heritage alluded to in Chapter 9 is only a sign of the historicality of consciousness, which Arab modernists thought they could ignore. Arab modernists did not see, early on, that the present life-situation of the society they were intent on reforming does not simply signify the objective continuation of past practices, but signifies also the subjective continuation of past forms of consciousness. They failed to see that while reinterpreting history may result in altering the written history of a people, it does not guarantee change in social behavior, for social behavior is rooted in heritage, i.e. in the forms of consciousness inherited from the past. Heritage is *not merely one's knowledge of the history of one's ancestors, but rather one's commitment to repeat and enhance past achievements, and remedy and redress past failures.* The past cannot be abandoned just because it is painful or problematic, unless one is willing to render one's life meaningless and purposeless. *A violent and wholesale rejection of the past can only suppress the unpleasant memories associated with it, and cover the problems rooted in it, but it will not make them go away.* The pain and failure of the past can be overcome and surpassed only through a sincere and honest encounter with the past, whereby the sources of pain and causes of failure are identified, mistakes and miscalculations are acknowledged, and future possibilities are projected from within the inherited life-situation.

The impact of heritage is by no means limited to the images one has of the past, or his sentiments towards it, but reaches into the very structure of one's consciousness. The human being becomes capable of self-consciousness, and self-evaluation at an advanced stage in the process of character formation. The basic structures of the individual character, his ideas and thoughts, values and beliefs, dispositions and ambitions, education and skills, shortcomings and contradictions, are formed at an early stage in life and molded into the cultural forms of his social environment. It is against this background that the human being would have to restructure and reform his life. And he has to do so by confronting head on the very ideas, values, and beliefs which lie at the foundation of the 'traditional' structures of consciousness. This also means that the subconscious has to be brought into the light so as to become conscious.

It follows from the preceding discussion that no social group can ever modernize by renouncing its past. Modernization must be attempted from within the realm of tradition and heritage. For authenticity's and modernity's demands need not stand in complete contradiction whereby the triumph of one can only be achieved at the expense of the other's defeat. Modernization and authenticity appear contradictory only when the former is used for denoting the process of Westernization and the latter is employed in reference to traditionalism. But authenticity denotes also another aspect of the current struggle for the future of the Arab society, viz. the call for distinguishing the positive from the negative aspects of Arab heritage, as the first step toward reinforcing the positive and repudiating the negative. As such, authenticity signifies a call for *originality*, a call for exploring solutions appropriate to the historical specificity of the Arab society, as opposed to implementing ready-made solutions borrowed from other cultural or historical settings. Similarly, modernization is not, and need not be, synonymous with Westernization, for it also refers to the need to be creative and innovative in dealing with contemporary problems, and developing future possibilities. Used in this sense, modernization (innovation) and authenticity (originality) are not only compatible with each other, but they are two integral parts of the process of modernization *qua* rationalization.

Bibliography

Abduh, Muhammad. Al-Islam wa al-Nasraniyyah ma' al-'Ilm wa al-Madaniyyah, 7th ed. Cairo, Egypt: Dar al-Manar, 1368 A.H.
--------. *Al-Islam Din wa Hadarah*, Tahir al-Tinaji, ed. (Cairo, Egypt: Al-Hilal, n.d.,
--------. Risalat al-Tawhid. Cairo, Egypt: Dar al-Ma'arif, 1966.
al-Afaghani, Jamal al-Din. *Al-A'mal al-Kamilah: Al-Kitabat al-Siyasiyyah, vol. 2, Muhammad 'Imarah, ed.*. Beirut, Lebanon: Al-Mu'assasah al-Arabiyyah Lil-Dirassah wa al-Nashir, 1981.
Aflaq, Michel. *Fi Sabil al-Ba'th.* Damascus, Syria: Dar al Tali'ah, 1959.
Alexander, Jeffery C. and Steven Seidman (eds.). *Culture and Society: Contemporary Debate.* Cambridge University Press, 1990.
Althusser, Louis. *For Marx*, trans. Ben Brewster. N.Y.: Pantheon Books, 1969.
Almond, Gabriel A. and James S. Coleman (eds.). *The Politics of Developing Areas.* N.J.: Princeton University Press, 1960.
-------- and Sidney Verba. *The Civic Culture: Political Attitudes and Democracy in Five Nations.* Princeton, N.J.: Princeton University Press, 1963.
-------- and G. Bingham Powell, Jr. *Comparative Politics: A Development Approach.* Boston: Little, Brown and Co., 1966.
Apter, David. *The Politics of Modernization.* The University of Chicago Press, 1965.
al-Bahrawi, Muhammad Abdul Latif. *Harakat al-Islah al-Uthmani fi 'Asir al-Sultan Mahmud al-Thani 1839-1808.* Cairo, Egypt: Dar al-Turath, 1398 A.H./1978 A.D.
Bellah, Robert N., et. al. *Habets of the Heart: Individualism and Commitment in American Life.* N.Y.: Harper & Row, 1985.
--------. (ed.). *Religion and Process in Modern Asia.* N.Y.: The Free Press, 1965.
Bennabi, Malek. *Mushkilat al-Afkar fi al-'Alam al-Islami*, trans. (French to Arabic) M. Abdul Azim Ali. Cairo, Egypt: Maktabat Ammar, 1391/1971.

--------. *Mushkilat al-Thaqafa,* 4th ed., trans. (French to Arabic) Abdul Sabur Shahin. Damascus, Syria: Dar al-Fikr, 1404/1984.

--------. *Ta'amulat.* Damascus: Dar al-Fikr, 1405/1985.

--------. *Fikrat Kamanwolth Islami,* 2nd ed. Cairo, Egypt: Maktabit Ammar, 1391/1971.

Berger, Peter L. *Pyramids of Sacrifice.* N.Y.: Basic Books, Inc., 1974.

Bernstein, Henry. "Modernization Theory and the Sociological Study of Development." *Journal of Development Studies,* October, 1971, 7:141-60.

Binder, Leonard et. al. *Crises and Consequences in Political Development.* Princeton University Press, 1971.

Boye, Roy. *Foucault and Derrida: The Other Side of Reason.* London: Unwin Hyman, 1990.

Brubaker, Rogers, *The Limits of Rationality: An Essay on the Social and Moral Thought of Max Weber.* London: George Allen and Unwin, 1984.

Cassirer, Ernst, *The Philosophy of the Enlightenment.* Princeton University Press, 1951.

Cudsi, Alexander S. and Ali E. Hillal Dessouki (ed.), *Islam and Power.* Blatimore: The Johns Hopkins University, 1981.

Descartes, Rene, *Meditations on First Philosophy,* trans. John cottingham. Cambridge University Press, 1986.

--------, *A Discourse on Method,* trans. John Veitch. N.Y.: Everyman's Liberary, 1969.

Eisenstadt, S. N., *Tradition, Change, and Modernity.* N.Y.: John Wiley and Sons, 1973.

--------, *Modernization: Postest and Change.* N.J.: Prentice-Hall, 1966.

-------- (ed.), *Patterns of Modernity,* Vol. 1. London: Frances Pinter, 1987.

Foucault, Michel, *Power/Knowledge,* trans. Colin Gordon, et. al. N.Y.: Pantheon Books, 1980.

--------, *The Order of Things: An Archaeology of the Human Sciences.* N.Y.: Vintage Books, 1973.

Gelven, Michael, *A Commentary on Heidegger's Being and Time.* Dekalb, Illinois: Nortrhern Illinois University Press, 1989.

Gadamer, Hans-Georg, *Truth and Method,* 2nd ed., trans. Joel Weinsheimer and Donald G. Marshall. N.Y.: Crossroad, 1989.

Habermas, Jurgen, *The Theory of Communicative Action,* 2 vols., trans. Thomas McCarthy. Boston: Beacon Press, 1984.

--------, *Knowledge and Human Interests,* trans. Jermy J. Shapiro. Boston: Beacon Press, 1971.

--------, *Theory and Practice*, trans. John Viertel. Boston: Beacon Press, 1971.

Halpern, Manfred, The Politics of Social Change in the Middle East and North Africa. Princeton, N.J.: Princeton University Press, 1963.

Hegel, G.W.F., *Faith and Knowledge*, trans. H. S. Harris. State Univeristy of New York Press, 1977)

--------, *The Phenomenology of Mind*, trans. J.B. Baillie. N.Y.: Harper and Row, Publisher, 1967.

--------, *The Science of Logic*, trans. William Wallace. Oxford: Clarendon Press, 1975.

Heidegger, Martin, *Being and Time*, trans. John Macquarri and Edward Robinson. London: SCM Press, 1961.

--------, *Kant and the Problem of Metaphysics*, trans. James S. Churchill. Indiana University Press, 1962.

--------, Nietzsche, Vol. IV.

Higgott, Richard A., *Political Development Theory: The Contemporary Debate*. London: Croom Helm, 1983.

Horkheimer, Max, *Eclipse of Reason*. New York: Continuum, 1947.

Hussain, Asaf. *Islamic Movement in Egypt, Pakistan, and Iran: An Annotated Bibliography*. London: Mansell Publishing Limited, 1983.

al-Hussari, Sati', *Abhath Mukhtarah fi al-Qawmiyyah al-Arabiyyah*, vol. 1. Beirut, Lebanon: Dar al-Quds, 1974.

Hussain, Taha, *Mustaqbal al-Thaqafa fi Misr* (1938), vol. 9 of al-Majmu'ah al-Kamilah. Beirut, Lebanon: Dar al-Kitab al-Lubnani, 1973.

--------, *Fi al-Adab al-Jahili*. Cairo, Egypt: Dar al-Ma'arif, 1927.

Husserl, Edmund. Cartesian Meditations: An Introduction to Phenomenology, trans. Dorion Cairns. M. Nijhoff, 1960.

Ingram, David, *Habermas and the Dialectic of Reason*. New Haven: Yale University Press, 1987.

Ismael, Tariq and Jacqueline. *Government and Politics in Islam*. London: Frances Printer, 1985.

al-Jabiri, Muhammad 'Abid, *Niqd al-'Aqil al-Arabi*, 2 vols. Beirut, Lebanon: Markaz Dirasat al-Wihdah al-Arabiyyah, 1989)

--------, *Ishkaliyyat al-Fikr al-Arabi al-Mu'asir*. al-Dar al-Bayda, Morocco: Mu'asasat Yanshurah Lil-Tiba'ah wa al-Nashr, 1989.

--------, *Al-Khitab al-Arabi al-Mu'asir*. Beirut, Lebanon: Dar al-Tali'ah, 1982.

--------, *Nahnu wa al-Turath: Qira'at Mu'asirah min Turathina al-Falsafi*. Beirut, Lebanon: Dar al-Tali'ah, 1980.

Kain, Philip J., *Marx and Ethics*. Oxford, England: Clarendon Press, 1988.

Kant, Immanuel, *Prolegomena to Any Future Metaphysics*. N.Y.: Macmillan Publishing Company, 1988.

--------, *Critique of Pure Reason*, trans. Norman Kemp Smith. N.Y.: Martin's Press, 1965.

al-Kawakibi, Abdul Rahman, *Al-A'mal al-Kamilah*, ed. Muhammad 'Imarah. Cairo, Egypt: Al-Hay'ah al-Misriyyah al-'Ammah Lil-Ta'lif wa al-Nashr, 1970.

Keddie, Nikkie R. ed. *An Islamic Response to Imperialism*. Berkely, CA: University of California Press, 1968

Kerr, Clark, et. al., *Indusrialism and Industrial Man*. Cambridge, Mass.: Harvard University Press, 1960.

Kolb, David, *The Critique of Pure Modernity: Hegel, Heidegger and After*. Chicago: The University of Chicago Press, 1986.

Konrad, George and Ivan Szelenyi, *The Intellectuals on the Road to Class Struggle*, trans. Andrew Arato and Richard E. Allen. N.Y.: Harcourut Brace Jovanovich, 1979.

Lash, Scott and Sam Whimster (eds.), *Max Weber, Rationality, and Modernity*. Boston, Mass.: Allen and Unwin, 1987.

Lenin, V.I., *Introduction to Marx, Engels, Marxism*. N.Y.: International Publishers, 1987.

Lerner, Daniel, *The Passing of Traditional Society*. Glencoe, Ill: The Free Press, 1958.

Lukacs, Georg, *History and Class Consciousness*, trans. Rodney Livingstone. Cambridge, Mass.: the MIT Press, 1971.

Mahmud, Zaki Najib, *Hadha al-'Asr wa Thaqafatuh*. Beirut, Lebanon: Dar al-Shuruq, 1400/1980.

Monaco, Paul, *Modern European Culture and Consciousness 1870-1980*. Albany, N.Y.: State University of New York Press, 1983.

Mannheim, Karl, *Ideology and Utopia*. New York: Harcourt, Brace & Co., 1940.

Marglin, Frederique and Stephan (eds.) *Dominating Knowledge*. Oxford: Claredon, 1990.

Marx, Karl, *Capital: A Critique of Political Economy*, vol. 1, trans. Ben Fowkes. N.Y.: Vintage Books, 1977.

--------, *Karl Marx Selected Writings*, see listing under David McLellan.

--------, *Marx-Engels Reader*, seel listing under Robert Tucker.

McLellan, David (ed.), *Karl Marx Selected Writings*. Oxford University Press, 1977.

Nash, Manning, *Unified Agenda: The Dynamics of Modernization in Developing Nations.* London: Westview Press, 1984.

Nietzsche, Friedrich, *On the Geneology of Morals,* trans. Walter Kaufmann and R.J. Hollingdale. N.Y.: Vintage Books, 1969.

--------, *The Will To Power,* trans. Walter Kaufmann and R.J. Hollingdale. N.Y.: Vintage Books, 1967.

--------, *Beyond Good and Evil: Prelude to a Philosophy of Future,* trans. Walter Kaufmann. N.Y.: Vintage Books, 1966.

O'Sullivan (ed.), *The Structure of Modern Ideology.* England: Edward Elgar, 1989.

Parsons, Talcott, *The Social System.* Glencoe, Illinois: The Free Press, 1951.

-------- and Edward Shils, *Toward a General Theory of Action.* Cambridge, Mass.: Harvard University Press, 1967.

Qutb, Sayed, *Ma'alim fi al-Tariq,* 9th ed. Beirut, Lebanon: Dar al-Shuruq, 1402/1982.

--------. *Milestones,* Cedar Rapids. Iowa: Unity Publishing, Co., n.d.

--------. *Hadha al-Din.* Cairo: Dar al-Qalam, n.d.

--------. *Al-Mustaqbal li-Hatha al-Din.* Cairo n.d.

--------. *Khasa's al-Tasawur al-Islami.* Al-'itihad al-Islami al-'Alami Lil-Munazamat al-Tulabiyyah, 1398/1978.

al-Rafi'i, Abdul Rahman, *'Asr Muhammad Ali,* 4th ed. Cairo, Egypt: Dar al-Ma'arif, 1402/1982.

al-Rafi'i, Mustafa Sadiq, *Tahta Rayat al-Quran.* Cairo, Egypt: Al-Maktabah al-Tijariyyah al-Kubrah, 1383/1963.

Rasmussen, David M., *Reading Habermas.* Cambridge, Mass.: Basil Blackwell, 1990.

Reiss, Hans (ed.), *Kant's Political Writings,* trans. H. B. Nisbet. Cambridge University Press, 1970.

Rigby, S. H., *Marxism and History: A Critical Introduction.* Manschester University Press, 1987.

Riziq, Jabir. *Madhabih al-Ikhwan fi Sujun Nasser.* Cairo: Dar al-Nasir Lil-Tiba'ah al-Islamiyyah, 1987.

Rostow, W.W., *Politics and the Stages of Growth.* Cambridge University Press, 1971.

Sharabi, Hisham (ed.), *The Next Arab Decade.* Boulder, Colorado: Westview Press, 1988.

Shils, Edward, *Tradition.* The University of Chicago Press, 1981.

--------, "The Intellectuals and the Powers: Some Perspectives for Comparative Analysis," in *On Intellectuals,* ed. Philip Rieff. Garden City, N.Y.: Doubleday and company, Inc., 1969.

Shklar, Judith N., *Freedom and Independence: A Study of the Political Ideas of Hegel's Phenomenology of Mind.* Cambridge University Press, 1976.

Shutz, Alfred, *The Phenomenology of the social World,* trans. George Walsh. N.Y.: Northwestern University Press, 1967.

So, Alvin Y., *Social Change and Development.* Newbury Park, CA.: Sage Publications, 1990.

al-Tahtawi, Rafa'ah Rafi', *Takhliss al-Ibriz fi Talkhiss Bariz* (1265 A.H.), printed with commentary in Mahmud Fahmi Hijazi, *Usul al-Fikr al-Arabi al-Hadith 'ind al-Tahtawi.* Cairo, Egypt: Al-Hai'ah al-Misriyyah al-'Ammah Lil-Kitab, 1974.

Tizini, Tayyib, *Min al-Turath ila al-Thawra: Hawla Nazariyyah Muqtaraha fi al-Qdiyyat al-Turath al-Arabi.* Damascus, Syria: Dar Dimashq, 1979.

Tucker, Robert C., *The Marx-Engels Reader,* 2nd edition. N.Y.: W.W. Norton & Company, 1978.

Turner, Bryan S., *Weber and Islam.* Boston: Routledge & Kegan Paul, 1974.

Vehelst, Thierry, *No Life Without Roots,* trans. Bob Cumming. London: Zed Books Ltd., 1987.

Velkley, Richard L., *Freedom and the End of Reason.* Chicago: University of Chicago Press, 1989.

Voegelin, Eric, *Order and History: In Search of Order,* vol. 5 . Louisiana State University Press, 1987.

Wahl Jean, *Philosophies of Existence.* N.Y.: Schocken Books, 1969.

Weber, Max, T*he Protestant Ethic and the Spirit of Capitalism,* trans. Talcott Parsons. London: George Allen & Unwin, 1976.

--------, *Economy and Society,* ed. Guenther Roth and Claus Wittich. N.Y.: Bedminister Press, 1968.

--------, *From Max Weber: Essays in Sociology,* trans. H.H. Gerth and C. Wright Mills. N.Y.: Oxford University Press, 1946.

Weiner, Myron and Samuel P. Huntington (eds.), *Understanding Political Development.* Boston: Little, Brown & Co., 1987.

Wilson, H.T., *Tradition and Innovation: The Idea of Civilization as Culture and its Significance.* Boston, Mass.: Routledge and Kegan Paul, 1984.

Index